T0305694

Online Learning Systems

This book discusses the newest approach to online learning systems in higher education. As e-Learning platforms change their mechanisms for data processing and storage, there is a need to move these systems toward being more efficient and smarter. This book covers online learning systems and their application to large-scale data along with the technological aspects of these processes and problem-solving methods.

Online Learning Systems: Methods and Applications with Large-Scale Data discusses the efficiency measurement and environmental impact of online education. The book offers a parametric evaluation and categorization of online learning systems and provides an exploration of big data ecosystems in cloud computing. Descriptive analytical methods that assist in finding solutions for big data challenges are also covered within the book.

The book is written for academicians, which includes teachers, students, and higher education policymakers who believe in transforming the education industry, as well as research scholars and those working in education technology and artificial intelligence. Industry professionals involved in education management and those working in e-Learning companies will also find this book useful.

Online Learning Systems
Methods and Applications with Large-Scale Data

Edited by
Zdzislaw Polkowski, Samarjeet Borah,
Sambit Kumar Mishra and Darshana Desai

CRC Press
Taylor & Francis Group
Boca Raton   London   New York

CRC Press is an imprint of the
Taylor & Francis Group, an **informa** business

First edition published 2023
by CRC Press
6000 Broken Sound Parkway NW, Suite 300, Boca Raton, FL 33487–2742

and by CRC Press
4 Park Square, Milton Park, Abingdon, Oxon, OX14 4RN

CRC Press is an imprint of Taylor & Francis Group, LLC

Library of Congress Cataloging-in-Publication Data
Names: Polkowski, Zdzislaw, editor. | Borah, Samarjeet, editor. | Mishra,
    Sambit Kumar, editor. | Desai, Darshana, editor.
Title: Online learning systems : methods and applications with large-scale
    data / edited by Zdzislaw Polkowski, Samarjeet Borah, Sambit Kumar
    Mishra, and Darshana Desai.
Description: First edition. | Boca Raton, FL : CRC Press, 2023. | Includes
    bibliographical references and index.
Identifiers: LCCN 2022037359 (print) | LCCN 2022037360 (ebook) | ISBN
    9781032225081 (hardback) | ISBN 9781032225104 (paperback) | ISBN
    9781003272823 (ebook)
Subjects: LCSH: Internet in higher education—Research. | Web-based
    instruction—Research.
Classification: LCC LB2395.7 .O66 2023 (print) | LCC LB2395.7 (ebook) |
    DDC 378.1/7344678—dc23/eng/20220922
LC record available at https://lccn.loc.gov/2022037359
LC ebook record available at https://lccn.loc.gov/2022037360

ISBN: 978-1-032-22508-1 (hbk)
ISBN: 978-1-032-22510-4 (pbk)
ISBN: 978-1-003-27282-3 (ebk)

DOI: 10.1201/9781003272823

Typeset in Times LT Std
by Apex CoVantage, LLC

Contents

Chapter 9 Comparison between TRANSPOSE and MTF Algorithm with

*Tapaswini Dash, Alina Swain, Pradyumna Kumar Mohapatra
and Banoj Kumar Panda*

Chapter 10 An Advanced Transpose Algorithm Using the Hash Function

*Tapaswini Dash, Pradyumna Kumar Mohapatra
and Banoj Kumar Panda*

Chapter 11

*Jyoti Deshmukh, Sunil Wankhade, Pranali Khuspe
and Akshay Kedar*

Chapter 12 Prediction of Selection of Communication Tools and

Rajkamal C. Sangole and Darshana Desai

Chapter 13 A Detailed Review on 6G Technology: Online Learning

*Arun Agarwal, Suvransu Sekhar Mishra,
Banoj Kumar Panda and Gourav Misra*

Editor Biographies

Dr. Zdzislaw Polkowski is presently an adjunct professor in the Department of Business Intelligence and Management at the Wroclaw University of Economics and Business, Poland. He holds a Ph.D. degree in Computer Science and Management from the Wroclaw University of Technology, a postgraduate degree in Microcomputer Systems in Management from the University of Economics in Wroclaw, and a postgraduate degree in IT in Education from the Economics University in Katowice. He obtained his engineering degree in Industrial Computer Systems from the Technical University of Zielona, Gora. Dr. Polkowski has published more than 55 papers in various journals and 15 conference proceedings, including more than 8 papers in journals indexed in the Web of Science. He has served as a member of the Technical Program Committee at many international conferences in Poland, India, China, Iran, Romania and Bulgaria.

Dr. Samarjeet Borah is currently working as a professor in the Department of Computer Applications, SMIT, Sikkim Manipal University (SMU), India. Dr. Borah handles various academics, research, and administrative activities such as curriculum development, Board of Studies, Doctoral Research Committee, and IT Infrastructure Management at the Sikkim Manipal University. Dr. Borah is involved with various funded projects from AICTE (Government of India) and DST-CSRI (Government of India) in the capacity of Principal Investigator/Co-principal Investigator. He has organized various national and international conferences and is involved with various books and journals with various publishers in the capacity of Editor/Guest Editor/ Reviewer. Dr. Borah is Editor in Chief of the book/proceedings series Research Notes on Computing and Communication Sciences, Apple Academic Press, USA.

Dr. Sambit Kumar Mishra has more than 22 years of teaching experience in different AICTE-approved institutions in India. He obtained his bachelor's degree in Computer Engineering from the Amravati University, Maharashtra, India in 1991; his M.Tech. in Computer Science from the Indian School of Mines, Dhanbad (now IIT, Dhanbad), India, in 1998; and his Ph.D. in Computer Science and Engineering from the Siksha 'O' Anusandhan University, Bhubaneswar, Odisha, India, in 2015. He has more than 29 publications in different peer-reviewed international journals and is an editorial board member of different peer-reviewed indexed journals. Presently, Dr. Mishra is associated with the Gandhi Institute for Education and Technology, Baniatangi, Bhubaneswar, Odisha, India.

Dr. Darshana Desai is an associate professor and department head of the MCA Department at the Indira College of Engineering and Management, which is an affiliated institute of the Savitribai Phule Pune University, India. She received her Ph.D. degree from the Gujarat Technological University in August 2017 in the area of IT Management with the subject of website personalization. She has more than 17 years of experience in academia and industry and has published more than 21 research papers and book chapters with internationally recognized publishers indexed in Scopus, Pro-Quest, etc. and peer-reviewed journals. Dr. Desai is interested in interdisciplinary research in the areas of website personalization, machine learning, artificial intelligence, cognitive science, data science, and its applications.

Contributors

Arun Agarwal
Siksha 'O'Anusandhan University
Bhubaneswar, India

Akbar Ahmad
MI College
Malé, Maldives

Mahboob Ahmed
Maulana Mukhtar Ahmad Nadvi
  Technical Campus
Maharashtra, India

Mohd Akram
Maulana Mukhtar Ahmad Nadvi
  Technical Campus
Maharashtra, India

Salman Baig
Maulana Mukhtar Ahmad Nadvi
  Technical Campus
Maharashtra, India

Vinayak Ashok Bharadi
Finolex Academy of Management and
  Technology
Maharashtra, India

Samarjeet Borah
Sikkim Manipal University
Sikkim, India

Tapaswini Dash
Vedang Institute of Technology
Odisha, India

Dr. Darshana Desai
Pimpri Chinchwad College
  of Engineering
Pune, India

Jyoti Deshmukh
Rajiv Gandhi Institute of
  Technology
Andheri(W), Mumbai, India

Sunil Dhal
Sri Sri University
India

Paweł Greń
Jan Wyżykowski University
Poland

Mohamed Haleem
MI College
Malé, Maldives

Dilawar Husain
Maulana Mukhtar Ahmad Nadvi
  Technical Campus
Maharashtra, India

Dr. Anil W. Kale
MGM College of Engineering and
  Technology
Mumbai, India

Akshay Kedar
Rajiv Gandhi Institute
  of Technology
Andheri(W), Mumbai, India

Pranali Khuspe
Rajiv Gandhi Institute of Technology
Andheri(W), Mumbai, India

Dr. Priyanka M. Kothoke
MGM College of Engineering and
  Technology
Mumbai, India

Jyoti Prakash Mishra
Gandhi Institute for Education and
  Technology
Baniatangi, Bhubaneswar, India
and
BijuPatnaik University of Technology
Rourkela, Odisha, India

Sambit Kumar Mishra
Gandhi Institute for Education and
  Technology
Baniatangi, Bhubaneswar, India
and
BijuPatnaik University of Technology
Rourkela, Odisha, India

Suvransu Sekhar Mishra
Siksha O Anusandhan Deemed to be
  University
Bhubaneswar, Odisha, India

Gourav Misra
Dublin City University
Dublin, Ireland

Pradyumna Kumar Mohapatra
Vedang Institute of Technology
Bhubaneswar, India

Yogesh G. Mulye
Finolex Academy of Management and
  Technology
Maharashtra, India

Dr. Vaibhav E. Narawade
Adik Institute of Technology
Mumbai, India

Banoj Kumar Panda
Gandhi Institute for Education and
  Technology
Bhubaneswar, India

Zdzisław Polkowski
WSG University
Bydgoszcz, Poland

Ravi Prakash
Motilal Nehru National Institute of
  Technology
Allahabad, India

Kaushal K. Prasad
Finolex Academy of Management and
  Technology
Maharashtra, India

Saraju Prasad
IBCS, SOA University
India

Mr. Rajkamal C. Sangole
Pimpri Chinchwad College of
  Engineering
Pune, India

Alina Swain
Vedang Institute of Technology
Odisha, India

Janmejaya Swain
Senior Consultant, Deloitte
USA

Oliwia Tarasewicz-Gryt
University of Applied Science
  in Jelenia Góra
Poland

Dr Ashwin Tomar
MCASC-GK
Pune, India

Dr Manjusha Tomar
Indira College of Engineering &
  Management
Pune, India

Sunil Wankhade
Rajiv Gandhi Institute
  of Technology
Andheri(W), Mumbai, India

1 Classification of Slow and Fast Learners Using a Deep Learning Model

Vinayak Ashok Bharadi[1], Kaushal K. Prasad[2] and Yogesh G. Mulye[3]

1 Information Technology Department Finolex Academy of Management and Technology, Maharashtra, India

2 Mechanical Engineering Department Finolex Academy of Management and Technology, Maharashtra, India

3 First Year Engineering Department Finolex Academy of Management and Technology, Maharashtra, India

CONTENTS

1.1 INTRODUCTION

The learning ability of a student plays a crucial role in academics. Some students have got outstanding cognitive skills, and they learn the concepts at a faster rate than others. Some students face difficulties in coping with the teaching-learning process due to reasons such as low cognitive ability, low attendance and less time for the preparation because of preparing for an examination due to failure in other classes. Teachers have to give special attention and remedial work to such slow learners. If they are identified in the early stages of the academic year, their performance can be improved significantly [1].

In this research work the case study of an engineering college affiliated to Mumbai University is considered; the institute follows a semester pattern. In order to prepare students for better understanding concepts as well as to prepare them for examinations and further hone their expertise, the teacher has to know the students' learning level. This process is quite tedious, and after getting to know the students well, the teachers can accordingly plan the activities for the students. In case of the semester pattern, there is less time for this acquittance period, and it becomes a challenge to identify the cognitive learning level of the students.

Besides this, various accreditation bodies, such as National Assessment and Accreditation Council (NAAC) as well as National Accreditation Board (NBA), which accredit higher education institutions also stress on the identification of the learning levels of the students and accordingly molding the teaching-learning process for them. If weak learners are identified at the start of the semester, the respective subject teachers can plan their academic activity for students to better understand the subject matter and for their results to improve as they go to the next semester. To improve the students' performance with tailored teaching-learning activities for slow and fast learners is the main outcome of this research.

Machine learning enables computing devices to learn without being explicitly programmed. This is a subdomain of the artificial intelligence (AI) that makes software programs or applications capable of precisely predicting the outcome. Deep learning methods analyze the patterns in the data. Further, these patterns are modeled as complex multilayered networks; this is the most general way to model a problem. This makes deep learning capable of solving difficult problems which are otherwise not addressable by modular programming logic [3–4]. Deep learning refers to machine learning using deep (artificial) neural networks. There exist a couple of algorithms which implement deep learning using hidden layers other than conventional neural networks. The concept of "artificial" neural networks dates back to the 1940s. It consists of a network of artificial neurons programmed out of interconnected threshold switches. This network is referred to as an artificial neural network, and it can learn to recognize patterns like the human brain does [5].

For the classification of the learner as per their learning ability, conventionally, a method based on a mathematical formulation was used in the institute under consideration. This method simply weights the semester grade point average score and the internal assessment marks. This method is quite simple and linear. A method based on the deep learning technique is proposed here. The proposed method uses a deep neural network to classify the students as slow, average and fast learners. The performance of the proposed deep learning classifier is compared with other types of classifiers, such as linear regression, Naive Bayes, decision trees and support vector machines.

1.2   SLOW AND FAST LEARNERS

The teaching-learning process is highly dependent on the cognitive levels of the students. The methods followed and the assignments as well as the remedial work given to the students should be different for different student levels. In the report published by Hacettepe Üniversitesi Eğitim Fakültesi Dergisi (H. U. Journal of Education) [6], the influence of the constructivist learning approach on the cognitive learning levels of the students while learning trigonometry and on their attitudes towards mathematics was analyzed. The constructivist teaching-learning process based on the students' learning level was found to be better than the conventional method.

Anees Sehar [6] performed a study that measured the cognitive levels of examination questions to evaluate students' learning. Question papers from various teachers related to different subjects were collected for the analysis pertaining to the targeted cognitive levels. The analysis concluded that there are several teaching methodologies for the teaching-learning process, but the examinations were confined to the lower level of learning.

Koparan, Timur, and Bülent Güven [8] studied the effect of the project-based learning approach on secondary-school students' statistical literacy levels, and it was found that the project-based learning approach increases students' level of cognitive learning.

In the current research the cognitive level assessment of students is performed to give a specific type of remedial work for slow learners so that their understanding about the subject contents will improve; the fast learners will be given creative assignments to prepare them for higher-cognitive-level assignments. The overall process is to boost students' understanding about the subject and prepare them for the examinations as well as placements.

1.3   DEEP LEARNING FOR PATTERN RECOGNITION

Deep learning is quite a popular research domain with a variety of applications. Several studies support the prominence of deep neural networks (DNNs) which exceed the performance of the previous leading standards in diverse machine learning applications [9–13].

Deep learning is a set of machine learning methods designed to model data with a high level of abstraction without being explicitly programmed. Deep learning is derived from the articulation of architectures of various transformations in the nonlinear space [9, 14]. The rising interest in deep learning research is mainly because of its conceptual as well as its technological advances. Factually, the available deep learning solutions based on the models of learning are based on the consumption of an immense reservoir of compute power. This huge compute capacity is made available through actual modern computers as well as requesting the main processor (CPU) and the graphic dedicated processors (GPU) as well as cloud-based deployments [15–18].

Deep learning is considered to be the most significant innovation in the past decade in the field of pattern recognition and machine learning; it has influenced the methodology of related fields like computer vision and attained enormous progress in both academy and industry. Deep learning solutions accomplished an end-to-end pattern recognition, merging previous steps of pre- processing, feature extraction, classifier design and post-processing [19–20].

1.4 PROPOSED SYSTEM AND IMPLEMENTATION

The problem under consideration is to classify a student as either a slow, average or fast learner, given their cumulative performance, attendance in the current semester and total failures in the past semesters. For a classification problem of this kind, a training dataset is needed. The dataset used for this research work is explained below.

1.4.1 DESCRIPTION OF THE DATASET

For the current research, a dataset of 1,082 students is prepared; the dataset consists of the cumulative grade point average (CGPA) of the student, the attendance (ATTN) in the current semester till point of the evaluation and the number of failures (KT) till the current semester. The fourth column in this dataset is the class. For the training purpose the cognitive level of the students assessed by the teachers based on his/her performance is added. This data will be used for training as well as testing. Using this data the class of the student has to be predicted as "Class 1—Slow Learner", "Class 2—Fast Learner" or "Class 0—Average Learner".

The dataset elements and their correlation are shown in Figure. 1.1 and description of the dataset can be found in Table 1.1. The three classes and their candidate distribution can be seen there.

1.4.2 DEEP LEARNING MODEL

Deep learning overcomes the challenges of the classification problem's workflow management by simplifying workflows while also improving accuracy, at least in many contexts. For the classification of slow and fast learners using deep learning, a deep neural network using multilayered perceptron nodes is used [21]. MLP are universal approximators, and they are very good at modeling nonlinear functions. The multilayer perceptron finds common application in the classification and regression applications in many fields, such as pattern recognition, image, speech and biometric recognition and classification problems. The choice of the architecture has a great impact on the convergence of these networks [22].

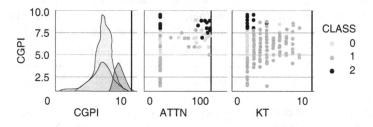

FIGURE 1.1   Dataset on the correlation of slow and fast learners.

TABLE 1.1

Description of Dataset

Parameter	CGPI	ATTN	KT	CLASS
count	1,081	1,081	1,081	1,081
mean	6.5211	6.1173	0.67068	0.59112
Std	1.23849	20.2052	1.37395	0.73237
Min	1.47	0.05	0	0
25%	5.785	0.73	0	0
50%	6.446	0.8	0	0
75%	7.22	0.9	1	1
Max	9.66667	100	8	2

For the implementation of the deep learning model, the Keras Deep Learning Library is used [23]. Keras Deep Learning Application Programming Interface is a high-level ANN library programmed in Python to build neural network models. The researchers do not have to work on the numerical techniques, tensor algebra and mathematical aspects of optimization methods. The Keras library is built on TensorFlow 2.0 and can scale to entire tensor processing unit (TPU) pods or a large cluster of graphics processing units (GPU). The focus of Keras library is to facilitate experimentations by allowing researchers to go for quick prototyping. They can start from the simple design of the model and quickly deploy the same in Keras with little delay to achieve the results, which is key for research. Keras gives a huge advantage to beginner developers, researchers and scientists. A person needs not worry about low-level computations and can directly delve into deep learning deployment using Keras.

A deep learning model having one input, three hidden layers and one output layer is designed in Keras. For the MLP nodes activation function used in rectified linear activation function (ReLU), the Keras model summary is given below. The model is of sequential type.

Once the model is ready, it is compiled and then trained. For training purposes out of 1,081 students' data, 75% of the data is used for model training and testing, and then the remaining 25% data is used for finding the accuracy. The deep learning network is trained with 400 epochs and a batch size of 5.

In the training phase the model has reached up to 95% accuracy, but the detailed analysis will be discussed in the next section.

1.4.3 MAKING THE MODEL ROBUST FOR THE VARIATIONS IN THE DATA

One of the most common problems faced by the deep learning researchers is the overfitting of the model [24]. Overfitting means the model is virtually remembering the training data, and the performance of the model degrades on real-life data beyond the training set. This problem is solved by regularization techniques.

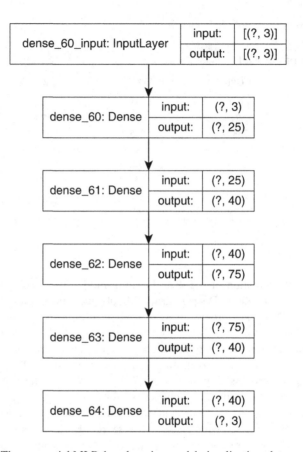

| dense_60_input: InputLayer | input: | [(?, 3)] |
| | output: | [(?, 3)] |

| dense_60: Dense | input: | (?, 3) |
| | output: | (?, 25) |

| dense_61: Dense | input: | (?, 25) |
| | output: | (?, 40) |

| dense_62: Dense | input: | (?, 40) |
| | output: | (?, 75) |

| dense_63: Dense | input: | (?, 75) |
| | output: | (?, 40) |

| dense_64: Dense | input: | (?, 40) |
| | output: | (?, 3) |

FIGURE 1.2   The sequential MLP deep learning model visualization plot.

Regularization is a technique in which slight modifications are made to the learning algorithm so that the model generalizes in a better way. This results in the improvement of the model's performance on the unseen data [25]. The Sequential MLP Deep Learning Model Visualization Plot in Figure 1.2. To improve the performance of the current model, the addition of gaussian noise and dropout layers is done, and the model is trained and evaluated. The results will be discussed in next section.

1.4.4 K-FOLD CROSS-VALIDATION

It is a general practice to use k-fold cross-validation for the evaluation of the performance of a classification algorithm. A model's performance is given by the accuracy estimate, and the reliability of the accuracy estimate is indicated by a relatively small variance over the various sets of input data. Several studies therefore recommended to repeatedly perform k-fold cross-validation [26]. Cross-validation (CV) is a technique based on resampling procedure; this is used to evaluate machine learning models on a limited data sample. To implement CV, it is required to keep aside a sample/

portion of the data; this sample should not be used to train the model; later this sample is used for testing/validating.

One variation of k-fold CV is the stratified k-fold approach. In this variation of the k-fold cross-validation, stratified folds are returned—i.e., the labels are equalized to have a uniform variation. Each set contains approximately the same ratio of target labels as the complete data.

K-fold CV has a single parameter referred to as "k" that indicates the number of groups that a given data sample is to be split into, hence the name k-fold cross-validation. A specific value for k is chosen—e.g., k=10, becoming 10-fold cross-validation.

This procedure shuffles the dataset randomly, then splits the dataset in k-folds, and on each such variation the model is tested, the final accuracy is averaged and the variance of accuracy is also calculated. For the evaluation of the model proposed in Figure. 1.3, k-fold cross-validation with K=10 is performed for both the normal as well as the regularized model. The results are given in the next section.

1.5 RESULTS

The sequential deep learning model with and without regularization is implemented and tested in Kears. To compare the performance of the model, other statistical classifiers are also implemented. The list is as follows:

- Support vector machines (SVM) [27]
- Logistic regression [28]
- Naive Bayes classifier [29]
- K-nearest neighbors [30]
- Decision tree [31]

Figure. 1.4 shows the final performance of deep learning and the statistical classifiers implanted as per the discussion in Section 1.4. The classifiers were implemented in Keras on the Google Colab Platform [32]. Deep learning classifiers have given the best performance as they have the ability to model complex nonlinear functions. The deep learning classifier has given 91.51% accuracy while classifying slow, fast and average learners. The regularized deep learning classifier has given 87.08% accuracy. The next best performance was given by logistic regression, K-NN classifier, logistic regression, decision tree and SVM.

The regularization technique and K-fold CV has further strengthened the findings, and the observed performance range is up to 90% for the deep learning ANN Classifier. Finally, the best performance is expected from the regularized DNN classifier; the expected range is 87 to 90% of accuracy. The summary of these results is given in Figure 1.5.

Once the classifier is trained and tested, this model can be saved as an H5 file format. These models can be called in Python script to predict the cognitive level of any student provided the required academic details are available. The code and the implementation for the previously mentioned research is available at DOI: 10.5281/zenodo.4153494 [33].

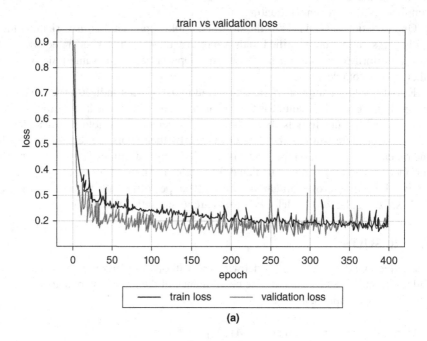

(a)

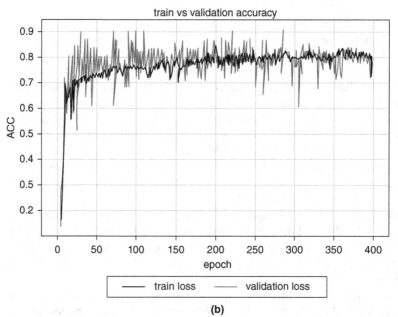

(b)

FIGURE 1.3 Deep network training details—(a) training and validation loss (b) training and validation. Accuracy for the model shown in Figure. 1.2

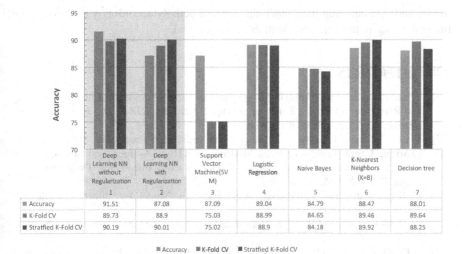

	Deep Learning NN without Regularization	Deep Learning NN with Regularization	Support Vector Machine(SVM)	Logistic Regression	Naive Bayes	K-Nearest Neighbors (K=8)	Decision tree
	1	2	3	4	5	6	7
■ Accuracy	91.51	87.08	87.09	89.04	84.79	88.47	88.01
■ K-Fold CV	89.73	88.9	75.03	88.99	84.65	89.46	89.64
■ Stratfied K-Fold CV	90.19	90.01	75.02	88.9	84.18	89.92	88.25

■ Accuracy   ■ K-Fold CV   ■ Stratfied K-Fold CV

FIGURE 1.4 Performance comparison of various classifier models implemented in the research.

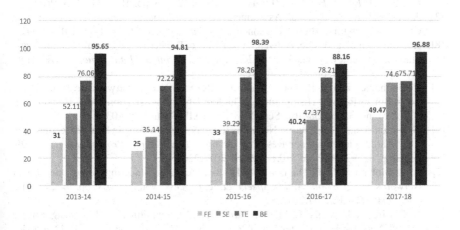

■ FE ■ SE ■ TE ■ BE

FIGURE 1.5 Improvement in students' performance as they go to higher years of their engineering degree.

1.6 CONCLUSION

In this paper a method was presented for classifying the cognitive levels of students based on their academic performance. The deep learning–based approach presented here has given an accuracy of 91.51%. Further, this model was regularized, and the accuracy of the regularized model was found to be in the range of 87% to 90%. K-fold and stratified K-fold cross-validation was also performed on the models proposed. This process will automate the work of teachers to classify students' cognitive levels, and they can plan their teaching-learning activity accordingly to improve the understanding of the concepts from the students' end.

1.7 REFERENCES

[1] Winn, Ariel S. et al. "Applying Cognitive Learning Strategies to Enhance Learning and Retention in Clinical Teaching Settings." *MedEdPORTAL: The J. Teach. Learn. Resour.*, vol. 15, p. 10850, 2019. Web.

[2] Visser, Lennart, Fred A.J. Korthagen, and Judith Schoonenboom. "Differences in Learning Characteristics between Students with High, Average, and Low Levels of Academic Procrastination: Students' Views on Factors Influencing Their Learning," *Front. Psychol.*, 9 May, 2018. Web.

[3] F. Rosenblatt, "The Perceptron: A Probabilistic Model for Information Storage Andorganization in the Brain,"

[4] W. S. McCulloch, and W. Pitts, "A Logical Calculus of the Ideas Immanent in Nervous Activity," 1990.

[5] T. Pham, T. Tran, D. Phung, and S. Venkatesh, "Predicting Healthcare Trajectories from Medical Records: A Deep Learning Approach," *J. Biomed. Inform.*, vol. 69, pp. 218–229, May 2017, doi: 10.1016/j.jbi.2017.04.001.

[6] "Influence of the Constructivist Learning Approach on Students' Levels of LearningTrigonometry and on Their Attitudes Towards Mathematics," *Hacettepe Üniversitesi Eğitim Fakültesi Dergisi*, vol. 28, no. 28–33, pp. 219–234, 2013. Print.

[7] Anees, Sehar. "Analysis of Assessment Levels ofStudents' Learning According to Cognitive Domain of Bloom's Taxonomy." *Online Submission*, pp. 1–14, 2017. Print.

[8] Koparan, Timur, and Bülent Güven. "The Effect of Project-Based Learning on Students' Statistical Literacy Levels for Data Representation," *Int. J. Math. Educ. Sci. Technol.*, vol. 46, no. 5, 2015, pp. 658–686. Web.

[9] H. Bouhamed and Y. Ruichek, "Deep Feedforward Neural Network Learning Using Local Binary Patterns Histograms for Outdoor Object Categization," *Adv. Model. Anal. B*, vol. 61, no. 3, pp. 158–162, Sep. 2018, doi: 10.18280/ama_b.610309.

[10] G. Hinton et al., "Deep Neural Networks for Acoustic Modeling in Speech Recognition: The Shared Views of Four Research Groups," *IEEE Signal Process. Mag.*, vol. 29, no. 6, pp. 82–97, 2012, doi: 10.1109/MSP.2012.2205597.

[11] A. R. Mohamed, G. E. Dahl, and G. Hinton, "Acoustic Modeling Using Deep Belief Networks," *IEEE Trans. Audio, Speech Lang. Process.*, vol. 20, no. 1, pp. 14–22, 2012, doi: 10.1109/TASL.2011.2109382.

[12] D. C. Cireşan, U. Meier, L. M. Gambardella, and J. Schmidhuber, "Deep, Big, Simple Neural Nets for Handwritten Digit Recognition," *Neural Comput.*, vol. 22, no. 12. pp. 3207–3220, Dec. 01, 2010, doi: 10.1162/NECO_a_00052.

[13] D. Yu and L. Deng, "Deep Learning and Its Applications to Signal and Information Processing [Exploratory DSP]," *IEEE Signal Processing Magazine*, vol. 28, no. 1, pp. 145–154, Jan. 2011, doi: 10.1109/MSP.2010.939038.

[14] Y. Bengio, "Learning Deep Architectures for AI," *Found. Trends Mach. Learn.*, vol. 2, no. 1, pp. 1–27, 2009, doi: 10.1561/2200000006.

[15] V. A. Bharadi, H. A. Mestry, and A. Watve, "Biometric Authentication as a Service (BaaS): a NOSQL Database and CUDA Based Implementation," 2019 5th International Conference on Computing, Communication, Control and Automation (ICCUBEA), Pune, India, 2019, pp. 1–5, doi: 10.1109/ICCUBEA47591.2019.9129570.

[16] V. A. Bharadi, and S. Tolye, "Distributed Decomposed Data Analytics of IoT, SAR and Social Network Data," 2020 3rd International Conference on Communication System, Computing and IT Applications (CSCITA), Mumbai, India, 2020, pp. 180–185, doi: 10.1109/CSCITA47329.2020.9137785.

[17]   V. A. Bharadi and M. Meena, "Novel Architecture for CBIR SAAS on Azure Cloud,"
       2015 International Conference on Information Processing (ICIP), Pune, 2015, pp. 366–
       371, doi: 10.1109/INFOP.2015.7489409
[18]   G. M. D'silva and V. A. Bharadi, "Modified Online Signature Recognition
       Using Software as a Service (SaaS) Model on Public Cloud," 2015 International
       Conference on Information Processing (ICIP), Pune, 2015, pp. 360–365, doi: 10.1109/
       INFOP.2015.7489408.
[19]   Zhang, Zhaoxiang, Shiguang Shan, Yi Fang, and Ling Shao. 2019. "Deep Learning
       for Pattern Recognition," *Pattern Recognit. Lett.* Elsevier B.V., doi: 10.1016/j.
       patrec.2018.10.028.
[20]   H. Bouhamed, "COVID-19 Deaths Previsions with Deep Learning Sequence
       Prediction," *Int. J. Big Data Anal. Healthc.*, vol. 5, no. 2, pp. 65–77, Aug. 2020, doi:
       10.4018/ijbdah.20200701.oa1.
[21]   Karlik, Bekir, and Av Olgac, "Performance Analysis of Various Activation Functions
       in Generalized MLP Architecturesof Neural Networks," *Int. J. Artif. Intell. Expert
       Systems(IJAE)*, vol. 1, no. 4, pp. 111–122, http://www.cscjournals.org/csc/manuscript/J
       ournals/IJAE/volume1/Issue4/IJAE-26.pdf.
[22]   Ramchoun, Hassan, Mohammed Amine, Janati Idrissi, Youssef Ghanou, and Mohamed
       Ettaouil, "Multilayer Perceptron: Architecture Optimization and Training," IJIMAI,
       vol. 4, no. 1, p. 26, 2016, doi: 10.9781/ijimai.2016.415.
[23]   F. Chollet, "Keras: The Python Deep Learning library," *Keras.Io*, 2015.
[24]   Tao, Zhou, Hou Muzhou, and Liu Chunhui, "Forecasting Stock Index with Multi-
       Objective Optimization Model Based on Optimized Neural Network Architecture
       Avoiding Overfitting," *Comput. Sci. Inf. Syst.*, vol. 15, no. 1, pp. 211–236, 2018. ComSIS
       Consortium, doi: 10.2298/CSIS170125042T.
[25]   D. Vasicek, "Artificial Intelligence and Machine Learning: Practical Aspects of
       Overfitting and Regularization," *Inf. Serv. Use*, vol. 39, no. 4, 2019, doi: 10.3233/
       isu-190059.
[26]   Wong, Tzu Tsung, and Po Yang Yeh, "Reliable Accuracy Estimates from K-Fold Cross
       Validation," *IEEE Trans. Knowl. Data Eng.*, vol. 32, no. 8, pp. 1586–1594, 2020,
       doi:10.1109/TKDE.2019.2912815.
[27]   Burges, Christopher J.C., "A Tutorial on Support Vector Machines for Pattern
       Recognition," *Data Min. Knowl. Discov.*, vol. 2, no. 2, pp. 121–167, 1998. Kluwer
       Academic Publishers, doi: 10.1023/A:1009715923555.
[28]   Sperandei, Sandro, "Understanding Logistic Regression Analysis," *Biochemia Medica*,
       vol. 24, no. 1, pp. 12–18, 2014, doi: 10.11613/BM.2014.003.
[29]   Chen, Shenglei, Geoffrey I. Webb, Linyuan Liu, and Xin Ma, "A Novel Selective Naïve
       Bayes Algorithm," *Knowledge-Based Systems*, vol. 192, Mar. 2020. Elsevier B.V, doi:
       10.1016/j.knosys.2019.105361.
[30]   Maillo, Jesus, Sergio Ramírez, Isaac Triguero, and Francisco Herrera, "KNN-IS: An
       Iterative Spark-Based Design of the k-Nearest Neighbors Classifier for Big Data,"
       Knowledge- Based Systems, vol. 117, pp. 3–15, Feb. 2017. Elsevier B.V., doi:10.1016/j.
       knosys.2016.06.012.
[31]   Song, Yan Yan, and Ying Lu, "Decision Tree Methods: Applications for Classification and
       Prediction," *Shanghai Arch. Psychiatry*, vol. 27, no. 2, pp. 130–135. Editorial Department
       of theShanghai Archives of Psychiatry, doi: 10.11919/j.issn.1002-0829.215044.
[32]   T. Carneiro, R. V. Medeiros Da NóBrega, T. Nepomuceno, G. Bian, V. H. C. De
       Albuquerque and P. P. R. Filho, "Performance Analysis of Google Colaboratory as a
       Tool for Accelerating Deep Learning Applications," *IEEE Access*, vol. 6, pp. 61677–
       61685, 2018, doi: 10.1109/ACCESS.2018.2874767.
[33]   Dr. Vinayak Ashok Bharadi, Dr. KaushalPrasad, and Dr. Yogesh Mulye, "Using Deep
       Learning Techniques for the Classification of Slow and Fast Learners(Version 1.0),"
       Zenodo, Oct. 29. 2020, http://doi.org/10.5281/zenodo.4153494

2 Transformative e-Learning
An IT Perspective on Education During Covid-19

Saraju Prasad[1] *and Sunil Dhal*[2]
1 IBCS
2 Sri Sri University

CONTENTS

2.1 INTRODUCTION

Covid-19 not only affected to community but also devastated the world economy through its rapid infection and deadly behavior. All sectors are equally affected, and the pandemic created a great panic and reduced regular activities in communities. The education sector is mostly affected by this because of its vulnerability in nature. The hidden behavior and virulent nature of Covid-19 forced the governments of many countries to close the educational institutions temporarily to reduce the speed of its spread. The principal governing body of various institutions in the world are in a panic to cover courses physically during the panic. The sudden closing of institutions created a challenge for authorities, teachers and students to think about their future course of action. As per the World Health Organization (WHO), guidelines to put mask and maintain social distancing became a great challenge for all sectors to follow.

Education systems in the world are struggling to develop platforms to deal with future challenges. The changing environment requires adequate planning in various educational institutions (Rieley, 2020). This situation compelled the world to unite for humanity. The unknown pandemic situation forced civilization to protect students, faculty, others of various fields and finally the whole nation.

E-learning is the latest educational platform and is associated with so many limitations. The limitations are mostly associated with the variables like accessibility, affordability, flexibility, learning pedagogy, etc., which affect a lot in online teaching. Most people have the opinion that an online mode of teaching has better accessibility and reach for students residing in distant areas. Offline education is associated with various costs like accommodation and transportation, which is nullified in online-based learning, and hence, the burden is less. More flexibility and control in terms of time and work is also present in online education. In order to enhance the effectiveness of learning, offline mode is quite successful through classrooms with a physical mode of education. But in e-learning platforms the students have the liberty to get knowledge anywhere at any time. The unpredictable pandemic situation forced the government to focus more on e-learning to deal rightly with the crisis. All over the world, schools and colleges were closed during the pandemic, and around 1.2 billion students were unable to get classroom education. This made a great challenge for the education system and increased the utility of the e-learning system, which was dormant for a period of time. The continuous changing behavior of the pandemic for a longer duration has increased the importance of online platforms, which enhanced the retention of information for a longer period with accessibility. The online platform of education is not only a step during Covid-19 but also a permanent solution in the post-Covid-19 era because of the unknown duration of the pandemic situation.

2.1.1 THE CHALLENGES OF ONLINE LEARNING

Initially it became a great challenge for students who are not tech-savvy. But from the research, it became evident that the average retention of students is more in the online mode of teaching than the offline one. The scope to read in more comfortable ways with greater learning values goes with e-learning platforms as students have the chance to learn more in their own way, like re-reading, skipping, going for more detail, etc. But it cannot be generalized that it can be effective for all age groups of students as younger students require more attention in a physical environment to reduce distractions.

2.2 LITERATURE REVIEW

Innovative technology through e-learning platform has reduced the difficulty of distance education (McBrien et al., 2009). The various forms of computer-based education through the internet are online education, web-oriented education, computer-mediated education, m-learning, etc., which created the platform to educate students anytime from anywhere with structured timing (Cojocariu et al., 2014). The online teaching platform became a major tool to teach students easily in more innovative and flexible ways. This platform became easy for the students because of its accessibility through computers or mobile phones with internet connectivity. Students from any corner can interact with their respective teachers independently (Singh & Thurman, 2019). The physical mode of learning is very much structured as the students and teachers' interactions are lively with an appropriate timing for learning and effective feedback for better understanding, whereas the online mode is unable to justify that extent. In online mode face-to-face interaction is not possible, and the level of learning cannot be judged because of the absence of responses and feedback from various students in different places (Littlefield, 2018). The physical mode of learning, otherwise called synchronous learning, has a great opportunity for social interactions (McBrien et al., 2009). As the pandemic situation continues in several countries, the online platform became necessary where (a) students can be engaged through video conferencing, (b) continuous interactions with the students can be made to avoid discontinuation of studies, (c) connections through internet will not be an issue, (d) learning accessibility can be possible through both the laptop and mobile, (e) there will be a scope for recorded contents of the teachers and (f) assignments or various activities of students can be taken regularly and instantly (Basilaia et al., 2020).

2.2.1 NECESSITY OF ONLINE MODE OF EDUCATION

The rapid spread of Covid-19 created havoc in majority of the countries of the world and forced the community to go through quarantines and closed down the schools, colleges and universities to check community infection. In order to maintain connectivity with students, the online mode of education became the only option to tackle the situation. The unknown behavior of Covid-19 compelled the government to think about the online mode of education, which was previously not a viable solution for better education. The contagious nature of the virus made online teaching a lucrative proposal for the governments of various countries. The online mode made an opportunity for institutions to accommodate more students in various part of the world with flexible times. It became a challenge for all institutions to make an appropriate pedagogy for teaching online. Digitalization in education systems started slowly in various institutions in the world to cope with the pandemic. This became a challenge in various institutions to prepare a qualitative online platform to educate students for a longer duration with greater efficacy. A number of e-classrooms have grown overnight to provide better solutions for an online platform. Major institutions started developing their own platform with changing pedagogy to cope with the changing environment. In this difficult situation institutions have a major focus area to provide an online platform which can accommodate the highest number of students with greater efficiency and learning values (Cathy, 2020).

In the entire world most of the institutions have not shown interest in any kind of resistance to online education. On the basis of affordability, they tried to change their platform to give more benefits of quality to students. In order to protect their reputation during the crisis majority of institutions tried to adopt qualitative online educational portals to increase learning values. Initially it was not possible to convert the entire curriculum to online mode. But with the passage of time they can transform the system to be at par with classroom teaching. The challenges will still remain with remote area connectivity, limitations of the online platform and personalizing the teaching pedagogy. Few institutions have innovative solutions to deal with situations very effectively during the pandemic (Liguori & Winkler, 2020). Few software companies developed various online platforms to provide education for various educational levels like schools, colleges and universities. Depending upon the teaching pedagogy the platforms are different and suitable for various stages of educational systems. Many institutions adopted various platforms from different software companies as per their requirements like Gmail, Google Forms, Google Calendars, Google Drive, Google Hangouts, Google Classroom, and Google Jam board and Drawings from google company. These online platforms of various form can able to solve the problem of offline classes (Basilaia et al., 2020).

2.2.2 CHALLENGES WITH ONLINE TEACHING AND LEARNING

Many online education platforms are available on the internet but not suitable for the exact requirements of learning. The cost common problems associated with these platforms are installation, login, issues with audio and video, etc. For students, online teaching is more boring and not encouraging. Online education is more time-consuming for the students and unable to engage them for any other personal activities. The two-way communication in classroom teaching is not possible in online classes, which hampers the real learning process and impacts students' understanding. Students are unable to practice and learn the content available online efficiently. Major issues in online learning are being unable to know the profile of students, technical problems associated with the location and gadgets and finally the level of understanding about the instruction for the portal (Song et al., 2004). It became a challenge for all students to balance their regular work at home and social activities with the online education. As students are unable get input in a physical platform, they are unable to achieve more success in e-learning or academic competencies. It equally affects their preparedness for various subjects, which reduces the total impact the learning system (Parkes et al., 2014).

2.3 HYPOTHESIS

Various research was conducted to find appropriate solutions for education during a pandemic like Covid-19. The online learning method became the most common method to avoid the pandemic. Many countries adopted the online teaching method to reduce the spread of the infection. Various issues related to teachers and students came to picture. This study identified through the literature review two issues: hardware related and software related. The hypothesis formulated on the basis of these two issues are given in hypotheses I and II.

2.3.1 HYPOTHESIS I

H0 = Students' and teachers' hardware issues affected them more in online education.
H1 = Students' and teachers' hardware issues affected them less in online education.

2.3.2 HYPOTHESIS II

H0 = Students' and teachers' online platform issues affected them more in online education.
H1 = Students' and teachers' online platform issues affected them less in online education.

2.4 OBJECTIVES

The e-learning system is the most accepted method of teaching during the pandemic. The literature review highlighted the focus area related to the infrastructure facilities and software-related difficulties associated with both students and teachers. The following objectives considered to evaluate real issues related to major stakeholders like students, teachers, government and finally parents. The objectives focus on whether the availability of hardware for online platforms can suffice for the requirement of students and teachers in their learning system. Finally, an appropriate online platform system must be designed which can be helpful for government, students, teachers and ultimately parents.

2.5 METHODOLOGY

The research paper is a descriptive study developed through a self-designed structured questionnaire. The structured questionnaire has questions related to the demographics and behavior of students and teachers. Various scales were utilized, but for the variables of behavior, the Likert scale or five-point scale was used to verify the degree of associations. A convenient sampling method was used to get responses from students and teachers of various schools, colleges and universities. The most developed cities like Khurda, Cuttack, Balasore, Berhampur and Sambalpur (districts of Odisha, an eastern State of India) were considered for the research. During the pandemic the easiest method was convenient sampling, which was implemented for its cost-effectiveness and to get a better rate of response (Eze et al., 2011; Ritchie et al., 2014).

The total respondents selected for this study was 300, who belong to different age groups of students from the various institutions of Odisha, out of which 270 gave their response in the survey, which gives a rate of response of 90%. The data was collected at various districts through personal contact in their homes during the lockdown period of the government. Out of 270 responses only 250 responses were valid to consider for further analysis. The data from the responses were codified and edited for the further analysis through the statistical software SPSS and AMOS.

2.6 ANALYSIS AND FINDINGS

2.6.1 DEMOGRAPHIC PROFILE

The data through questionnaire are analyzed on the basis of statistical tools to quantify the results and inferences. Data shown in the Table 2.1 contains the demographics of students in the e-learning process during Covid-19 in five districts of Odisha (Khurda, Cuttack, Balasore, Berhampur and Sambalpur).

In Table 2.1 the students' family income is above Rs. 60,000 per month not considered for the study as they can access all the facilities. Among the parents of the students selected, 38.0% are government salaried employees, 20.4% are private sector salaried employees, 19.2% are businesspeople and 22.4% are professionals. The

TABLE 2.1
Demographic Profile of the Students

Type	Particulars	Frequency	Percentage
Gender			
	Boys	174	70.4
	Girls	76	29.6
Age			
	Less than 15	120	48
	15–20	88	35.2
	20–25	42	16.8
	More than 25	0	0
Educational Qualification			
	School	37	14.8
	College	58	23.2
	University	95	38
	Professional Degree	60	24
Family Occupation			
	Govt. Salaried Employee	95	38
	Pvt. Salaried Employee	51	20.4
	Businessman	48	19.2
	Professionals	56	22.4
Family Income per Month			
	Less than 30K	58	23.2
	30K–60K	144	57.6
	Above 60K	48	19.2

age profile of respondents is 48% of age less than 15 years, 35.2% of age 15–20 years and 16.8% of 20–25 years.

2.6.2 CHI-SQUARE TEST-I

The Pearson chi-square value shown in Table 2.2 is 138.726, with the p-value of 0.016 less than 0.05. This rejects the null hypothesis and accepts alternative hypothesis with 95% level of significance, i.e.,

> *H1 = Students' and teachers' hardware issues affected them less in online education.*

That shows that the hardware or infrastructure issues are less associated with the effects of learning between students and teachers.

2.6.3 CHI-SQUARE TEST-II

The value of chi-square statistics in Table 2.3 is 17.325, with a p-value of 0.834, which is more than 0.05. Hence, the null hypothesis is accepted with 95% level of significance, i.e.,

> *H0 = Students' and teachers' software platform issues affected them more in online education.*

TABLE 2.2
Pearson Chi-Square Value

	Value	df	Asymp. Sig. (2-sided)
Pearson Chi-Square	138.726[a]	120	.016
Likelihood Ratio	135.404	120	.059
Linear-by-Linear Association	.547	1	.060
N of Valid Cases	222		

[a] 139 cells (96.5%) have an expected count of less than 5. The minimum expected count is .07.

TABLE 2.3
Chi-Square Statistics Values

	Value	df	Asymp. Sig. (2-sided)
Pearson Chi-Square	17.325[a]	24	.834
Likelihood Ratio	17.368	24	.833
Linear-by-Linear Association	.287	1	.592
N of Valid Cases	304		

[a] 11 cells (30.6%) have an expected count of less than 5. The minimum expected count is 1.30.

That shows that the software platform issues are more associated with the effect of learning between students and teachers.

2.6.4 INFRASTRUCTURE ISSUES IN ONLINE LEARNING

Countries like India always face major challenges in infrastructure, and education is not separated from that. The issues mostly faced by students and teachers in semi-urban and rural areas are issues related to infrastructure. Here the issues coming under the infrastructure or hardware are the availability of electricity, the compatibility of apps, financial status, strength of signal, phone operation, data storage, teachers' technology awareness, conversion of material to soft form and finally the appropriate configuration for cellphones or laptops. These variables' relative importance were studied through the data collected from both students and teachers. Confirmatory factor analysis through structural equation modeling gave the relative importance of each variable regarding students' and teachers' related issues.

2.6.5 MODEL-I (ISSUES RELATED TO HARDWARE DIFFICULTIES)

The data has gone through the multivariate normality test for regression analysis to check the normality by using the AMOS software (Arbuckle, 2012). The ratio of skewness, which is more than 1, and/or value of kurtosis, which is more than 2, rejects the normality of the data (Nunnally & Bernstein, 1994). The skewness and kurtosis of all these nine variables for both cognitive and emotional consumers are less than 1 and 2 respectively; they are accepted through the multivariate normality test (Figure 2.1).

Regression analysis was conducted to verify that the hypothetical statistical model will fit the data collected through the questionnaire. The chi-square value of 10.56 with the p-value of 0.004 signifies a goodness of fit of data in the model, having nine independent variables and two dependent variables for regression analysis. All the indices' value may not be acceptable for a model fit, but the strength of one index may compensate for the weakness of the others (March et al., 1995). For structural equation modelling the most acceptable indices are comparative fit index (CFI), the goodness of fit (GFI) and the incremental fit index (IFI), whose ranges are mostly between 0 to 1; more than 0.9 indicates the better fit (Wang et al., 1996). 'Acceptable model fit is indicated by a CFI value of 0.90 or greater' (Hu & Bentler, 1999). The normed fit index (NFI) and non-normed fit index (NNFI) are two other parameters to verify the extent of the model fit (Bentler & Bonet, 1980). The confirmatory factor analysis with the hardware-related issues of students and teachers is CFI=0.907, NFI=0.860 and IFI=0.910 respectively, which is quite acceptable for the goodness of fit. The RMSEA (root means square error of approximation) value of less than 0.05 describes a 'close fit', but the value of more than 0.05 is not acceptable for the model (Browne & Cudeck, 1989). For issues related to hardware for the students' and teachers' cases, the RMSEA value is 0.083, which is less or nearer to 0.05 and hence accepted for a good model. In order to construct the appropriate model fit, it can be advantageous to refer to a variety of fit indices.

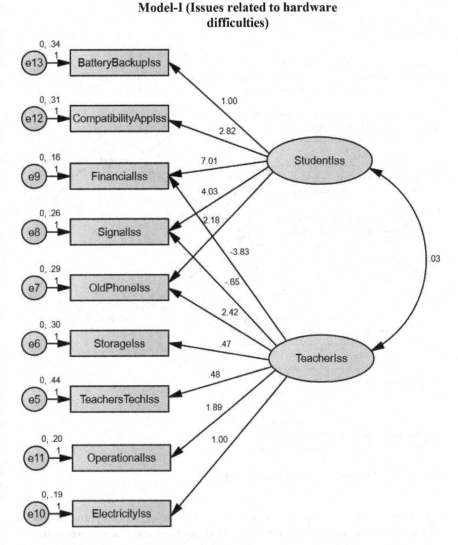

Model-I (Issues related to hardware difficulties)

FIGURE 2.1 Issues related to hardware difficulties.

2.6.6 Software Platform Issues in Online Learning

At the students' and teachers' level, introducing a new software platform and training them with a limited period of time and expecting 100% accuracy in learning is a great challenge for all the software companies. The software which was already designed for e-learning has certain limitations and is price sensitive (Figure 2.2). It was a great challenge to introduce a platform to reduce the burden on students and teachers for effective education. The software-platform-related issues considered here are download related, logging in to the platform, quantity of data consumption, online video,

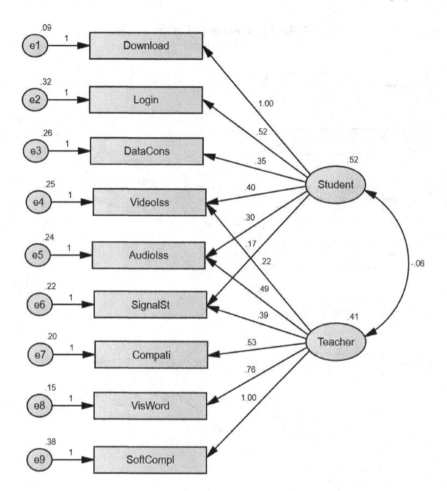

FIGURE 2.2   Software issues in online learning.

audio, signal related, compatibility with the phone, word visibility and finally the software's inability to perform. The opinions of students and teachers were taken on the basis of these platform-related issues, and the relative importance of those variables can be known through the confirmatory factor analysis. The following results came with the relative correlation with the variables.

2.6.7 MODEL-II (ISSUES RELATED TO SOFTWARE PLATFORM DIFFICULTIES)

For the issues related to the software platform, CFI=0.862, RFI=0.745, TLI=0.784 and IFI=0.865 respectively, which is quite acceptable for goodness of fit. For issues related to hardware for students' and teachers' cases, the CFA RMSEA value is 0.017, which is less or nearer to 0.05 and hence accepted for good model. In order to construct the appropriate model fit, it can be advantageous to refer to a variety of fit indices.

2.6.8 POSSIBLE SOLUTIONS FOR PROBLEMS

Instant difficulties in communication due to new technology adoption can be reduced through prerecorded contents and early experimentation with the digital platform with audiences. Social media is one of the most common mediums to communicate information to students. Communication directly becomes important when texts, messaging through various applications and videos are unable to fulfill the requirement of the students. The improvement of the quality of education should be done continuously to give support to teachers for a better learning platform. Courses' quality can be improved through continuous upgrade and academic research activities. Greater focus should be given to e-learning systems to make them more creative, relevant to students, interactive in nature and finally related to group education (Partlow & Gibbs, 2003). Continuous information related to instructions must be developed by educators for the effectiveness of e-learning systems. Online instructions can create a better feedback system with effective question and answer sessions (Keeton, 2004). 'Institutions must focus on pedagogical issues and emphasize collaborative learning, case learning, and project-based learning through online instructions' (Kim & Bonk, 2006). The challenge for educational institutions is not only to develop new technology to make better system for students and teachers but also to make their association with a digital education system for future uncertainty.

2.6.9 MODEL-III (CONCEPTUAL FRAMEWORK FOR e-LEARNING)

The previous model is a conceptual model designed to reduce the hardware- and software-related issues faced by the students and teachers during the effective learning process. This model has given higher importance to the third party who will

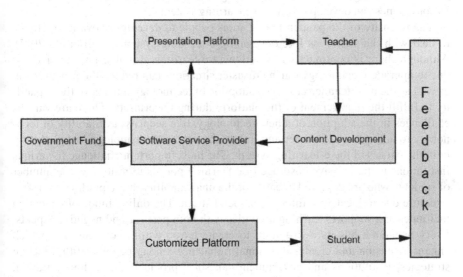

FIGURE 2.3 Conceptual framework for e-learning.

take responsibility for the risk associated with hardware and software technology. Government will fund the third party, mostly the software developers, to prepare the interactive software which will not only be a platform for interaction but also a storage device for the lectures missed by the students during any kind of difficulties. It will equally receive the lectures from the teacher without any huddle or disconnection. It will also record the lecture during internet connectivity failure and can upload during the reconnection. This will help the entire system to operate without the barrier of platform or internet or issues. Students can access the lectures anytime they need. The role of a third party will be to provide a platform with limited space consumption that will work or record without the internet connectivity.

2.7 CONCLUSIONS AND SUGGESTIONS

Depending upon the intensity of the havoc, respective plans will be formulated accordingly by government. The unpredictable environment due to the pandemic has given a lesson to students to become a warrior to solve problems, to develop the skill of critical thinking and to adapt to unconventional situations. Educational institutions should develop a plan to recover quickly from unanticipated situations to normalize their education system and increase the learning values. Educational institutions should have contingency strategies to tackle situations arising due to various natural uncertainties (Seville et al., 2012). The authenticity of available information through various sources available on the internet can help a lot to deal with drastic situations created from natural disasters (Huang et al., 2020). 'Instruction, content, motivation, relationships, and mental health are the five important things that an educator must keep in mind while imparting online education' (Martin, 2020). Most pedagogy methods like lectures, learning through case-study discussion, debates and discussions among students, learning through experience, brainstorming and playing various games can develop an effective learning system.

The intensity of the pandemic motivates people to develop innovative methods to deal with the situations like developing e-learning systems (Tull et al., 2017). Although there is continuous innovation in e-learning systems, its effectiveness due to upgraded technology during disaster situations can reduce the procurement as well as the maintenance cost. The adoption of technology must have the capability to fulfill the requirement of the platform during uncertainty. There are various challenges in the adoption of a new technology, like security, availability of technology to all, speed of internet and finally the extent of technology knowledge by both the parties of the e-learning system. The most important challenge to various institutions is the massive coverage of e-learning portals to minimize the number of students who are deprived because of the unavailability of the platform or infrastructure due to location, ethnicity or social strata. The online mode of education facilitates and supports learning activities with both positive and negative aspects. Every pandemic has its own tenure to create havoc within communities, which enhances tension and creates emotional imbalance among people. With effective strategies, institutions and government can solve problems for a short duration, which further develops an innovative system to handle long-term instability in the environment.

2.8 REFERENCES

Arbuckle, J. L. (2012). *IBM SPSS Amos 21*. Amos Development Corporation.

Basilaia, G., Dgebuadze, M., Kantaria, M., & Chokhonelidze, G. (2020). Replacing the classic learning form at universities as an immediate response to the COVID-19 virus infection in Georgia. *International Journal for Research in Applied Science & Engineering Technology*, 8(III).

Bentler, P. M., & Bonnet, D. G. (1980). Significance tests and goodness of fit in the analysis of covariance structures. *Psychological Bulletin*, 88, 588–600.

Browne, M. W., & Cudeck, R. (1989). Single sample cross-validation indices for covariance structures. *Multivariate Behavioral Research*, 24, 445–455.

Cathy, Li. *Head of media, entertainment and sport industries.* World Economic Forum, Farah Lalani, Community Curator, Media, Entertainment and Information Industries, World Economic Forum. https://www.weforum.org/agenda/2020/04/coronavirus-education-global-covid19-online-digital-learning/

Cojocariu, V.-M., Lazar, I., Nedeff, V., & Lazar, G. (2014). SWOT analysis of e-learning educational services from the perspective of their beneficiaries. *Procedia-Social and Behavioral Sciences*, 116, 1999–2003.

Eze, U. C., Manyeki, J. K., Yaw, L. H., & Har, L. C. (2011). Factors affecting internet banking adoption among young adults: Evidence from Malaysia. In *International conference on social science and humanity, IPEDR* (Vol. 11, pp. 377–381).

Hu, L., & Bentler, P. M. (1999). Cutoff criteria for fit indexes in covariance structure analysis: Conventional criteria versus new alternatives. *Structural Equation Modeling*, 6, 1–55.

Huang, R. H., Liu, D. J., Tlili, A., Yang, J. F., Wang, H. H., Zhang, M., Lu, H., Gao, B., Cai, Z., Liu, M., Cheng, W., Cheng, Q., Yin, X., Zhuang, R., Berrada, K., Burgos, D., Chan, C., Chen, N. S., Cui, W., Hu, X., et al. (2020). *Handbook on facilitating flexible learning during educational disruption: The Chinese experience in maintaining undisrupted learning in COVID-19 outbreak.* Smart Learning Institute of Beijing Normal University.

Keeton, M. T. (2004). Best online instructional practices: Report of phase I of an ongoing study. *Journal of Asynchronous Learning Networks*, 8(2), 75–100.

Kim, K.-J., & Bonk, C. J. (2006). The future of online teaching and learning in higher education: The survey says. *Educause Quarterly*, 4, 22–30.

Liguori, E. W., & Winkler, C. (2020). *From offline to online: Challenges and opportunities for entrepreneurship education following the COVID-19 pandemic.* Entrepreneurship Education and Pedagogy. https://doi.org/10.1177/2515127420916738

Littlefield, J. (2018). The difference between synchronous and asynchronous distance learning. https://www.thoughtco.com/synchronous-distance-learning-asynchronous-distance-learning-1097959

March, J. (1995). Cognitive-behavioral psychotherapy for children and adolescents with OCD: A review and recommendations for treatment. *Journal of the American Academy of Child & Adolescent Psychiatry*, 34, 7–18. [PubMed] [Google Scholar]

Martin, A. (2020). How to optimize online learning in the age of coronavirus (COVID-19): A 5- point guide for educators. https://www.researchgate.net/publication/339944395_How_to_Optimize_Online_Learning_in_the_Age_of_Coronavirus_COVID-19_A_5-Point_Guide_for_Educators

McBrien, J. L., Cheng, R., & Jones, P. (2009). Virtual spaces: Employing a synchronous online classroom to facilitate student engagement in online learning. *The International Review of Research in Open and Distributed Learning*, 10(3), 1–17.

Nunnally, J. C., & Bernstein, I. H. (1994). *Psychometric theory* (3rd ed.). McGraw-Hill.

Parkes, M., Stein, S., & Reading, C. (2014). Student preparedness for university e-learning environments. *The Internet and Higher Education*, 25, 1–10. https://doi.org/10.1016/j.iheduc.2014.10.002

Partlow, K. M., & Gibbs, W. J. (2003). Indicators of constructivist principles in internet-based courses. *Journal of Computing in Higher Education*, 14(2), 68–97.

Rieley, J. B. (2020). *Corona Virus and its impact on higher education*. Research Gate.

Ritchie, J., Lewis, J., Nicholls, C., McNaughton, J., & Ormiston, R. (2014). *Qualitative research practice: A guide for social science students and researchers*. SAGE Publications. doi:10.4135/9781452230108

Seville, E., Hawker, C., & Lyttle, J. (2012). *Resilience tested: A year and a half of ten thousand aftershocks*. University of Canterbury.

Singh, V., & Thurman, A. (2019). How many ways can we define online learning? A systematic literature review of definitions of online learning (1988–2018). *American Journal of Distance Education*, 33(4), 289–306.

Song, L., Singleton, E. S., Hill, J. R., & Koh, M. H. (2004). Improving online learning: Student perceptions of useful and challenging characteristics. *The Internet and Higher Education*, 7(1), 59–70.

Tull, S. P. C., Dabner, N., & Ayebi-Arthur, K. (2017). Social media and e-learning in response to seismic events: Resilient practices. *Journal of Open, Flexible and Distance Learning*, 21(1), 63–76.

Wang, L., Fan, X., & Willson, V. (1996). Effects of non-normal data on parameter estimates and fit indices for a model with latent and manifest variables: An empirical study. *Structural Equation Modeling*, 3, 228–247.

3 Ecological Footprint Assessment of E-Learning in India

Mohd Akram[1], Salman Baig[1], Mahboob Ahmed[2],
Dilawar Husain[2], Akbar Ahmad[3],
Mohamed Haleem[4] and Ravi Prakash[5]

1 Department of Computer Science and Engineering,
  Maulana Mukhtar Ahmad Nadvi Technical
  Campus, Malegaon, Maharashtra, India
2 Department of Mechanical Engineering,
  Maulana Mukhtar Ahmad Nadvi Technical
  Campus, Malegaon, Maharashtra, India
3 Faculty of Science and Information
  Technology, MI College, Malé, Maldives
4 Faculty of Language Education and Arts,
  MI College, Malé, Maldives
5 Department of Mechanical Engineering, Motilal Nehru
  National Institute of Technology, Allahabad, India

CONTENTS

DOI: 10.1201/9781003272823-3

3.1   INTRODUCTION

According to United Nations Sustainable Development Goals (SDGs), a sustainable education system enables upward socioeconomic mobility and is key to removing poverty (SDGs, 2015). A sustainable education system also helps to develop overall community and protect our planet. The education system can play significant role for the global progress toward sustainability (Ceulemans et al., 2015). This is accredited to the prediction of continuous development for the comprehensive education system (HM Government, 2013) and intensifying learner outlooks for sustainability actions incorporated by academic institutions all over the world (SOS, 2018). In their capacity, the key contributors of academic institutions are progressively recognized as dynamic players and supporters of the global agenda for United Nations SDGs (Figueiro and Raufflet, 2015).

Academic institutions represent significant architects of sustainable growth; they can also prominently contribute to environmental impact on the planet (Lozano et al., 2013). Academic institutions contribute energy and natural resource consumption during their operation and their associated harmful ecological externalities, particularly global warming (Scheuer et al., 2003). Academic institutions emit directly or indirectly huge amounts of greenhouse gas (GHG) emissions due to on-campus energy consumption, water use, stationary use, transportation, etc. (Shields, 2019; Wynes et al., 2019; Hawkins et al., 2012; Parece et al., 2013). Various academic institutions use different types of laboratory equipment, appliances, machineries, etc. in the campus, the carbon footprint of which may be huge and problematic upon overall assessment (Robinson et al., 2018). Institutions obtain widespread inventories of goods and services, and these academic activities can be energy-intensive (Filho et al., 2019). However, institutions generate a significant amount of waste, whose assimilation involves energy and corresponding GHG emissions (Ridhosari and Rahman, 2020).

The global spread of the pandemic COVID-19 has enforced education systems to transform from offline to online teaching-learning, the distinctive rise of e-learning being the result in an unprecedented increase in data transmission over networks (Pokhrel and Chhetri, 2021). COVID-19 has resulted in academic institutions closing due to complete nationwide lockdowns being implemented all over the globe (Gettleman and Schultz, 2020). In general, 1.2 billion students were out of the classroom during the global lockdown (WEF, 2021). Research suggests that online learning has been shown to increase retention of information and takes less time, meaning that the changes the coronavirus has caused might be here to stay. Although, these changes have an environmental impact, they have received less attention. The carbon intensity of online teaching and learning was found to be almost equal to that of staff and student commute in the pre-lockdown period

TABLE 3.1
Differences between Offline and Online Teaching-Learning Processes

Parameters	Offline Teaching-Learning	Online Teaching-Learning
Teaching Methodology	Conventional systems are used during teaching-learning	Digitized tools such as laptop, desktop, tablet, and mobile etc. are used during teaching-learning
Accessibility	Only location specific learning is possible	Connect through cloud from anywhere in the world
Affordability	Transportation cost, overall cost of institution become these learning expensive	Relatively low-cost learning
Flexible	Dependent on location and proper schedule	Based on convenience of students and teachers
Tools	Traditional tools (i.e., board, chalk, papers and pen, etc.)	Digitalized tools (internet communication system and digital teaching aid appliances, etc.)
Efficiency	Less efficient and relatively time taking teaching-learning process	More efficient and time saving teaching-learning process
Environmental impact	Relatively high environmental impact teaching-learning process	Relatively low environmental impact teaching-learning process

(Filimonau et al., 2021). There is environmental impact through sustainable tools. One of the main advantages of the online mode of teaching and learning is that it can easily be accessed from rural and remote areas. In comparison, it is relatively cheaper in terms of transportation cost and overall cost for the institution (Dhawan, 2020). The parameters associated with online teaching and learning are listed in Table 3.1.

3.1.1 ONLINE/OFFLINE TEACHING-LEARNING PROCESS

Technological development enhanced the quality of e-learning. Online teaching-learning is a learner-centric practice that increases learners' interest and involvement in virtual studies. Teaching assistance plays a significant role in effective communication with learners. Various digital platforms are used by teachers to share knowledge to learners in online teaching-learning. It offers the liberty to each individual to study, teach and develop skills according to learners' capacity. It provides face-to-face interaction with the learners. It needs computing devices with high-speed network facility.

Although offline teaching-learning offers a physical learning environment for learners within the academic institution's buildings, it provides face-to-face interaction between learners and teachers. Active communication is only possible in offline teaching-learning. The schematic diagrams of online and offline teaching-learning are depicted in Figure 3.1 (a. b).

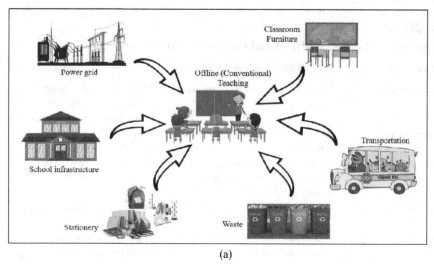

(a)

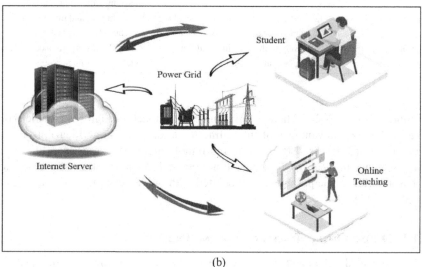

(b)

FIGURE 3.1   (a) Schematic representation of offline teaching-learning; (b) Schematic representation of online teaching-learning.

3.1.2 ECOLOGICAL FOOTPRINT (EF)

Mathis and Rees developed the ecological footprint analysis for the quantitative environmental assessment of human activity (Wackernagel and Rees, 1996). The assessment tool can be applied to different sustainable measures for the feasibility of the proper distribution of the bio-capacity of the zone/country/planet. The analysis considered all resources such as energy, materials, water, human activities, etc. considered as input and converts into a single parameter. The unit of EF (i.e., global hectare) is defined as "one gha is equivalent to one hectare of bio-productive land with world average productivity".

The study endorses United Nations Sustainable Development Goal 4 (Quality Education). A quantitative assessment of two different (offline and online) teaching-learning techniques has been done in this case study. The literacy rate in India is about 75%, and most of the population (70%) live in rural areas; there is a scarcity of internet connection. This study may help to assess the overall estimation of resource use as well as the environmental impact due to online/offline teaching-learning in India. It also helpful to explore the feasibility and imprint reduction potential in the education system of the country.

3.2 METHODOLOGY

The ecological footprint assessment of online/offline teaching learning modes has been done in this study. The globalization and communication techniques help to enhance the teaching- learning processes; therefore, a comparative assessment of online/offline teaching-learning processes is required to understand global education systems.

3.2.1 EF OF TEACHING-LEARNING

The offline/online teaching systems are responsible for different types of resource uses; therefore, the environmental impact of offline/online teaching systems should be examined. The ecological footprint of online/offline teaching systems depends on four factors: (1) internet use, (2) teaching tools, (3) stationary and (4) transportation of teachers/students. The system boundary for the estimation of the ecological footprint of offline/online teaching is depicted in Figure 3.2. The ecological footprint of teaching-learning process as calculated by Eq. 3.1 is as follows:

$$EF_E = EF_i + EF_{ta} + EF_s + EF_a + EF_t \tag{3.1}$$

where EFm represents EF of internet use during teaching-learning process; EFta represents EF of direct energy consumption in teaching appliances like laptops, desktops, tablets, mobiles, etc.; EFs represents EF of stationary consumption; and EFt represents transportation impact of teachers/students.

3.2.1.1 EF of Internet Use (EFi)

The information communications and technology industries provide internet and other cloud services. The electricity demand reaches up to 1% of the global energy demand to maintain data centers (Masanet et al., 2020); it is also responsible for up to 3.6% of the total global emissions. Internet use has GHG emissions ranging from 28 to 63 gCO_2 equivalent per gigabyte (Obringer et al., 2021). The imprint of internet use on the planet should be examined through sustainability tools. The ecological footprint of internet use in online/offline teaching-learning processes as calculated by Eq. 3.2 is as follows:

$$EF_i = \sum t_i . a_i . \frac{(1 - Aoc)}{Af} . e_{CO_{2\,land}} \tag{3.2}$$

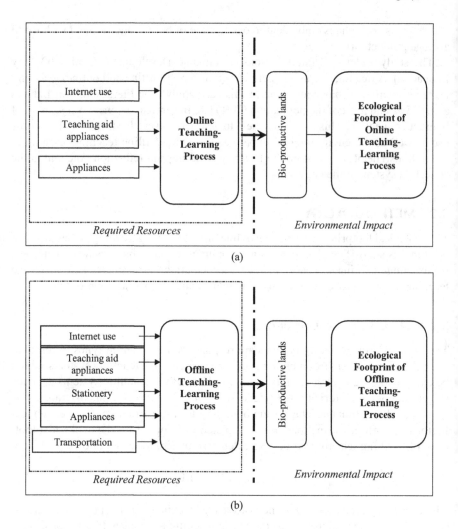

FIGURE 3.2   (a, b) System boundary for offline/online teaching-learning.

where ti represents the time of internet use (in hour) and ai represents the carbon emissions per hour during internet use. Carbon emissions depend on the mode of internet use like video streaming, without video streaming, general surfing etc. Aoc represents the fraction of annual oceanic anthropogenic CO_2 sequestration, and Af is the annual rate of carbon uptake/hectare of forestland at world average yield. eCO2 land represents the equivalence factor of carbon absorption land. All the parameters and ecological footprint of internet use are mentioned in Table 3.2.

3.2.1.2 EF of Teaching Aid Appliances

Electronic devices like laptops, desktops, tablets, projectors, smart boards, etc. are necessary for education systems. These important/supporting equipment help

TABLE 3.2
Details about the Different Parameters and Their Ecological Footprint

Parameters	Capacity	Emissions Rate	Ecological Footprint
Standard videoconferencing	2.5GB/hr (Obringer et al., 2021)	0.157 kgCO$_2$/hr	5.21 × 10^{-5} gha/hr
Ultra HD or 4K		0.441 kgCO$_2$/hr	0.000146347 gha/hr
Video turned off		0.02513 kgCO$_2$/hr	8.34 × 10^{-6} gha/hr
Laptop	60–90 watt per hour (DEB, 2017)		2.36–3.54 × 10^{-5} gha/hr
Desktop	60–200 Watts per hour (DEB, 2017)		2.36–7.87 × 10^{-5} gha/hr
Mobile		0.17260274 kgCO$_2$/hr	5.73 × 10^{-5} gha/hr
Tablet	2.5–10 Watts per hour (HXED, 2021)		9.84 × 10^{-7}–2.46 × 10^{-6} gha/hr
Internet use	60–150 MB/hr	28–63 gCO$_2$/GB (Obringer et al., 2021)	1.55 × 10^{-6} gha/hr
Transportation			
Bike (petrol)		0.0385 kgCO$_2$/km	1.2 × 10^{-5} gha/km
Car (diesel)	5–7 person	0.2676 kgCO$_2$/km	8.89 × 10^{-5} gha/km
Car (CNG)	5–7 person	0.2306 kgCO$_2$/km	7.65 × 10^{-5} gha/km
Car (electric)	5–7 person	0.1562 kgCO$_2$/km	5.18 × 10^{-5} gha/km
Car (petrol)	5–7 person	0.2376 kgCO$_2$/km	7.89 × 10^{-5} gha/km
Bus	50 persons	3.17 kgCO$_2$/kg of fuel; 0.238 kg of fuel/km (EEA, 2013)	2.5 × 10^{-4} gha/km
Appliances			
Light	9W		3.54 × 10^{-6} gha/hr
Fan	70 W		2.76 × 10^{5} gha/hr
Air-conditioning	1450–1650W		3.80–4.1 × 10^{-4} gha/hr
Exhaust fan	200W–300W		7.8 × 10^{-5}–1.18 × 10^{-4} gha/hr
Projector	250W–350W		9.83 × 10^{-5}–1.38 × 10^{-4} gha/hr
Smart board	150W–220W		5.90 × 10^{-5}–8.66 × 10^{-5} gha/hr
Stationary			
Papers		3.73 kgCO$_2$/kg (ICE, 2016)	0.0123 gha/kg
Pen/pencil		0.02155 kgCO$_2$/unit	7.15 × 10^{-5} gha/unit
Chalk			0.000107 gha/kg

(Continued)

TABLE 3.2 *(Continued)*

Details about the Different Parameters and Their Ecological Footprint

Equivalence Factor (ei)	Bio Productive Land	Value (GFN, 2016)
$e_{crop\ land}$ $e_{pasture\ land}$ $e_{forest\ land}$	Cropland, pastureland, forestland, CO_2 land	2.52 gha/ha
$e_{CO2\ land}$ $e_{marine\ land}$		0.43 gha/ha
$e_{built\text{-}up\ land}$	Marine/sea productive land, built-up land	1.28 gha/ha
		1.28 gha/ha
		0.35 gha/ha
		2.52 gha/ha
A_{oc}		0.3 (SIO, 2017)
A_f		2.68 tCO_2/ha (Husain and Prakash, 2019)

to enhance the teaching-learning process. The ecological footprint of teaching aid appliances in online/offline teaching-learning process as calculated by Eq. 3.3 is as follows:

$$EF_{ta} = \sum k_i . b_i . \frac{(1-Aoc)}{Af} . e_{CO_2\ land} \qquad (3.3)$$

where k_i represents the time of teaching aid appliances use (in hour) and b_i represent the carbon emission factor of different appliances. The ecological footprint of different types of teaching aids are mentioned in Table 3.2.

3.2.1.3 EF of Stationery (EFs)

The ecological footprint of stationary use is an important parameter; it has a significant impact on the teaching-learning process (offline). The ecological footprint of stationery use in online/offline teaching-learning process as calculated by Eq. 3.4 is as follows:

$$EF_s = \sum S_i . c_i . \frac{(1-Aoc)}{Af} . e_{CO_2\ land} \qquad (3.4)$$

where S_i represents the consumption of different types of stationery (in tonne) and c_i represents the embodied emissions factor of corresponding stationery. The ecological footprint of different types of stationery are mentioned in Table 3.2.

3.2.1.4 EF of Appliances (EFa)

All the appliances use such as light, fan, exhaust fan, heating/cooling systems, etc. (except teaching aids) during offline/online teaching-learning are considered to assess the impact of appliances. The ecological footprint of appliances used in online/offline teaching-learning processes as calculated by Eq. 3.5 is as follows:

$$EF_a = \sum A_i . P_i . \frac{(1-Aoc)}{Af} . e_{CO_2\ land} \qquad (3.5)$$

where A_i represents the time of different appliances use (on hour) and P_i represents the embodied emissions factor of corresponding appliances use during online/offline teaching-learning process. The ecological footprint of different types of appliances is mentioned in Table 3.2.

3.2.1.5 EF of Transportation (EFt)

The EFt depends on student/teacher transportation from their houses to the lecture room in an institute. The EFt is estimated by Eq. 3.6:

$$EF_t = \Sigma \left\{ (T_i . D_i) E_v . \left(\frac{1 - A_{OC}}{A_f} \right) . e_{CO_2 \, land} \right\} \tag{3.6}$$

where Ti represents the total number of students/teachers involved in theteaching-learning process. Di represents the average distance traveled by students and teachers. Ev represents the emissions rate of vehicles used by students and teachers. The ecological footprint of different types of transportation mediums are mentioned in Table 3.2.

3.3   CASE STUDY

The case study considered the teaching-learning system of Maulana Mukhtar Ahmad Nadvi Technical Campus (MMANTC), Malegaon (Maharashtra), India. The institute provides different courses in engineering streams; however, engineering education is always considered as an outcome-based learning process. The education system of the institute transformed from offline mode to online mode during the pandemic's (due to COVID-19) spread all over the state. The environmental impact of the offline to online shift has been considered in this study. The ecological footprint assessment of the one-hour teaching-learning process has been evaluated for the 40 students of the institute. The modes of online/offline teaching-learning processes are mentioned as follows:

3.1   Online teaching-learning is the process of educating others on virtual platforms. This type of teaching involves virtual classes, videoconferencing, webinars and other online tools. The online applications are developed and designed to facilitate easy learning and better understanding. To carry out the case study, two modes of online teaching have been considered in MMANTC during the lockdown period.

Mode I: In this scenario, the internet used for the remote conduction of teaching without video streaming has been considered for a one-hour lecture in the MMANTC. The teaching aids such as laptops, desktops, tablets, etc. have been taken into account by the students and teachers. Appliances (i.e., lighting, fan, HVAC system, etc.) for a better environment for the attendees of online lectures are also considered.

Mode II: In this scenario, all the factors of Mode I have been considered, with video-streaming facilities incorporated during the online lectures.

3.2 **Offline teaching-learning** also refers to traditional/conventional teaching-learning process. In this teaching-learning process: learners/students need to go to the academic institution physically to interact with teachers. To carry out the case study, two modes of offline teaching-learning for one hour has been considered in MMANTC during the lockdown period.

Mode I: In this scenario, a conventional teaching methodology considered that provided during normal conditions. Techers take physical classes through chalk and board, and students use paper and pen to record lecture notes during lectures.

Mode II: In this scenario, to assess the physical teaching through smart classrooms that consist of projectors/smart boards and teaching aid appliances used with internet access.

3.4 RESULTS

The main difference between the online and offline teaching-learning processes is the communication medium and location. In the online teaching-learning process, the student and teacher only need to log on to the internet from anywhere. There is no need to travel to the institute location. In the offline teaching-learning process, the student and teacher are required to travel to the institute location. The ecological footprint assessment of the online/offline teaching-learning process for the case institute is evaluated as follows:

3.4.1 EF OF TEACHING-LEARNING

The ecological footprint of online teaching-learning for Mode I and Mode II are 2.82×10^{-3} gha/hr and 4.62×10^{-3} gha/hr, respectively. The ecological footprint of offline teaching-learning for Mode I and Mode II are 3.86×10^{-2} gha/hr and 3.88×10^{-2} gha/hr, respectively. The results indicate that the online teaching-learning has a comparatively lower environmental impact than offline teaching-learning (i.e., 7.2% to 11.9% of the offline teaching-learning). The details of the ecological footprint assessment are explained as follows:

3.4.1.1 EF of Internet Use (EFi)

The ecological footprint of internet use depends on the communication medium, speed of data consumption, data transfer, etc. The ecological footprint of online teaching-learning for Mode I and Mode II are 3.42×10^{-4} gha/hr and 2.13×10^{-3} gha/hr, respectively. In offline teaching-learning Mode I, the internet was not used during the lecture; therefore, the internet impact is zero for this mode of teaching. The ecological footprint of internet use in offline teaching-learning for Mode II is 1.55×10^{-6} gha/hr.

3.4.1.2 EF of Teaching Aid Appliances

The ecological footprint of teaching aid appliances in the online teaching-learning process for Mode I is a range of 1×10^{-4} gha/hr to 2.1×10^{-3} gha/hr. The average value of the ecological footprint of teaching aid appliances is the same (i.e., 1.2×10^{-3} gha/hr) for both Mode I and Mode II of the online teaching-learning process. In offline teaching-learning Mode I, the teaching aid appliances were not used during the lecture; therefore, the impact of teaching aid appliances is zero for this mode of teaching. However, the ecological footprint of teaching aid appliances in the offline teaching-learning process for Mode II is a range of 2.45×10^{-6} gha/hr to 7.28×10^{-5} gha/hr. The average value of the ecological footprint of teaching aid appliances is about 1.48×10^{-4} gha/hr for Mode II of the offline teaching-learning process.

3.4.1.3 EF of Stationery (EFs)

Stationary use has a significant impact on the offline teaching-learning process. The ecological footprint of stationary use is estimated as 8.3×10^{-4} gha/hr (Mode I) and 8.1×10^{-4} gha/hr (Mode II). In online teaching-learning, stationary was not used during the lecture; therefore, the stationary use impact is zero for online teaching-learning.

3.4.1.4 EF of Appliances (EFa)

The ecological footprint of appliances used during the offline teaching-learning process is about 1.87×10^{-4} gha/hr for both the modes. In the lecture room, 6 LED bulbs and 6 fans are used during offline lecture and without the use of a heating/cooling system. During online teaching, only a single LED bulb and single fan were used; therefore, the EF of appliances used during online teaching-learning is about 1.27×10^{-3} gha/hr for both the modes.

3.4.1.5 EF of Transportation (EFt)

The significant difference between the online and offline teaching-learning processes is transportation. In the online teaching-learning process, the student and teacher only need to log on to the internet from anywhere. However, during offline teaching-learning, the student and teacher need to travel to the institute location. The details of the transportation medium and pattern for the institute members (student/teacher) are mentioned in Table 3.3. The ecological footprint of transportation for offline teaching-learning for the students and teachers of the institute is about 0.0377 gha for both the modes.

The EF distribution analysis for offline teaching-learning and online teaching-learning of Modes I and II are demonstrated in Figure 3.3 (a-d). The EF of transportation has a major impact on Modes I and II of offline teaching-learning, as shown in Figure 3.3 (a) and (b). The EF of transportation for offline teaching-learning is about 97.4% in Mode I and 97% in Mode II. The other parameters, stationery and appliances, contribute about 2.1% and 0.5% respectively both in Mode I and Mode II. The teaching aid appliances and internet access contribute about 0.8% and 1%, respectively.

There is no contribution of transportation in online teaching-learning, as the student and teacher can access and log on to the internet from any location. The only contributions in Modes I and II of online teaching-learning are appliances, teaching aid and internet use. The EF of appliances contribute more in Mode I at about 45.1% than in Mode II at about 27.6. Also, the EF of teaching aids contributes more in Mode I at about 42.8% than in Mode II at about 26.2%. There in an increase in the EF of internet use in Mode II at 46.2% due to video streaming and 12.1% in Mode I due

TABLE 3.3
Details of Transportation Ecological Footprint of MMANTC Students/Teachers

S.No	Medium	Percentage	Range	EF (gha)
1	Public transport (bus)	25%	0–2 km	0.002.5
			2–5 km	0.01
			5–10 km	0.02
2	Bike	70%	0–2 km	0.00035
			2–5 km	0.0014
			5–10 km	0.0028
3	Car	1%	0–2 km	3.5×10^{-5}
			2–5 km	1.4×10^{-4}
			5–10 km	2.8×10^{-4}
4	Bicycle	4%	0–2 km	-
			2–5 km	-
			5–10 km	-
Total EF of transportation				**0.0377 gha**

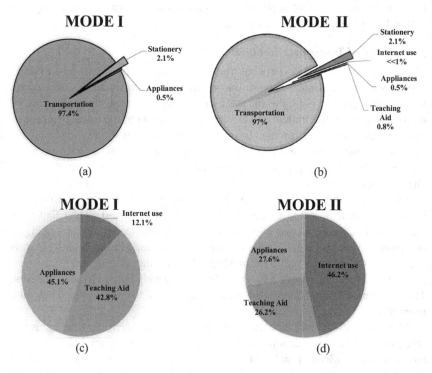

FIGURE 3.3 (a) EF distribution in offline teaching of Mode I in MMANTC; (b) EF distribution in offline teaching of Mode II in MMANTC; (c) EF distribution in online teaching of Mode I in MMANTC; (d) EF distribution in online teaching of mode II in MMANTC.

to low data involved in this mode of teaching-learning. It is also seen that the EF of appliances varies in Modes I and II of online teaching-learning, whereas it remains the same in Mode I and Mode II of offline teaching-learning. There is a significant increase of 34.1% of internet use in Mode II of online teaching-learning in comparison to Mode I. Conversely, only 1% of internet use in seen in Mode II of offline teaching-learning.

3.5 CONCLUSIONS

The study represents an effort to rise sustainability issues in offline/online teaching-learning processes, and it estimates the environmental impact of offline/online teaching-learning processes. The research work helps to identify a sustainable education system with statistical data that emphasizes to achieve the United Nations Sustainable Development Goal 4. Regarding the known promise toward the SDGs, the ecological footprint assessment of offline/online teaching-learning processes is promoted as knowledge multipliers on SDGs. The research work has a limit in estimating the overall impact of online/offline teaching processes on the planet. It has not considered the impact of the building infrastructure, water use and the life cycle impact of appliances used during the teaching-learning process.

For suggestions to policy makers, the research has recognized some sections which need attention. Transportation and appliance use play a significant role in the teaching-learning process; it should be efficient for a sustainable education system.

3.6 REFERENCES

Ceulemans, K., Molderez, I., van Liedekerke, L., 2015. "Sustainability reporting in higher education: A comprehensive review of the recent literature and paths for further research". *Journal of Cleaner Production* 106, 127–134.

Dhawan, S., 2020. "Online learning: A panacea in the time of COVID-19 crisis". *Journal of Educational Technology Systems* 49 (1), 5–22. https://doi.org/10.1177/0047239520934018

Direct Energy Business(DEB), 2017. https://business.directenergy.com/blog/2017/november/laptops-vs- desktops-energy-efficiency (Accessed on 25/01/2021)

European Environment Agency (EEA), 2013. "EMEP/EEA Air Pollutant Emission Inventory Guidebook—2013". http://www.eea.europa.eu/publications/emep-eea-guidebook-2013

Figueiro, P. S., Raufflet, E., 2015. "Sustainability in higher education: A systematic review with focus on management education". *Journal of Cleaner Production* 106, 22–33.

Filho, W. L., Skouloudis, A., Brandli, L. L., Salvia, A. L., Avila, L. V., Rayman-Bacchus, L., 2019. "Sustainability and procurement practices in higher education institutions: barriers and drivers". *Journal of Cleaner Production* 231, 1267–1280.

Filimonau, V., Dave A., Bellamy, L., Smith, N., Wintrip, R., 2021. "The carbon footprint of a UK University during the COVID-19 lockdown". *Science of the Total Environment* 756, 143964. https://doi.org/10.1016/j.scitotenv.2020.143964

Gettleman, J., Schultz, K. (24 March 2020). "Modi Orders 3-Week Total Lockdown for All 1.3 Billion Indians". *The New York Times.* ISSN 0362–4331

Hawkins, D., Hong, S.M., Raslan, R., Mumovic, D., Hanna, S., 2012. "Determinants of energy use in UK higher education buildings using statistical and artificial neural network methods". *International Journal of Sustainable Built Environment* 1 (1), 50–63.

HM Government, 2013. *International Education–Global Growth and Prosperity: An Accompanying Analytical Narrative.* UK's Department for Business, Innovation and Skills.

Husain, D., Prakash, R., "Ecological footprint reduction of built envelope in India". *Journal of Building Engineering* 21 (2019), 278–286. https://doi.org/10.1016/j.jobe.2018.10.018

HXED. https://www.h3xed.com/mobile/how-much-power-does-a-phone-or-tablet-use-while-charging (Accessed on 27/05/2021)

Geoff Hammond and Craig Jones. Sustainable Energy Research team, "*Embodied energy and Carbon construction materials*", Proc. Instn. Civil Engrs., 2008.

Lozano, R., Lukman, R., Lozano, F.J., Huisingh, D., Lambrechts, W., 2013. "Declarations for sustainability in higher education: Becoming better leaders, through addressing the university system". *Journal of Cleaner Production* 48, 10–19.

Masanet, E., Shehabi, A., Lei, N., Smith, S., Koomey, J., 2020. "Recalibrating global data center energy-use estimates". *Science* 367 (6481), 984–986.

Obringer, R., Nateghi, R., Rachunok, B., Madani, K., 2021 "The overlooked environmental footprint of increasing Internet use". *Resources, Conservation & Recycling* 167, 105389.

Parece, T., Grossman, L., Geller, E., 2013. "Reducing carbon footprint of water consumption: a case study of water conservation at a university campus". *Climate Change and Water Resources* 25, 199–218.

Pokhrel, S., Chhetri, R., "A literature review on impact of COVID-19 pandemic on teaching and learning". *Higher Education for the Future* 8 (1), 2021133–2021141.

Ridhosari, B., Rahman, A., 2020. "Carbon footprint assessment at Universitas Pertamina from the scope of electricity, transportation, and waste generation: Toward a green campus and promotion of environmental sustainability". *Journal of Cleaner Production* 246, 119172.

Robinson, O.J., Tewkesbury, A., Kemp, S., Williams, I.D., 2018. "Towards a universal carbon footprint standard: A case study of carbon management at universities". *Journal of Cleaner Production* 172, 4435–4455.

Scheuer, C., Keoleian, G., Reppe, P., 2003. "Life cycle energy and environmental performance of a new university building: Modeling challenges and design implications". *Energy and Buildings* 35 (10), 1049–1064.

Scripps Institution of Oceanography (SIO), 2017. "The keeling curve". https://scripps.ucsd.edu/programs/keelingcurve/2013/07/03/how-much-co2-can-the-oceans-take-up/ (Accessed on 23/3/2020)

Shields, R., 2019. "The sustainability of international higher education: Student mobility and global climate change". *Journal of Cleaner Production* 217, 594–602.

Students Organising for Sustainability (SOS), 2018. "Student expectations for action on sustainability as strong as ever". https://sustainability.nus.org.uk/articles/student-expectations-for-action-on- sustainability-as-strong-as-ever (Accessed on 12/8/2021)

United Nations Sustainable Development Goals (SDGs), 2015. https://www.un.org/sustainabledevelopment/education/

Wackernagel, M., Rees, W., 1996. *Our ecological footprint: Reducing human impact on the earth*. New Society, Gabriola Island, British Columbia.

World Economic Forum (WEF), 2021. "The COVID-19 pandemic has changed education forever. This is how". https://www.weforum.org/agenda/2020/04/coronavirus-education-global-covid19-online-digital-learning/

Wynes, S., Donner, S.D., Tannason, S., Nabors, N., 2019. "Academic air travel has a limited influence on professional success". *Journal of Cleaner Production* 226, 959–967.

4 The Environmental Impact of Online Education

Manjusha Tomar and Ashwin Tomar
Indira College of Engineering & Management
Pune, India

CONTENTS

4.1 INTRODUCTION

In this day and age, education has become unimaginable without technology, which has now become as essential as pen and paper for students. Twenty-first-century students are growing up with affinity for technology. The technology is easy, comfortable and helpful because it elevates learning.

Under traditional learning, which is face-to-face learning, children passively absorb information by skimming through textbooks and sitting for classes. Many of the factors that create physical constraints and infrastructural demands in traditional face-to-face teaching become less relevant in the online mode of teaching. The time and effort required in face-to-face learning is more compared to an online system. It is teacher-based rather than learner-centric. Teaching and learning depend on both the element of the system (i.e., teacher, student) and their relationship. To win a battle a Lord Krishna–like teacher and Arjuna-like student are required with a very good interaction and relationship between them. The quality of traditional classroom learning in India is affected due to its huge population, poor infrastructure (like bad roads, ill-equipped schools and colleges), poverty, child labor, lack of awareness, inadequacy of good and qualified teachers, poor educational system and unemployment.

It targets the local audience. The paper incorporates a literature review, a SWOC analysis and the predicted environmental impact of online education.

4.2 LITERATURE REVIEW

Distance education, also known as distance learning, is the education of students who may not always be physically present at a school. Distance learning means education and training is beyond the limits of time and place for learner and teacher (i.e., anyone, anyway, anywhere and anytime separated physically) [1].

An online school (virtual school or e-school or cyberschool) teaches students through the internet. Virtual education is the use of information and communication technologies to deliver educational programs and courses [2].

Online learning may refer to e-learning in education. *E-learning* refers to the intentional use of computers, the internet and networked information and communications technology in teaching and learning [3]. Data can be accessed using computers. A number of other terms are also used to describe this mode of teaching and learning. They include *online learning, virtual learning, distributed learning, network* and *web-based learning.*

The letter "e" in e-learning stands for the word "electronic". E-learning would incorporate all educational activities that are carried out by individuals or groups working online or offline and synchronously or asynchronously via networked or standalone computers and other electronic devices. *E-learning* is all about learning with the use of technology, presumably computers and other modern-day tools (technology and communication infrastructure) for teaching and learning delivery [4]. The rapid growth of information and communication technology (ICT) has made teaching and learning delivery easy. Technologies like augmented reality, virtual reality, cloud computing, mobile applications and cybersecurity are bringing impact and forcing society to change. The brick university has to be replaced with click technology due to the World Wide Web. Advances in open-source software cheap hardware have led to an e-learning revolution where students can access a plethora of learning materials easily and conveniently. Computer technology plays a significant role in promoting e-learning in India. Revolution in mobile technology has brought knowledge and information to our fingertips by smartphones. A mathematical model, Web-Based Virtual Classroom System (WebVCS), was developed to provide a viable medium through which sound education can be offered in tertiary institutions that can cater a variety of learners irrespective of their abilities, dispositions and geographical locations [5].

In online classes, students can benefit from flexible access to lectures and instructors and can engage with the learning material at their own convenience. The degree to which the efficiency gains positively influence them needs further study [6]. The *learning outcomes* of information technology in face-to-face learning and online learning varies from student to student. The learning outcome is seen in terms of performance. The *performance outcome* of students in face-to-face learning is said to be better than online e-learning for adult students.

The aim of this work is to measure the service quality of online teaching delivered during the COVID-19 period. Universities need to redefine their online format by integrating methodological and technological decisions and involving collaboration between teachers, students and administration staff and services [7].

There are 3 aspects in designing such a system: system quality, information quality and service quality. The system should be designed in such a way that it should deliver slides, audio, scripts, case studies, practice problems, tutorials, assignments and practice exams. This will lead to user satisfaction. The outcome of this system is enhanced learning, time savings and academic success [8].

4.3 SWOC ANALYSIS

Education and training are strategic tools that a society needs to continuously apply to sustain a global competitive advantage and create a better standard of living and development. Increasingly, several universities worldwide, including some in India, are making positive attempts to implement e-learning strategies in order to enhance equity and quality, share instruction technology resources, compete in the global environment of higher education and meet the rising demand for tertiary education.

There are various tools used for online education, which are face-to-face communication, videoconferencing tools, audioconferencing tools, telephone/mobile, net radio, chat/instant messaging, e-mail, Moodle (i.e., LMS tool), blackboard and downloaded course lectures [9–10].

The new apps available for online education or learning are the following:

[a] *Google Classroom*: Calendar is a time-management and scheduling calendar service developed by Google. Google Calendar is used for videoconferencing. It also allows users to create and edit events [11]. It is said that it is not accessible for people in China. Click Google Classroom, Create Classroom, Class Work. A whiteboard is also available. There is also an eraser. Teaching notes can also be typed.

[b] *Zoom*: Zoom Meetings (commonly shortened to Zoom and stylized as zoom) is a proprietary video teleconferencing software program developed by Zoom Video Communications. The free plan allows up to 100 concurrent participants, with a 40-minute time restriction. Users have the option to upgrade by subscribing to a paid plan. The highest plan supports up to 1,000 concurrent participants for meetings lasting up to 30 hours [12]. It is an interactive virtual classroom for online teachers in distance learning mode. It is very user-friendly. There is also a calendar app. A virtual background can be used. Slide shows and PDF files can be used to deliver online classes. Students' faces can also be seen here. It is the best app for small kids. All teaching material can be uploaded here, so there is no need to panic at any time.

[c] *Microsoft Teams*: Microsoft Teams is a proprietary business communication platform developed by Microsoft, as part of the Microsoft 365 family of products. Teams primarily compete with the similar service Slack, offering workspace chat and videoconferencing, file storage and application integration [13]. Teams are replacing other Microsoft-operated business messaging

and collaboration platforms, including Skype for Business and Microsoft Classroom. It is better than Zoom and Google in terms of security [14].
[d] Use *VEDAMO* interactive Virtual Classroom and Learning Management System for successful online tutoring. One can conduct live online classes with a virtual classroom regardless of one's location. One can create their own online academy to manage courses, content and learners [15].

A *SWOC analysis* is a strategic planning tool and can be used as a powerful framework to discuss and clearly identify strengths, weaknesses opportunities. The objective of conducting a SWOC analysis is to develop key areas of focus for improvement [16]. Online education is conducted by some education or training companies. *Strength* involves the factors which the company holds expertise in and contributes to the continued success of the organization. These are the basics for the continued success of the organization and will assist in gaining the organization's mission. *Weaknesses* are factors that prevent an organization from meeting its mission and achieving full potential. These weaknesses hamper organizational success and growth. *Opportunities* involve the environment within which our organization operates and offers opportunities. An organization can identify such opportunities and enjoy benefits arising from them by planning and executing required strategies. *Threats* are the factors existing in the external environment that jeopardize the profitability and reliability of the organization. Such threats are uncontrollable and prove to be a risk to the stability and survival of the organizations. SWOC analysis for this system has been listed in Figure 4.1.

4.3.1 BENEFITS OR STRENGTHS OF ONLINE EDUCATION [S]

Online education should be seen as offering solutions to several challenges. [s] represents the strength of online education. Following are the strengths collected from various papers:

a) Reduces the cost for instructor fees and materials.
b) Reduces the time spent on learning due to the use of audio, multimedia, internet, information.
c) Easy access of educational resources from anywhere, anytime using the internet.
d) Students become independent as all material is available through interne.
e) It helps the job person to enroll for degrees.
f) It increases interaction with students through email, discussions.
g) E-learning has made it easy to eliminate illiteracy by reaching to populations.
h) Reduces employee's absence from duty.
i) Makes learning takes place anytime, anywhere and greatly increases knowledge retention.
j) Assist learners to create access, view, modify, print or send documents.
k) Lectures can become interesting by using new advanced technology like virtual reality, augmented technology, data science, robotics, machine

learning and artificial intelligence. The course material can be integrated with graphics, multimedia and text, thereby building quality materials.

l) Lectures can be uploaded on the ERP system [LMS] of the college or university using cloud technology.

m) E-learning improves behavior performance among others.

n) Delivers content beyond state and country with high quality.

o) The use of new technology is associated with crimes against women like cyberstalking, cyberdefamation, cybersex, dissemination of obscene material and trespassing into one's private domain. So parents feel comfortable with online teaching from home for their daughter.

4.3.2 DISADVANTAGES OR WEAKNESSES OF ONLINE EDUCATION [W]

a) It is seen that quality is not improved till the instructor is serious about the content being delivered.

b) with Continuous education for 7–8 hours, small children may find difficult to concentrate. Teacher has to be very interactive.

c) Continuous exposure to radiation emitted by mobile phones may create cancers in children and students, which will be reflected after some years.

d) Internet problem, strength of signal may not be good in case of remote places.

e) Some technical courses like BE, mechanics and electronics cannot be understood as they must be demonstrated in offline mode only.

f) Small children and students accessing smartphones through the internet, which is not uncontrolled, may become dangerous for families, society and the nation (if not checked and controlled). Life is beautiful in a disciplined and controlled form.

g) In coming years, it is likely that the offline pattern will change into two parts: easy and difficult part. The easy part will be conducted in an online mode, and the other difficult part like practicums can be conducted in an offline mode.

h) Students were demanding smartphones. It was seen that if the smartphone was not given by some parents, the children committed suicide.

i) The education system will have to change with the needs and satisfaction of student. If only online modes are going on in that case, students may become isolated and may not learn and understand the concept of team work, culture, unity in diversity, leadership and hard work. Physical and mental issues will be created. It may also lead to lack of patience and sustainability problems.

4.3.3 OPPORTUNITIES [O]

a) No age limit.

b) Critical and creative thinking is required.

c) A problem-solving attitude is needed.

d) Innovation and digital development needs time.

e) A technical person is required.

4.3.4 CHALLENGES FACED [c]

a) Lack of funds[c].

b) Inadequate ICT infrastructure including computer hardware, software, internet bandwidth/access (i.e., signal strength), electric power supply, telecommunication (i.e., network), mobiles, LAN, routers, etc.

c) Lack of skilled manpower to manage available systems and inadequate training facilities for ICT education.

d) High cost of software would not encourage and permit online education to succeed.

e) Resistance to change from traditional face-to-face methods to more innovative, technology-based teaching and learning methods, by both students and academics.

f) The overdependence of educational institutions on government for everything has limited institutions' ability to collaborate with the private sector or seek alternative funding sources for ICT educational initiatives.

g) Ineffective coordination of all the various ICT for education initiatives.

h) Cost of internet connectivity. Most students make use of cybercafes.

4.4 PREDICTED ENVIRONMENTAL IMPACT OF ONLINE EDUCATION

Online education has impacted the following areas:

[A] **Education** [school, colleges, universities]
The environmental impact in online education is of a mixed type. Some have gained; some have lost. Some have gained in business; others have lost. Due to the pandemic situation globally, all schools, colleges and universities

Strength [21]	Weakness [21]
➢ Anywhere, anytime	➢ Personal attention
➢ Wider accessibility	➢ Internet access not for all—rural, urban
➢ Dynamic interaction between learner and instructor	➢ Computer knowledge required
	➢ Technical knowledge
➢ Student-centered	➢ Frustration, confusion
➢ Emphasis is on content other than age, dress, appearance, race, gender	➢ Not appropriate for younger students
	➢ Lack of essential online qualities for facilitator
➢ Creative teaching	
➢ Access to resources from anywhere	➢ Not all subjects can be taught
Opportunities	**Challenges**
➢ No age limits	➢ Quality education needed
➢ Critical thinking	➢ Digital literacy required
➢ Problem-solving	➢ Development of e-resources, e-content
➢ Innovation and digital development	➢ Technology cost

FIGURE 4.1   SWOC analysis.

shifted to online mode by their respective governments. No one has the information on how long this pandemic will remain (it began in March 2020 in India], and hence, the teaching method was shifted to online mode.

It is seen that the *learning outcome* has affected students of early class (kg to 5th std) age groups, who need live interaction with instructors. Students from 6th to 9th std are less impacted during COVID-19. Some of the students could not be covered as the schools did not take the lead to take regular classes. In schools the computer subject was considered optional. Students with classes from 10th to 12th made up their loss by working hard. Some students were impacted during COVID-19. But overall, all students have gained due to an online system of examinations.

In colleges UG students have scored high due to online examination systems. These students are adults, belong to the age group 18–22 years, self-dependent and more understanding and can make up if they are determined to do so. They have scored more in university exams due to an online mode of education and the MCQS exam system. UG students passed, and hence, all PG (age group 21–25 years) seats of colleges are full. Colleges have gained, but some are at a loss. Their fees are decreased marginally, but salaries of teachers are not increased. Overall, all students in education systems have passed (gained) due to changes in the educational pattern and examination system, government relaxing rules, supporting policies and many other factors (due to COVID-19). The learning outcome is seen in terms of performance, which is considered the outcome of students. As the learning outcome increases, the performance also increases.

Impact depends on many factors; some are considered. *Some factors affecting the teaching-learning process are instructor quality, student satisfaction, feedback for improvement and design of curriculum* [17]. Instructor quality is the most prominent factor that affects student satisfaction during online classes. Instructors should be enthusiastic and efficient and should understand students' psychology to deliver the course content, which will bring satisfaction and better performance in them. Students' expectations, if fulfilled, brings satisfaction and results.

After delivering the course, appropriate feedback should be taken by the instructors to plan future courses. There must be a proper feedback system for improvement because feedback is the course content's real image.

The course content and practicums designed should be effective and easily understandable. Easy content leads to satisfaction and better performance in the exams. Online instructors must be enthusiastic about developing genuine instructional resources that actively connect learners and encourage them toward proficient performances. In case of difficult topics, the instructor should have interactive sessions with learners.

In IT and education, ambitious people have sped up their process during the lockdown. They worked hard to access internet and YouTube materials to keep updated with the world. Smart people have enrolled in new courses online and updated themselves to change their job opportunities.

The world survived this pandemic due to IT inventions in the last 20 years, like the internet, networks, LAN, WAN, routers and open-source software. Computers and the internet kept people working from their houses. The IT companies started giving people work from home due to the lockdown, and companies survived this pandemic due to IT and vaccination. Online learning is an excellent educational option that offers convenience, reduced costs and a personalized experience. Online learning boosts productivity [18].

[B] **IT Industry**

IT industry employers are developers of software; they have started working from home. Many employees living as tenants have shifted to their own homes and are working from their places. Sleeping, working and washing can be done with jobs done from home. Many are enrolled for courses and certificates in colleges to get degree benefits. IT training is going on online mode.

[C] **Manufacturing, Transportation and Other Industry**

Online learning reduces the negative environmental impacts that come from manufacturing and transportation. The materials needed for traditional education institutions (textbooks, desks, electricity, buildings) are dramatically reduced. This reduces waste and conserves natural resources.

[D] **Saving Natural Resources, Raw Goods**

Four more things can be saved by choosing online learning: gas, pollution and emission, natural resources and paper. Online education reduces the demand for natural resources such as raw goods like plastic, metal, wood and other building materials, which protects the environment. Curriculums, assignments and textbooks have become digital [18].

[E] **Reducing Problems due to Transportation**

Online degrees are a perfect fit to reduce the carbon footprint and have a lower impact on the environment. Climate change leads to environmental degradation and transportation problems [19–20, 22–23].

[F] **Health Issue**

Online education increases eye and backbone problems and exposure to radiation from mobile phones. Exercise is required to become fit. People working online more can become lazy. Their weight and obesity can increase. If they do not work out, it will lead to many diseases.

[G] **Reduces Greenhouse Gas Emissions**

It is good for the environment as it reduces the emission of carbon dioxide gas, thereby reducing the temperature of the environment. This prevents climate change [24].

4.5 CONCLUSION

Humanity has survived the pandemic due to IT, work from home and the vaccination of population. This has led to online education, which is good for the environment as it reduces greenhouse gas emissions. Society is looking at it as a boon, and in coming years, there will be growth in online virtual classrooms, training centers, videoconferencing tools and open-source software, with improvement in their functionalities. Online education is a very big market.

4.6 REFERENCES

[1] https://en.wikipedia.org/wiki/Distance_education.
[2] https://en.wikipedia.org/wiki/Virtual_school
[3] https://en.wikipedia.org/wiki/Online_learning
[4] A Mohammed, "Evolution of E-Learning as a Strategy of Improving Teaching and Learning in Nigerian Universities: Challenges and Prospects," *Journal of Education and Practice*, vol. 4, no. 26, pp. 53–62, 2013.
[5] Olumide S. Adewale, Emmanuel O, "A Web-Based Virtual Classroom System Model," *IBAM Turkish Online Journal of Distance Education-TOJDE*, vol. 13, no. 1, pp. 211–223, January 2012, ISSN 1302–6488, Article 14.
[6] Martin, M. Parker, "Use of Synchronous Virtual Classrooms: Why, Who, and How?" *Journal of Online Learning and Teaching*, vol. 10, no. 2, p. 192, 2014.
[7] J. M. Amírez-Hurtado, A. G. Hernández-Díaz, A. D. López-Sánchez, V. E. Pérez-León, "Measuring Online teaching service quality in higher education in the covid-19 environment," *International Journal of Environmental Research and Public Health*, vol. 18, no. 5, pp. 1–14, 2021.
[8] T. Saba, "Implications of E-learning systems and self-efficiency on students outcomes: A model approach," *Human-centric Computing and Information Sciences*, vol. 2, no. 1, pp. 1–11, 2012.
[9] https://www.talentlms.com/elearning/technologies-used-in-elearning
[10] Shadi Aljawarneh, Zahraa Muhsin, Ayman Nsour et al., "E-learning Tools and Technologies in Education: A Perspective," *MIT LINC*, May 2010, DOI: 10.13140 / 2.1.1017.9847, https://www.researchgate.net/publication/266078239
[11] https://en.wikipedia.org/wiki/Google_Calendar
[12] https://en.wikipedia.org/wiki/Zoom_ (software)
[13] S. Dhawan, "Online Learning: A Panacea in the Time of COVID-19 Crisis," *Journal of Educational Technology Systems*, vol. 49, no. 1, pp. 5–22, 2020.
[14] https://en.wikipedia.org/wiki/Microsoft_Teams
[15] www.VEDAMO.com
[16] Tarbiat Modares, Mansoureh Abdi, Mandana Azadegan-Mehr, "Swot Methodology, a State-of- the Art Review for the Past, a Framework for the Future," *Journal of Business Economics and Management*, vol. 12, no. 1, pp. 24–48, April 2011, DOI: 10.3846/16111699.2011.555358, https://www.researchgate.net/publication/254214770
[17] Ram Gopal, Varsha Singh, Arun Aggarwal, "Impact of Online Classes on the Satisfaction and Performance of Students During the Pandemic Period of COVID 19," *Education and Information Technologies*, vol. 26, pp. 6923–6947, 2021, https://doi.org/10.1007/s10639-021-10523-1.
[18] https://www.triplepundit.com/story/2015/4-unsung-environmental-benefits-Online-education/35151F.
[19] https://www.pewresearch.org/science/2019/11/25/u-s-public-views-on-climate-and-energy
[20] Shivangi Dhawan, Online Learning: A Panacea in the Time of COVID-19 Crisis.
[21] M. Siva Durga Prasad Nayak, K. A. Narayan, "Strengths and Weaknesses of Online Learning," *University Illinois*, vol. 24, no. 5, pp. 1–10, 2015.

[22] R. Roy, S. Potter, K. Yarrow, "Designing low carbon higher education systems: Environmental impacts of campus and distance learning systems," *International Journal of Sustainability in Higher Education*, vol. 9, no. 2, pp. 116–130, 2008.

[23] M. Versteijlen, F. Perez Salgado, M. Janssen Groesbeek, A. Counotte, "Pros and cons of online education as a measure to reduce carbon emissions in higher education in the Netherlands," *Current Opinion in Environmental Sustainability*, vol. 28, pp. 80–89, 2017.

[24] J. Campbell and D. Campbell, "Distance Learning is Good for the Environment: Savings in Greenhouse Gas Emissions," *Journal of Distance Learning Administration*, vol. 14, no. 4, pp. 1556–3847, 2011.

5 Transformation of Communication Rituals in Remote Learning

Paweł Greń and Oliwia Tarasewicz-Gryt
Jan Wyżykowski University
University of Applied Science in Jelenia Góra

CONTENTS

5.1 INTRODUCTION

The modern world is undergoing constant modifications. The broadly understood technological development is considered the basic determinant—deciding upon their form and shape. Permanent dynamization of newer and newer technical solutions significantly influences the change not only of nature but also of the organizational culture of societies. They are observable in most sectors of life.

As mentioned by Mirosława Pluta-Olearczyk [2004], the factors regulating changes determine, among others, the level of advancement of the information society and the knowledge-based economy, which, in a way, forces the implementation of innovative solutions. Over the last dozen years, unprecedented offers related to *e-business* or *e-shopping* have started to appear in the labor market. New technical possibilities began to be used also in the education process. Human activity—including many activities related to the search for new forms of teaching—set new standards over time. Remote learning has been implemented, also referred to as *e-learning* or *e-education*. This process successively supported the previously known forms of education and evolved along with technical development. Over time, the transfer of knowledge from the most distant corners of the world—and in real-time with the help of image and sound—has become a fact. Earlier, the concentration of the scientific community was dictated by visiting different places worldwide to gain knowledge. Nowadays, distances are no longer a problem. The same applies to talent shortage due to the creation of remote teams—collaborating effectively despite the distance between their members. It has turned out that people can act effectively by communicating remotely and overcoming the limitations related to the transformation of the way of communication—from face-to-face to virtual. As Gajaraj Dhanarajan writes [Kubiak, 2000]:

> Reaching those hungry for education at the highest level anywhere on Earth is just a matter of imagination. We already have the necessary knowledge, experience, and skills to attract people and establish contact with them. We also have the necessary technology. We still need an overall vision that would show us how to implement it all.

It is therefore worth considering at this point whether substitute communication rituals have developed during the implementation of a substitute form of education. The ritual approach to communication positions its value above the basic function, which is the classical transmission of information. Communication should be defined more broadly. It is a social practice focusing around, inter alia, activities aimed at transferring values or creating relationships. The goal of communication is therefore constructing sense and building meaning through (mediated) media. The creation of communication rituals is of particular importance in remote learning, where apart from the transmission of information, a relationship should be created between the teacher and the learner. Otherwise, it is impossible to motivate students to learn and to effectively manage the educational process by the teacher.

5.2   DIACHRONY OF REMOTE EDUCATION

Teaching and learning with the use of the latest ICT technologies are becoming an integral part of the educational process in the world. The history of distance education has a rich tradition, and the teaching systems functioning in particular periods were subject to modifications from the very beginning. From the dawn of time, communication has played an important role in human life. Initially, sounds and non-verbal communication were the only forms of communication between people. Presumably, the first and most basic functions were the sound signals they produced. They informed about hunger, anger, or fear and also influenced the environment— that is, family, kinsmen, and coexisting group [Zwoliński, 2013]. The overriding purpose of the vocal messages sent at that time was to elicit a reaction from the recipient. As Adam Skibiński mentions [2012]:

> Every behavioral manifestation communicates something each time, and since the behavior has no opposite, we cannot help but communicate. Also, the lack of a message . . . eg silence . . . is a kind of message in the context of the expected behavior. . . . All behavior means something in a specific situational and relational context.

Cognitive descriptions not directly related to defining desires and influencing the environment have become a much more complex form of communication. The description that functions as a message is detached from the currently felt need, so to create it, it is necessary to distance yourself from the currently experienced state and the accompanying emotions. Over time, the basic messages being sent became insufficient. People began to see the benefit of getting more and more accurate information. This tendency influenced the development of language, and the people used the possibilities of this organism by verbally modulating the original signal. The diachronic approach to the signals was situational. Producing short and varied phonetic effects was possible thanks to the scale of sound modulation. As Andrzej Zwoliński [2013] writes:

> The basic imperative of living organisms is the economization of effort, which in the case of language, as a communicative activity, led from the language of certain separated signals denoting holistically perceived situations to an articulated language in which individual sounds influence the content of the message, as is the case in contemporary languages.

As the author adds, the articulated language changed the way of thinking—from pictorial to discursive thinking—which constituted a fundamental change in the scope of human mental efficiency. In discursive thinking, individual words have an independent meaning and are "carriers" of specific contents. At its core, there is an elementary weakness of human cognition and the possibility of departing from the perception of reality to the path of self-perception, often composed of a mental structure. The invention of speech and language meant crossing the signal boundary in communication between people. Man differs from animals in that he uses articulated speech and thus uses words to express thoughts and feelings. As Walery Pisarek wrote [1976]:

> The ability to convey all our thoughts to other people is an essential and existential feature of . . . language as the most perfect system of signs. It is hard to argue that the language reflects the extra-linguistic reality available to people. . . . When we say that the emergence of human speech is associated with the beginning of collective work for people, this does not mean that "primitive" man felt the need to express a message like "this stone is heavy." It seems incomparably more likely is that in this instance the message that a given person needed to express was: "help me move it."

Therefore, language has always been an integral part of the culture and has penetrated it, becoming present in all areas, including economy, education, law, magic, religion, art, or play, determining their shape and image at the same time. Linguistic reception and interpretation of the surrounding reality significantly influenced the development of societies and the world. With the progress of civilization, communication was expanded to include ever-changing tools that not only transmitted information but also materialized it. The development of civilization, and with it interpersonal communication, took various forms, the consequence of which is, among others, the appearance of the writing (around 3,500 BC). Thus, the formation of a literate culture took place not thanks to the creation of any writing system but due to the shaping of the phonetic alphabet [Sitkowska, 2012]. This invention has therefore become a constitutional form of storing our thoughts and speech. It began to constitute a set of conventional symbols using which it became possible to graphically represent the spoken language. Platon, among others, has been critical of this invention. As Jarosław Barański writes [2003]:

Platonic reflection on the written sign (as well as on the iconic sign) is full of contradictions, even paradoxes, which arise from the theoretical matrix formed by the concept of memory and recall. Moreover, the interpretation according to which Plato bestowed the cognitive privilege of speech over writing, seeing in the former the means of reaching for the truth, and in the latter - a tool of simulation. And yet this epistemological restoration was doomed to failure, which, paradoxically, turned out to be a creative discovery of the hermeneutic aura of the sign.

In dialogue, Plato expressed his concerns about the writing. He believed that it would significantly weaken memory by "infecting" it with forgetfulness. The philosopher assumed that people who would no longer trust their memories would trust the signs of writing instead. He also saw a specific danger in the distribution of materialized content. Plato was afraid that lofty philosophical considerations would reach the undesirable hands of the members of the "wide circles"—that is, to put it bluntly, the mob. Time has shown that writing significantly influenced the development of civilization and became an indispensable ingredient in everyday communication between people. It also turned out to be the first tool used in remote learning.

It may seem that distance learning via the Internet is an invention of the twentieth and twenty-first century, which enables people to gain knowledge outside the walls of universities. J. D. Łuszkiewicz [2003] says that the said phenomenon happened much earlier and left its mark at the beginning of our era. St. Paul, who taught the first Christian communities, is considered a forerunner of this form of education. This apostle popularized the content of the Christian faith with the help of letters. The actual and institutional form of distance learning began in 1700 in the United States. It was then that the first advertisement for the correspondence course appeared. The educational model focused on sending materials between the teacher and students via mail. Similar educational traditions in the eighteenth century can also be found in other academic centers, including Poland. In 1776, the University of Kraków—as the first university in the country—offered craftsmen a correspondence course. A few years later, an extramural course for physicists was conducted at the University of Warsaw [Heba, 2009].

With the appearance of newer devices—used for remote communication—the range of offered forms of education has expanded. This is exemplified by the story of the English photographer Isaac Pitman, who in 1837, using a transcript, monitored the effects of students' work. The extramural cooperation consisted in delivering to the lecturer—by post—the Bible fragments copied on the transcript, which in turn were subject to evaluation. Several years later, Pitman's brother introduced remote shorthand courses in the United States. The project was met with great interest, and it has been translated into several languages. That moment also marked a new direction in the history of extramural education. In 1850, the University of London—as the first university in the world—included specialist correspondence courses in its offer. They were dedicated to the British living in India and Australia. At the same time, extramural forms of language learning were developing in the United States.

A breakthrough in the historiography of distance learning turned out to be the establishment in 1873 in Boston of the institution entitled *The Society to Encourage Study At Home*. Its activities focused on compiling a reading list, the content of lectures and tests, which in turn were sent in printed form to participants. People participating in the training were obliged to read the material and deliver the completed tests by post. Twenty-four subjects were taught this way [Heba, 2009].

A kind of renaissance in distance learning took place in the 1920s. Since the invention of the radio, part-time learning has taken a very different form. The auditory affordances of the medium, as well as connecting the tutor with the students, significantly revived and made the teaching methods functioning up to that point far more realistic. Educational radio courses were first provided by the University of Iowa. They were used mainly by students from rural or sparsely populated areas, far from academic and industrial centers. Similar solutions were also used, among others, in Australia. Less than three decades later, media with audiovisual properties appeared. The mass media, which functioned until the 1950s, were dominated by a new medium—television. Its heyday caused the expansion of visual civilization and set new trends in the mass communication system. It was originally perceived as an elite medium that only a few could afford [Myślak, 2017]. Soon the price of receivers became more affordable, and over the years, television began to regularly fill the time in the lives of most people. What's more, it "settled" and attracted viewers to such an extent that the so-called TV room had been often arranged to accommodate the device. Television successfully annexed the most important areas of human activity, including science. Knowledge has already begun to be transmitted using image and sound - by engaging the recipient's eyesight and hearing receptors. In 1945, an educational television was established in the United States, and in the late 1950s, the first program, "Sunrise Semester," was broadcast in Chicago. Initially, TV education was passive [Juszczyk, 2002]. The knowledge provided by the teacher was materialized on video cassettes, and then the recording was played during classes. Direct broadcasts of educational programs were equally popular at that time. The aforementioned technical solution made it possible to conduct didactic classes on a large scale. At the end of the 1960s, the British Open University was founded, which introduced distance learning. With time, the TV classes became interactive, which significantly made the educational process more attractive. The year 1962 should be considered a breakthrough; it was then that the American telecommunications satellite Telestar 1 was put into orbit. The event marked a new era in distance learning using audio and videoconferencing. The image transmitted in real time, combined with the acoustic layer, was possible to transmit using satellites. The new technical possibilities quickly found application in the distance learning process. In the 1970s and 1980s, they were used by large academic centers. The pioneer in this matter was the University of Alaska, which since 1985—via a satellite link—offered many remote courses also to other universities.

In the 1990s, the Internet and multimedia developed. Although the term "new media" has been used in social sciences since the 1960s, it was in the 1980s, which coincided with the birth of the Internet, it has taken on a much wider meaning. It has also marked a new reality. Hubert Marshall McLuhan's thesis that the world has become a global village had become true: metaphorically, space and time have completely "shrunk." Sending information to the recipient from the most distant parts of the world, without time limits, was no longer a problem. Contrary to the previously functioning media, the Internet was able not only to coexist in the media system but also did not eliminate other forms of communication. Instead, in a sense, it had become an "incubator" thereof, allowing them to develop in the way that their offer corresponded to the expectations of the market and recipients. Thus, electronic forms of publishing newspapers, Internet broadcasts of radio programs, or video reports have appeared. However, the most important of the changes brought about by the development of new media concerns their interactivity. In the case of traditional media, the message was mostly one-sided. With the development of new technologies and the Internet, this has changed. The sender and the recipient could already alternate roles in the communication process. The revolution in social communication did not remain indifferent in the sphere of science. Distance learning attracted widespread attention. This moment can be described as the birth *of e-learning*. The popularization of the Internet turned out to be a breakthrough for distance learning, and its technical capabilities enabled global communication and guaranteed a high level of interaction. Synchronized communication (verbal and non-verbal) between the facilitator and the participants was therefore no longer a problem. It has also become a natural determinant regulating the shape and technical capabilities of tools used for distance learning. Society adapts to life through modern communication and information techniques but also has a certain set of expectations.

Before 2020, remote education was offered by many universities and institutions around the world. In most cases, they were treated as an interesting supplement to the stationary offer. With time, universities, taking the trouble to modernize the teaching process, decided to combine the traditional form with the remote one. However, the outbreak of the Covid-19 pandemic has changed our habits and forced changes in functioning in all sectors of social and economic life. As a result, distance learning ceased to be an innovative form of education and even became a necessity.

5.3 FROM AN ANONYMOUS COMMUNITY TO A VIRTUAL CLASSROOM

At the beginning of the twenty-first century, Manuel Castells (2008a) described the network society as a type of information society, where for a group of people the essence is building interpersonal relations, taking place via the Internet in various circles of interest, constituting the main axis of contacts. However, communication mediated by the network is undergoing a constant and rapid transformation. The community participating in remote lessons should be defined in terms other than the "network," as it is proposed by Manuel Castells because its members are connected not only by a virtual network of connections.

Marek Graszewicz and Dominik Lewiński [2010], criticizing Castells' (2008b) concept, argue that on the Internet—if only because of the anonymity of users— communication is devoid of systemic responsibility for the content transmitted and may be interrupted without social consequences. It is possible to simply not communicate, while normally, in social interactions, that kind of lack of communication is not possible. We can only talk about socializing when online ties lead to offline meetings. Describing the hypothetical participation in a scientific conference via the Internet, Graszewicz and Lewiński recognize that the participating community is still a scientific community, not a network. They also prove that it is impossible to create a network community like a virtual kindergarten because social and symbolic capitals, hierarchies, sanctions, and coordination of behavior (such as joint lunch) cannot be built among children.

We encounter a situation similar to participation in the virtual scientific conference described by Graszewicz and Lewiński during distance learning, which in 2020 has temporarily replaced stationary learning. The community learning during remote lessons is still a school community, not a network, so we will call it a virtual class because it has not been elusively constituted around a topic interesting for its members but has been transferred to virtual reality from the real world. Thus, can the virtual classroom build "social and symbolic capitals, hierarchies, sanctions, and coordination of behavior" among students? It seems that building social capital is not the main goal of communication in remote group learning; this constitutes the disadvantage of this communication. This kind of communication is oriented toward knowledge transfer and student work management rather than relationship building. However, observing how new communication rituals are created, transferred, and adapted to the virtual environment from a traditional classroom setting, it can be assumed that shortly, this transformation will be aimed not only at making distance learning more effective—through appropriate and appropriate remote tools tasks, work coordination and enforcement of tasks—but also the skillful motivation of students to building commitment by forming relationships. This is also noticed by the creators of remote work tools, gradually equipping them with functionalities that allow one to work in small groups, enriching written communication with non-verbal signals, such as emoticon reactions to text written in a chat.

The learning community (virtual classroom) differs from the network society—i.e., a group of anonymous users gathered around a topic of interest to them, and the differences are as follows:

- The lack of anonymity of its members—which increases the responsibility for communication and the content transferred;
- Fixed timeframe—which makes it impossible to suddenly break the continuity of the community by interrupting communication because the lesson is scheduled at a specific time and repeats itself cyclically;
- The synchronicity of communication—communication takes place during the lesson. The synchronization interruption may take the form of simultaneous speaking and writing in chat; however, this modification does not introduce significant changes to the communication;
- Persistence—tools for remote work allow not only communication but also storing knowledge, gathering opinions, and extra-substantive conversations. A virtual class community does not disappear once the computer is turned off;
- The existence of a common goal and responsibility for the tasks and atmosphere in the group (especially when working in smaller groups);
- Possibilities for the teacher to establish and enforce compliance with the rules of remote work;

- Building a sense of belonging by assigning a user (student) to a virtual team, the repetition of events (lesson plan, ritualism of meetings, etc.), and other communication rituals, such as integration games at the beginning of meetings.

Despite the existence of tools enabling the creation of virtual communities, Polish teachers mainly point to the consequences of one-way communication, consisting essentially in transmitting information from the sender to the recipient as the main challenge of remote work with students. There is a talk of a lack of interaction with students (Romaniuk and Łukasiewicz - Wieleba, 2021). Participants of remote lessons cannot see each other (if cameras are not turned on during the meeting), which limits the possibility of receiving feedback and two-way communication. If teachers do not create conditions for remote cooperation—e.g., in the form of shared documents, visible to all participants in the lesson, they do not know if the students are working during the lesson. Making communication one-way deprives the process managers—that is, teachers—of the tools of control. In such conditions, participants focus solely on completing the tasks. The relationship is reduced to the learner handing over the assignment and feedback from the teacher.

On the other hand, when asked about the disadvantages of remote learning, students mention the difficulty in determining priorities ("we don't know what is important"). This means that teachers are not able to effectively set tasks, set the work schedule, and are not able to overcome these deficiencies—e.g., when specifying tasks—because such clarification does not take place. Other disadvantages of remote education identified by students include the inaccessibility of the teacher, the inability to ask instant questions and get feedback, chaos, a sense of isolation, a disturbed sense of security, and difficulty in motivating oneself to work. This clearly proves that the mere transmission of knowledge is not enough to create a remote education-friendly environment.

5.4   FROM SUBSTITUTION TO REDEFINITION

By perfecting the distance learning workshop, the teacher moves along the levels of the SAMR model developed by Ruben Puentedura (2014). The SAMR model categorizes four different degrees of technology integration in the classroom. It is designed to share a common language across disciplines, in response to the needs of teachers who seek to personalize learning and help students visualize complex concepts. It is assumed here that during remote or hybrid learning, the biggest challenge is building relationships and using remote work tools that will simultaneously ensure effective work and integrate a virtual team. The acronym SAMR comes from the first letters of the words "substitution," "augmentation," "modification," and "redefinition," and it reflects the four levels of technology used in the teacher's work. The lowest level and currently the most frequently used one in classroom lessons that use the ICT is substitution, consisting in the use of technology to perform basic tasks that could and can be performed without the use of digital tools (e.g., the use of an interactive whiteboard for writing only or use of Keynote, PowerPoint, Prezi, Slides, or a similar presentation program). The second level of the model is augmentation, understood as the extension and use of digital tools to solve basic problems and economize the teacher's work (e.g., using the application to check presence, verify content, test students, or include interactive materials such as a virtual poll during the lesson). Substitution and augmentation are the first steps in strengthening and improving the skills of both teachers and students, as well as shaping new attitudes. In the third level, one moves on to modifying the teaching process and enriching the workshop. Technology makes it possible to create tasks that were previously impossible in a classroom lesson. An example is the work of a group of students on a joint document, presenting its effects and asking for feedback from other students in the comment section of the presented material. The top level of the SAMR model is redefinition. In this approach, technology allows one to carry out tasks that could not have been predicted before. For example, after working in a group and getting feedback from classmates, students can use the technology to engage with students in another country to see how regional differences affect how others feel about the problem. Modification and redefinition are transformative approaches toward remote education. Both of these levels assume not only the replacement of traditional tools with virtual ones but also require the use of communication rituals that allow for effective remote work and at the same time building and maintaining relationships.

5.5   A TRANSFORMATIVE APPROACH TO COMMUNICATION IN REMOTE EDUCATION

Similar shifts to the ones used when implementing increasingly perfect tools and taking advantage of the opportunities offered by distance learning, instead of treating it as a substitute for stationary learning, may concern communication. Substitution consists in replacing face-to-face communication with communication using information and communication technology. The substitution was correspondence learning, where the message was saved and sent; transformation is the creation of new codes and rituals that would not be possible in a communication situation other than an application for online meetings, a group created on a messenger or a remote learning application, such as MS Teams, Google Classroom, etc.

The researchers of the method of communication on dating websites argue that functioning in the virtual world cannot be based solely on the transmission of information (Kotlyar and Ariely, 2013). They showed that despite massive infrastructure investments enabling users to choose partners, the quality of communication was neglected. The lack of non-verbal cues has made it difficult for virtual dating users to form relationships, whereas mimicking face-to-face communication by adding non-verbal cues through avatars helps to improve the quality of online interaction and relationship building. Compared to simple text chat, versions that contained a greater variety of non-verbal cues due to the use of avatars were associated with a more favorable perception of the other person and a stronger desire to establish a relationship.

Similarly, in the case of remote education, the challenge is to find and use virtual tools to replace non-verbal signals that make remote communication similar to natural. The communication and project management tools used in corporations are evolving in this direction, as exemplified by Slack, where a whole system of non-verbal signs has been created to maintain the commitment and motivation of the virtual team. In this application, it is possible to virtually celebrate the team's successes, and non-substantive thematic channels are also created—for example, sports or hobby channels—which enable employees to "drink coffee virtually" and chitchat, which mimics the office life. All this is to make the team integrate also outside the office. The ultimate goal is to improve the effectiveness and efficiency of employees. Instead of replacing face-to-face communication with imperfect virtual tools, users move to the next rung of the SAMR ladder and create codes specific to virtual communication, substitutes for non-verbal communication such as the "hate dot" (i.e., using a period at the end of a sentence written in an online messenger not to follow the rules of punctuation but to show attitude and force the interlocutor to end the topic or break the contact).

"Everything OK?"
- Yes. vs. Yes

Communication via remote communicators caused a transformation in the understanding of written language as different from spoken language (W. Ong, 2002). This is not a written language despite it being in writing, but rather, as the linguist, John McWorther proves, "fingered speech," which resembles natural spoken language. Thus, there is a certain modification of the language, the formation of a completely different language that is neither written nor spoken. This method of communication is also constantly evolving and influences the way of face-to-face communication is. As a living and flexible language, it also has the potential to build relationships between telephone or computer users communicating in this way. Thurlow Crispin and Poff (2013) write about this potential, postulating a departure from thinking about computer-mediated communication as anti-social. They believe that SMS is a "social technology," and it is impossible to accurately separate relational intention from transactional intention—relationship building from information exchange. The text messages analyzed in their research were predominantly relational. They pursued goals such as friendly greetings, concluding social contracts, and maintaining friendships. Transactional messages, consisting in sending information, constituted only 15% of all analyzed messages. Even these apparent exchanges of information (e.g., practical arrangements) have invariably served to solve more social problems, such as finding some company for a night out or politely letting someone know they will be late. The predominantly relational, often phatic function of SMSs also manifested itself in the use of humor and the passing on of chain letters (jokes, memes). The authors argue that many text messages correspond to small talk. In its ephemeral and immediate nature, sending text messages (as well as chat and e-mails) is speech rather than writing, and their defining feature is ultimately their social function. Even if they seem to be dominated by the informational function, they will most often serve relational purposes, to the extent that this function is a genre-defining property of texts to a greater extent than other properties of this type of messages—such as the length or the use of abbreviations, emoticons, homophones in letters and digits, etc.

It works in a similar way in the virtual classroom, where the teacher's task is to use ICT in a way that not only transmits knowledge but also builds relationships. The informational function and remote work tools subordinated to it should be enriched with communication rituals and non-verbal signals. In order to at least partially reduce the distance, virtual interactions must be made as similar to in-person interactions as possible. The most important and the most natural is the contact via video channels, which makes remote communication similar to *face-to-face* communication. Then there is the audio channel (i.e., a telephone or conference with the exclusion of video, especially with a weaker connection), chat, and e-mail (as the most impersonal and least liked form of communication by students, enforcing the official style and hindering building of relationships). The sense of security in a virtual classroom can be partially created by taking care of the constant rhythm of the day—it is best to do it by entering remote lessons in the schedule, ensuring their repetition is analogous to lessons at school. It is also important to create a place for storing knowledge and gathering materials available for all team members. A consistent method of communication is also important (descriptions of groups, classes) and precise determination of the information exchange channel (e.g., had chat, "tasks," application, etc.). It is also good practice creating less formal channels in remote learning teams, equivalent to a virtual break, where informal, non-classroom conversations, corresponding to *small talk, can take place.*

5.6 SUMMARY

Humanity has come a long way from sending letters through anonymous network communities to virtual teams collaborating on a project or learning in a virtual classroom. Technological progress and subsequent inventions enable more and more perfect implementation of the goal of communication, which is constructing sense and building meanings. A direction has been set out, clearly moving from the substitution and descent of real relations to transformation and a complete redefinition of the way of communication, so that the processes implemented with it—such as teaching—can be effective. This direction is confirmed in research on text messages and dating websites—people have natural needs that communication must satisfy. If there are no tools currently available, they will appear over time, adapting to constantly changing realities and new challenges.

5.7 SOURCES

Barański J. (2003), *Pismo-farmakon i paradoksy myśli Platona: o twórczym niepowodzeniu restauracji epistemologicznej*, Prace Naukowe Akademii Ekonomicznej we Wrocławiu. Humanities, vol. 8, no. 1008.

Castells M. (2008a), *Siła tożsamości*, Warszawa: Wydawnictwo Naukowe PWN.

Castells M. (2008b), *Społeczeństwo sieci*, Warszawa: Wydawnictwo Naukowe PWN.

Graszewicz M. and Lewiński D. (2010), *Co to Jest społeczeństwo Sieciowe I Dlaczego Ono Nie Istnieje?* Nowe Media. Czasopismo Naukowe, vol. 1, pp. 13–21. https://doi.org/10.12775/NM.2010.001.

Heba A. (2009), *Nauczanie na odległość—wczoraj i dziś,* Nauczyciel i Szkoła, vol. 3–4, no. 44–45.

Juszczyk S. (2002), *Edukacja na odległość. Kodyfikacja pojęć, reguł i procesów*, Toruń: Multimedialna Biblioteka Pedagogiczna, Wydawnictwo Adam Marszałek.

Kotlyar I. and Ariely D. (2013), *The effect of nonverbal cues on relationship formation*. Computers in Human Behavior, vol. 29, no. 3.

Kubiak M.J. (2000), *School, internet, intranet. Wirtualna edukacja*, Warszawa: Wyd. Mikom.

Łuszkiewicz J.D. (2003), *Kształcenie na odległość—współczesne tendencje oświatowe*, Warszawa: Edukacja Ustawiczna Dorosłych, 4.

Myślak D.A. (2017), *Telewizja cyfrowa i jej cyfrowe pochodne a oczekiwania współczesnego odbiorcy*. Media—Kultura—Komunikacja Społeczna, t. vol. 13, pp. 31–55.

Ong W.J. (2002), *Orality and Literacy the Technologizing of the Word*, London: Routledge.

Pisarek W. (1976), *Język służy propagandzie*, Kraków: Ośrodek Badań Prasoznawczych RSW Prasa-Książka-Ruch, s. 1–3.121.

Pluta-Olearczyk M. (2004), *Rozwój nowych form edukacji na poziomie wyższym—wyzwania i szanse dla polskich uczelni*, Poznań: Marketing szkół wyższych, pod red. G. Nowaczyk, M. Kolasiński, p. 169.

Puentedura R.R. (2014), *Building transformation: An introduction to the SAMR model*, Blog Post. http://www.hippasus.com/rrpweblog/archives/2014/08/22/BuildingTransform ation_AnIntroductionToSAMR.pdf

Romaniuk M. and Łukasiewicz-Wieleba J. (2021), *Zdalna edukacja kryzysowa w APS w okresie pandemii COVID-19. Z perspektywy rocznych doświadczeń. Raport z badań*, Warszawa: Akademia Pedagogiki Specjalnej im. Marii Grzegorzewskiej.

Sitkowska K. (2012), *Kulturowy wymiar ewolucji mediow w ujęciu przedstawicieli „Szkoły Toronto"*, Kultura—Media—Teologia, nr 11, 42–54.

Skibiński A. (2012), *Gregory Bateson i kontekstowa teoria komunikacji. Różnica, która czyni różnicę, i wzorzec, który łączy*, Poznań: Komunikologia. Teoria i praktyka komunikacja,red. Kulczycki E., Wendland M.

Thurlow, Crispin and Poff. (2013), *The language of text messaging. Handbook of the pragmatics of CMC*. https://www.researchgate.net/publication/237406258_The_language_of_ text-messaging

Zwoliński A. (2013), *Słowo w relacjach społecznych*, Kraków: Wydawnictwo WAM, pp. 13–17.

6 Analysis of Large-Scale Data Linked to Online Platforms Using Evolutionary Computing Mechanisms
A Case Study

Jyoti Prakash Mishra[1], Sambit Kumar Mishra[1], Zdzislaw Polkowski[2] and Samarjeet Borah[3]

1 Gandhi Institute for Education and Technology, Baniatangi, Bhubaneswar, affiliated to Biju Patnaik University of Technology, Rourkela, Odisha, India

2 WSG University, Bydgoszcz, Poland

3 Sikkim Manipal Institute of Technology, Sikkim Manipal University, Sikkim, India

CONTENTS

6.1 INTRODUCTION

Particularly in the present pandemic situation while being associated with large-scaled data, it has been observed that data has been more and more sequenced and available. For instance, educational institutions or research organizations can gain more meaningful information, relevant knowledge and vision from this huge data based on decision-making. Sometimes mining this data can give the ability to retrieve valuable information from a huge and complex set of data or data streams. Sometimes there may be difficulties to adopt specific techniques because of enormous amount of data on a continual basis. In such situations, it is essential to analyze the specialties from the datasets. Also it is required to focus on the computational parameters, including processing time and cost. In this application, data retrieved from any source can be analyzed to acquire the responses and obtain the results with minimized cost factors with proper decision-making. Particularly, in this application, it is intended to accumulate large-sized heterogeneous data implementing evolutionary computing mechanisms toward the optimal analysis of data. The reason behind the same is its efficiency and power of handling complex and growing datasets with numerous, self-directed sources.

6.2 ANALYSIS OF LEARNING MECHANISMS

The mechanisms associated with learning can not only be viewed to gather information or meta knowledge but also several interactions with other entities or domains along with the skill to access independently. For instance, student-content interaction can focus on interactive accessibility, and the mentor with student accessibility can lead to the representation of contents with skilled knowledge in interactive way. As reflected in Figure 6.1, interactivity is the basic technique toward acquiring knowledge and enhancing the cognitive expertise being provisioned with linked interactions. Though it is not so easy to define the term based on learning, it still depends on the ability in response to specific tasks. Probably, it initiates the mechanism to construct knowledge.

Prioritizing the equivalency interaction mechanism, it is observed that in case of deep learning studies, the interaction with the most advanced proficient demonstration is better compared to traditional ones. As shown in Figure 6.2, it is understood

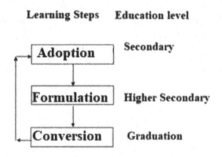

FIGURE 6.1   Specified traditional learning steps.

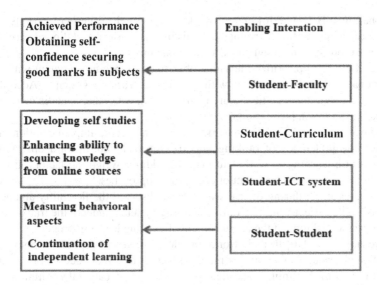

FIGURE 6.2   Conceptualization of learning mechanisms.

that minimizing the physical interaction of the basic tutors may enhance other specific interactions by adopting the features of online learning systems. Of course, connectivity in social aspects is very much required during the implementation of supervised learning approach.

6.3   LITERATURE SURVEY

Kuo Y et al. [1] in their work have focused on interactivity as well as pedagogy impacting significantly on the learning. Of course, the lack in interactivity may link to the gap affecting the quality of learning.

Croxton et al. [2] during their research observed that to obtain a better performance toward achieving the learning goals, the gap between the pedagogical aspects of traditional as well as e-learning systems should be maintained, and probably it is possible by enhancing interactivity in e-learning systems. Based on the demand in the higher level education, the challenges in this regard should be resolved through e-learning.

Conrad et al. [3] in their work have focused on enhancement of the overall effectiveness of the e-learning system provisioned with feedback. Therefore, confirmation in such cases may be preserved toward constituting the learning process as e-learning.

Aljabre et al. [4] in their work focused on the aspects of e-learning. They have also prioritized the advancement linked to recent technology and support of cognitive software on participation in simulations.

Basak et al. [5] in their study observed the flexibility of e-learning with a positive aspect towards enhancement of quality of education. In fact, the implementation of e-learning technologies can improve the intercommunication with better knowledge exchange and also strengthen the learning community.

Mohammed H.J. et al. [6] in their work focused on the criteria of various significant approaches of online learning mechanisms. They prioritized flipped classrooms, which are more specific provisioned with online modules.

Ince M et al. [7] prioritized learning objectives of specific e-content with online educational materials associated with web-based learning systems. Accordingly, they accumulated the analytic hierarchy mechanism with other specific mechanisms to make the selection process more convenient.

Andayani S et al. [8] in their work focused on specific implementation criteria adopting the preference of ranking organization technique toward observing the readiness of e-learning as well as to map the additive weighting factors. It is more essential toward the enhancement of e-learning approaches.

Naveed et al. [9] during their research have observed the flexibility and accessibility as well as effectiveness of online learning systems. Indeed, the transformation system is essential toward the enhancement of existing learning processes.

Dweiri, F et al. [10] in their work considered more the process inclusive of the allocation of resources with proper management. In fact, they focused on the critical factors linked to the limits of academic integrity of educational institutions. Also, they have done research on the essential factors of e-learning.

Al Mulla et al. [11] during their research experienced distance learning in connection with the online learning. They observed major quality factors in connection to distance education like adequate infrastructure and physical as well as human expertise with quality of technology.

G. Marinoni et al. [12] in their work focused on the impact linked to teaching and learning systems. In the pandemic situation, it of course impacted many institutions, and gradually majority of the institutions have adopted online learning systems.

Affouneh S et al. [13] in their work prioritized specific learning strategies provisioned to summarize the present online teaching methodologies. They focused on high-impact principles linked to online education, i.e., linkages among online educational design as well as student learning and emergency plans to deal with unexpected incidents of online learning platforms.

Favale T et al. [14] observed the significance of online learning which may be supportive toward switching the online systems in most educational institutions. Of course, it will help to focus on the fruitful side of e-learning technologies.

Tull S. P. C. et al. [15] in their work focused on the mechanism of the adoption of online learning systems as well as the enhancement of the quality of virtual courses. Accordingly, they have also realized the requirement of effective and efficient educational system. So toward enhancing the effectiveness of e-learning, they prioritized some specific techniques and minimized procurement as well as maintenance costs.

Brianna D et al. [16] in their work prioritized on EdTech start-ups to minimize the distractions observed Iin the lecture deliberation. So to maintain consistency and to make more effective and meaningful learning environment, this startup can help to enhance instructions.

Maity S et al. [17] during their research focused on specific mutation operators and tried to implement them in testing routines with specified small-scale instances. Also, they prioritized a modified genetic algorithm along with a new selection and crossover operations.

Wang Y et al. [18] in their work focused on hybrid genetic algorithm along with local optimization strategies. During their research, they focused on improved genetic algorithm with two-part chromosome crossover to implement over small- and medium-scale instances.

X. Zeng et al. [19] in their research have observed and prioritized large-scale data being produced by the rapid enhancement of the internet of things. The primary linkages in such applications are through different types of sensors along with high-dimensional, random and strong interferences.

C.-J. Tsai et al. [20] in their work have implemented statistics to quantify class attribute correlation toward maximizing operations. Somehow, optimizing operations based on a single attribute interval may not be sufficient to maintain consistency in the original data.

H. S. Hassanein et al. [21] in their work prioritized efficient and influential data preprocessing technologies. The main intention is to minimize the complexity of data by transforming the continuous features in massive data to discrete features. In fact, they focused on specific mechanisms to improve the efficiency of data mining as well as machine learning applied on the data.

K. Sriwanna et al. [22] in their research focused on the complexity of multidimensional data along with predefined features. In their work implementing genetic algorithm toward the optimization of multidimensional data, they observed the primary challenges because of cross fragments and diversity linked to multidimensional data.

6.4 APPLICATION OF EVOLUTIONARY MECHANISMS

Initially large-sized heterogeneous data being provisioned can be divided into small groups, and each group may be considered a population. Using genetic operators applied iteratively on the population, an optimum solution can be obtained. Of course, the search initiation process may be initiated either locally or in random, which may help to explore the entire solution and is proficient in avoiding reaching a local optimum, while local search helps in exploring all the local possibilities and reaching the best solution. It is understood that the genetic algorithm is quite effective while searching the problem domain as well as solving complex problems. Typically, it performs search and is provisioned with near optimal solutions for an objective function. Practically, the chromosomes can be referred to as a population, and within each chromosome, it may link to the parameters in the search space. Initially it is required to formulate the population randomly representing feasible solutions in the search space. After that, some part of the chromosomes may be selected based on the fitness values, and also the same may be linked to the next generation. After that focus may be given on a generation of new candidate solutions after recombination is performed upon candidate solution selection. Specifically, the selection operation is based on the evaluation of individual fitness parameters, and the individuals with higher fitness in general may be selected. Also, the probability of the individual is dependent on the population size and fitness values. Somehow, the individuals with large fitness are more likely to be selected, which may result indirectly in the population diversity. It is seen that these individuals may not be linked towards optimality but may be close approximately to the optimal feasible solution. Therefore, it may be required for the expansion of the fitness of functional parameters to obtain the factors.

6.5 BASIC STEPS TOWARD OBTAINING OPTIMALITY USING EVOLUTIONARY TECHNIQUES

Step 1: Determine the number and size of the clusters with permissible data sets.

Step 2: Obtain the population size Psize with maximum iterations.

Step 3: Initialize the chromosomes accumulated from the set of data for i=1 to Psize for every chromosome j. Allocate the data sets to the cluster.

Step 4: Compute the fitness value of chromosome j.

Step 5: Generate the offspring and new parametric values of chromosomes implementing the selection and crossover as well as mutation operation.

Step 6: Based on the size of the population, determine the fitness parameters of individual chromosome fitness(t) = 2. (qi - 1)/T-1, where t may be have unique value, qi denotes the positional occurrence and T is a group of unique parametric values.

Step 7: Satisfying the conditional achievement of fitness values, obtain the solution. Step 8: Determine the level of fitness aggregating all the fitness parameters.

Step 9: Apply the crossover as well as mutation operations on each part of the population.

6.6 EXPERIMENTAL ANALYSIS

In general, most of the systems linked to large-scale data have been focused on processing unstructured data. Accordingly, the indices may be created, and of course, these are required to enhance the internet search capabilities. So, the benefits toward processing unstructured data can lead in the implementation of processing structured data (Table 6.1). While involving the queries with the joining databases as well as aggregation, and as reflected in Figure 6.3, it is obvious that the results of the join can require multiple iterations associated with join indices. Also, the join key may not be similar with the group-by aggregation key. In such situations, some of the partial aggregations can be the part of saving the significant input/output along with the runtime sequence costs by preventing unnecessary intermediate data during the operation (Table 6.2).

TABLE 6.1
Linked Databases with Response Time

Sl.No.	Number of Linked Databases	Response Time (m.sec.)
1	20	0.47
2	29	0.51
3	35	0.56
4	40	0.61

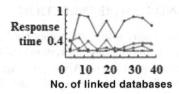

FIGURE 6.3 Linked databases with response time.

TABLE 6.2
Deployed Servers with Response Time

Sl.No.	Size of Deployed Servers	Response Time (m.sec.)
1	20	0.34
2	35	0.47
3	44	0.51
4	55	0.61

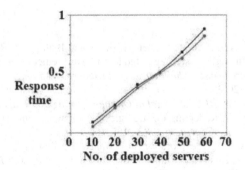

FIGURE 6.4 Deployed servers with response time.

Sometimes the system may be responsible to transform the aggregation operators into multiple stages and compute these partial aggregations focusing the cardinalities of the join key values with the entire databases of concern. In fact, the schema implementation on datasets depends on the loading mechanism interception with the mapped tasks and parsing logic. Therefore, the data organized in some situations can be linked with only those processes that generate the data and help in facilitating the optimization process. Considering the nested or semi structured data and as cited in Figure 6.4, it is observed that unifying the relations and databases as a unique entity can enhance the semantics as well as the performance of the system. Also the optimality of the schema values of the datasets can be more beneficial especially to the nested datasets. Therefore, the statistical properties of specific attribute expressions can be preserved, and the automatic generation of a complete normalized schema can be obtained.

6.7 DISCUSSION AND FUTURE DIRECTION

Earlier platforms with prerequisite information may not be adequate in the present situation due to inflexibilities. But making the system customized may adopt toward implications on online learning systems. Also, using the system, many content-based parameters can be influenced traversing the customized learning paths. Of course, the necessary steps and mechanisms should be more involved in the generation of new learning paths. Basically, the mechanism implemented in this learning scheme generation seems to be genetic, as maximum context parametric values can be viewed as constraints, and the genetic algorithm is suitable for handling multiple constraint satisfaction problems.

6.8 CONCLUSION

To obtain the optimality linked to the complex queries is a tedious task, and it is required to find a solution for the optimization of complex queries. Therefore, evolutionary algorithm is better toward implementation and to resolve NP-hard optimization problems. Therefore, the genetic programming approach has been applied to optimize complex queries linked to the databases of the deployed servers.

6.9 REFERENCES

[1] Kuo, Y.-C., Walker, A. E., Schroder, K. E. E., and Belland, B. R. (2014). Interaction, Internet self-efficacy, and self-regulated learning as predictors of student satisfaction in online education courses. *The Internet and Higher Education*, 20: 35–50.

[2] Croxton, R.A. (2014). The role of interactivity in student satisfaction and persistence in online learning. *MERLOT Journal of Online Learning and Teaching*, 10(2): 314–325.

[3] Conrad, D. (2008). Reflecting on strategies for a new learning culture: Can we do it? *Journal of Distance Education*, 22(3): 157–162.

[4] Aljabre, A. (2012). An exploration of distance learning in Saudi Arabian universities: Current practices and future possibilities. *International Journal of Business, Humanities and Technology*, 2(2): 132–137.

[5] Basak, S.K., Wotto, M., and Bélanger, P. (2016). A framework on the critical success factors of e-learning implementation in higher education: A review of the literature. *International Journal of Science Education*, 10: 2409–2414.

[6] Mohammed, H.J., Kasim, M.M., and Shaharanee, I.N. (2018). Evaluation of E-learning approaches using AHP- TOPSIS technique. *Journal of Telecommunication, Electronic and Computer Engineering (JTEC)*, 10: 7–10.

[7] Ince, M., Yigit, T., and Isik, A.H. (2017). AHP-TOPSIS method for learning object metadata evaluation. *International Journal of Information and Education Technology*, 7: 884–887.

[8] Andayani, S., HM, B.S., and Waryanto, N.H. (2020). Comparison of Promethee–Topsis method based on SAW and AHP weighting for school e-learning readiness evaluation. *Journal of Physics: Conference Series*, 1581: 1–8.

[9] Naveed, Q.N., Muhammad, A., Sanober, S., Qureshi, M.R.N., and Shah, A. (2017). A mixed method study for investigating critical success factors (CSFs) of e-learning in Saudi Arabian universities. *International Journal of Advanced Computer Science and Applications (IJACSA)*, 8(5): 171–178.

[10] Dweiri, F., Kumar, S., Khan, S.A., and Jain, V. (2016). Designing an integrated AHP based decision support system for supplier selection in automotive industry. *Expert Systems with Applications*, 62: 273–283.

[11] AA. (2016). AL MULLA: Evaluation of two distance education experiments: The Open University of Malaysia and the colleges of education for girls in Saudi Arabia based on the quality assurance agency for higher education (UK). *International Journal of Educational Research/UAE University*, 39: 123–168.

[12] Marinoni, G., Land, H. V., and Jensen, T. (2020). *The Impact of COVID-19 on Higher Education Around the World*. IAU Global Survey Report.

[13] Affouneh, S., Salha, S. N., and Khlaif, Z. (2020). Designing quality e-learning environments for emergency remote teaching in coronavirus crisis. *Interdisciplinary Journal of Virtual Learning in Medical Sciences*, 11(2): 1–3.

[14] Favale, T., Soro, F., Trevisan, M., Drago, I., and Mellia, M. (2020). Campus traffic and eLearning during COVID-19 pandemic. *Computer Networks*, 176: 107290.

[15] Tull, S. P. C., Dabner, N., and Ayebi-Arthur, K. (2017). Social media and e-learning in response to seismic events: Resilient practices. *Journal of Open, Flexible and Distance Learning*, 21(1): 63–76.

[16] Brianna, D., Derrian, R., Hunter, H., Kerra, B., and Nancy, C. (2019). Using EdTech to enhance learning. *International Journal of the Whole Child*, 4(2): 57–63.

[17] Maity, S., Roy, A., and Maiti, M. (2015). A modified genetic algorithm for solving uncertain constrained solid travelling salesman problems. *Computers & Industrial Engineering*, 83: 273–296.

[18] Wang, Y. (2014). The hybrid genetic algorithm with two local optimization strategies for traveling salesman problem. *Computers & Industrial Engineering*, 70: 124–133.

[19] Zeng, X., Xu, G., Zheng, X., Xiang, Y., and Zhou, W. (2019). E-AUA: An efficient anonymous user authentication protocol for mobile IoT. *IEEE Internet of Things Journal*, 6(2): 1506–1519.

[20] Tsai, C.-J., Lee, C.-I., and Yang, W.-P. (2008). A discretization algorithm based on class-attribute contingency coefficient. *Information Sciences*, 178(3): 714–731.

[21] Hassanein, H. S., and Sharief, M. A. O. (2017). Big sensed data challenges in the Internet of Things. Proceedings of the 2017 13th International Conference on Distributed Computing in Sensor Systems (DCOSS), Ottawa, Canada.

[22] Sriwanna, K., Boongoen, T., and Iam-On, N. (2016). An evolutionary cut points search for graph clustering- based discretization. Proceedings of the 2016 13th International Joint Conference on Computer Science and Software Engineering (JCSSE), Khon Kaen, Thailand, July.

7 A Study on Online Learning Systems' Identification with Security Schemes and Applications

Anil W. Kale[1], Vaibhav E. Narawade[2]
and Priyanka M. Kothoke[1]
1 MGM College of Engineering and
  Technology, Mumbai, India
2 Ramrao Adik Institute of Technology, Mumbai, India

CONTENTS

7.1   INTRODUCTION

Information sharing and feedback is part of the online community. On the one hand, web technology offers this functionality, but due to the increasing number of daily internet users and their increasing knowledge of basic information, it is very difficult for website providers to provide information and personal data of the user on request and on demand without the knowledge of the website user. After the current practice of designing web services in relation to the customer was studied, it was found that all the information available in the data is heterogeneous in different forms such as audio, video, text, multimedia, etc. Intelligence is a unique model given to man, and artificial intelligence is the asset that man has been trying to integrate into the computer system for fifty years, and the journey continues. The Semantic Web technology is a new innovation in web technology developed by Mr. Tim Berners Lee, president of the W3C, to distribute information in an intelligent way. The Semantic Web is a new WWW platform that not only supports web browsing but is also related to formal semantics. Information is presented in a descriptive way using the semantic network that positively enables computers and people to work together. The idea of the semantic network is to leave most operations and decisions in the machine [1]. It is a task to increase the knowledge of the network system. But to develop a good semantic web technology, the ontology must be developed. The ontology describes an intimate part of the world in a way that can be understood by a machine. Ontology is designed as a tool to define other concepts placed on web pages and provide them for use by software and web applications [2]. The innovation included the e-learning system was used for higher education via the internet. Traditional e-learning provides instructional information only in the form of robust electronic data that demonstrates the online system or the use of built-in independent personal computer software and CD/DVD. However, this era of information technology can go even further, as information in the form of text or multimedia is not only presented but presented intelligently, according to the Knowledge of a Web Educator standard as well as a human educator. This document is organized according to the views of various researchers on learning systems and semantic web services described in section 2. The main model of e-learning is explained in section 3. Read the comparative study of learning institutions in section 4. Research and design issues for e-learning system improvements are discussed in section 5, then the authors complete the work in section 6.

With the advent of the internet and the WWW, the world has become a global city. In the past, the dissemination of information was very difficult around the world. But today it is easier to share and learn than to use the internet. The internet has greatly helped the education system to introduce a concept called Learning Management System (LMS) based on e-learning. Many schools have started using these systems to meet a variety of business needs. A standard e-learning system (LMS) is introduced. Typically, an LMS has several different components or modules. The class management module provides the tools to add new courses, browse or update existing courses and provide teachers with course and course details. The student administration module includes student registration for regular and elective courses. This module is important for the other modules to work properly. A web-based test section is often used to separate the assessment process from students and is a great help for the teacher to save time. Since character is not required in this module, it provides 100% accuracy. On the online assessment board, the student can upload the course electronically, so there is no need to submit it on paper. The teacher can download tutorials, videos and other resources using the web-saving module. Using this module, students will be able to view and download these study materials. Students will be able to provide feedback on each of the topics and topics, and only the other party will consider the idea. It is a valuable aid for the basic assessment. It provides faster and better output compared to manual response systems. There are several LMS

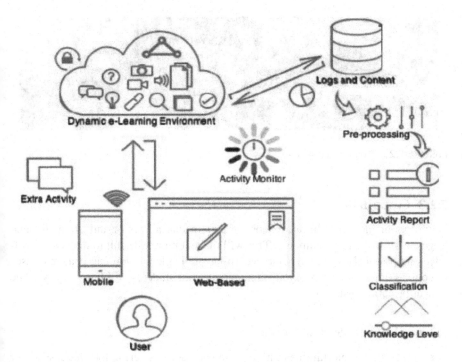

FIGURE 7.1   Online e-Learning system architecture.

systems based on Bayesian networks, ontology, artificial intelligence, multi-agent, fuzzy knowledge, Multimedia Assistive Environmental Instruction (MATE), and the Model Driving Approach. LMS e-learning systems can also help with project management and content management. An e-learning system architecture can be found in Figure 7.1 and Figure 7.2.

7.2   APPLICATION

7.2.1   MICROLEARNING

Microlearning is where you learn and learn using simple methods to remember knowledge. Few people have access to education in a classroom or classroom, but its distribution in small groups is guaranteed to work well. Microlearning is more than traditional training, and you should make sure it's an integral part of any e-learning system you use for business training or general education of any kind.

7.2.2   MOBILE PHONE: LEARN FIRST

Almost everyone in the developing world has a mobile phone these days—many people work in global commerce. By allowing students to use their own phone, they can schedule classes and training at their convenience anywhere in the world.

FIGURE 7.2   Cloud-based system.

7.2.3 Cloud-Based

Few parts of the world have a telephone system that allows organizations to send large class files to large numbers. This will make it more difficult to manage knowledge and power. However, if your e-learning site is global, you can change classes or courses quickly whenever you want, and all your students will have access to the new information instantly.

7.2.4 e-Learning System Products

For all e-learning entertainment, it's easy to get stuck answering lots of questions or false positives. A well-designed power supply offers a wide range of types of power supply equipment that is a type of mineral meaning. This way, you can ask students to answer any type of question in different ways. You can use scratch to explain questions, look up words, do the right thing, and more. This way you can add a part of each to the small lessons and engage the students.

7.3   PREVIOUS WORK

These previous works provide information on security schemes that provide security in OLS. Some of the schemes are mentioned as follows:

The authors developed a multi-agent mobile learning system architecture based on a 3-tier framework involving mobile applications, the base layer and the information center. In this case, a telemarketer continuously monitors the student's performance to determine the best learning opportunities and to identify the user's weaknesses [1]. The developer supports the process of creating personal information for a single phone user, rapid map development and integration.

Design for the development and implementation of a regional framework for e-learning systems is based on the presentation of educational resources using the World Wide Web [2].

One of the most common challenges faced by researchers is the development of an e-learning system that requires a variety of components, such as developing questions, screening students, training blogs, web knowledge and psychology (i.e., self-ishness, self-discipline), communication and the ability to multitask with all these tools in one building [3].

Agent-Based Technology (ABIS) is an application framework designed for e-learning. The authors examine the methods and techniques used to transmit the data. It aims to create collaborative and technological approaches to data discovery through the integration and coordination of extensive research in the field of e-learning [4].

One of the benefits of the online learning process is the ability to access new learning materials while creating unique learning plans for students. Another advantage of the online learning system is that it can help teachers track student progress and improve the relationship between the teacher and the students who are struggling with a problem [5].

The problem with the current online learning system is the lack of isolation due to learning disabilities [6]. The theoretical aspects of web services technology are not enough to make it difficult to obtain improved web services based on perceived user demand [7]. Online learning is slowly becoming an important part of learning in modern society. It is especially important to know how to present students with relevant and effective learning resources from a wide range of learning resources. Technical recommendations are one of the best solutions. However, due to a lack of consideration of learning environment data, learning resource counseling methods may not be able to effectively address issues such as loss of educational mobility and entering the subject of learning. To answer these questions, this article recommends an instructional counseling method based on the learning environment. By building a map of the learning environment and a "learning-focused" contextual accommodation system, combined with personalized counseling technology, learners and learning resources are maintained according to learning goals. This approach can help students understand the process of learning and the direction of learning and improve their academic achievement.

In response to the emergence and permanent solution to the Covid-19 outbreak, this study offers a theoretical framework based on literature and design to determine the success of an e-learning website. The study compared men and women using [8] the e-learning channel. The purpose of the study was to examine gender differences across online learning access to student environments. The research covers service quality, system quality, data quality, user satisfaction, system usage and success of the e-learning channel. The actual data of 280 students was obtained from various Malaysian universities through a Google search which was analyzed using the framework of the underlying system. The study further divided the complete model into two categories, namely women and men. In a male model, data quality and system quality are directly related to user satisfaction. Data quality also supports compatibility with system usage. At the same time, there is a positive relationship between user satisfaction and e-learning networks. Similarly, in the female model, the quality of the electronic service and the quality of the information support both the use of the system and the satisfaction of the users. Similarly, system quality has a good relationship with user satisfaction, and user satisfaction has a good relationship with e-learning methods. The study further assists Malaysian university policymakers such as senior management, the Ministry of Higher Education, and the Association of Malaysian Universities to formulate effective education policies.

7.4   RESEARCH METHODOLOGY

There are six parts in this e-learning system as shown in Figure 7.3. Learner entity is a graphical interface for the learner or student who wants to learn from the online learning system. The trainer is the heart of this model, which provides tutorials, reviews, questions answered añd more. The resources section contains statistical data, which determines the information provided to a student through the transcripts section. The most important part of this product is the evaluation section, which continuously evaluates the student's behavior, learning progress through the evaluation of an experience or some other form of evaluation by the system. The final section contains the student records that will preserve the student's knowledge

7.5   CONCLUSION

While e-learning is a continuous process and the demands of e-learning are changing every day, every online training center is known to have certain limitations. It is a very difficult task for administrators and researchers to meet the needs of international students. One of the solutions to this problem is the combination of semantic web technology and smart software technology which provides the advantage of student privacy. With their help, truly effective e-learning applications can be developed. A cloud-based learning management system (CLMS) must be developed, which can integrate all the topics covered in the previous section with the latest features, such as simple performance analysis with the addition of a plagiarism detector as well as the comparison of words, navigation in the virtual workshop on the web and unique signage.

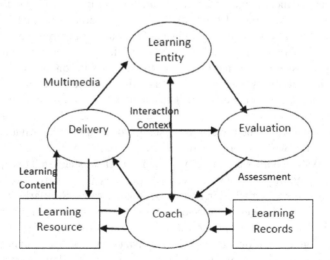

FIGURE 7.3   Online learning systems of the proposed model.

7.6　EXPECTED OUTCOME

- Explore the growth of EdTech start-ups and e-learning.
- Lead strengths, weaknesses, opportunities and challenges.
- Emphasize e-learning during coronavirus disease and natural disasters.
- Provide ideas and suggestions for website success.
- How to learn in times of crisis.

7.7　REFERENCES

[1]　Omar Al-Sakran, Hasan, Bin Muhaya, Fahad, & Serguievskaia, Irina. (2010). Multi agent-based M- learning system architecture. *IEEE Region 8 SIBIRCON-2010*, Irkutsk Listvyanka, Russia, July 11–15, pp. 870–875.

[2]　S. Prakasam, Prof. R. M. Suresh. (2010). An agent-based intelligent system to enhance e-learning through mining techniques. *International Journal on Computer Science and Engineering*, 2(3), 759–763.

[3]　Axita Shah, Sonal Jain. (2011). An agent based personalized intelligent e-learning. *International Journal of Computer Applications (0975–8887)*, 20(3), 40–45.

[4]　Masrom, Suraya, & Sani Abd. Rahman, Abdullah. (2009). An adaptation of agent-based computer- assisted assessment into e-learning environment. *IJEIT*, 3(3), 163–170.

[5]　Dawn, G. (2007). Online e-learning agents. *The Learning Organization*, 14(4), 300–312.

[6]　Jamuna Rani, S., Marie, Stanislas Ashok, & Palanivel, K. (2009). Adaptive content for personalized e- learning using web service and semantic web. *International Conference on Intelligent Agent and Multi Agent System*, IEEE.

[7]　Li, Hao, Wang, Libin, Du, Xu, & Zhang, Mingyan. (2017). Research on the strategy of E-Learning resources recommendation based on learning context. In *2017 International Conference of Educational Innovation Through Technology (EITT)*. IEEE, pp. 209–213.

[8]　Shahzad, Arfan, Hassan, Rohail, Yusuff Aremu, Adejare, Hussain, Arsalan, & Nawaz Lodhi, Rab. (2021). Effects of COVID-19 in E-learning on higher education institution students: The group comparison between male and female. *Quality & Quantity*, 55(3), 805–826.

8 A Study on the Impact of Mobility on the Performance of Routing Protocols in MANET-Based Online Learning Platforms

Banoj Kumar Panda[1],
Pradyumna Kumar Mohapatra[2],
Arun Agarwal[3] *and Janmejaya Swain*[4,1]

1 Gandhi Institute for Education and Technology, Bhubaneswar, India

2 Vedang Institute of Technology, Bhubaneswar, India

3 Siksha 'O'Anusandhan University, Bhubaneswar, India

4 Deloitte USA

CONTENTS

8.1 INTRODUCTION

An online learning platform based on MANET [1] is created by gathering of numerous wireless communicating devices without having any fixed centralized server. Here each learning node can behave as a source node, destination node or intermediate node. These learning nodes move randomly, and the network topology varies continuously. The mobility of every online learning node acts as a key factor for the performance variation of the routing protocols. Hence, the examination of some parameters may give us the causes of the performance variation. We can improve the MANET-based online learning performance by taking proper majors to causes. The mobility characteristic of the learning nodes in a network chooses the suitable routing protocol for better network online performance [1–4]. Nodes in a MANET-based online network move arbitrarily with different speed, so it is difficult to get a path to the destination. In this work, we have used Direct Source Routing (DSR) as the routing protocol, and the performance evaluation has been done at several pause-times and different network traffic.

8.2   DIRECT SOURCE ROUTING PROTOCOL

DSR uses 'source routing'; that means sender learning nodes know the details about the route for the sink learning nodes. The route details are kept in a routing table of every learning node. The DSR protocol does two functions: route path discovery and path maintenance [5]. If a source learning node wants to send some data to a particular destination learning node, it copies the route information in different field of packet header. Normally the route search process is initiated when a route for a particular destination is not available in its route cache. A new route search is done by broadcasting a special packet to the network known as route request packet (RREQ). When a learning node in the network obtains a RREQ packet, it checks whether the packet is for itself or not. If the packet destination is the learning node itself, then it sends the Route Reply packet (RREP); otherwise, it is rebroadcasted toward next neighboring nodes [6–8]. When it reaches at the destination, learning node replies RREP packets, which are sent back toward the source node in same path in the reverse direction. The fresh route is memorized at the source node for further use. When a link breaks, the sending node is informed by sending a route error (RERR) packet [9–11]. When an RERR packet is received at a source node, the particular path is cleared from route cache.

8.3   ENVIRONMENT FOR SIMULATION

Simulation analysis is done using Global Mobile Simulator (Glomosim) as the network simulator [12–13]. Here the simulation is done using the DSR routing protocol. The Random Way Point model is used as mobility model in this simulation [14–16]. The parameters that we have assumed for the simulation are listed below in Table 8.1.

The network simulation is done for a total of 15 minutes or 900 seconds. Every simulation is regarded as a seed. For a given set of parameters, five has been taken. A point on performance plot is the average of these five seeds.

8.3.1   PERFORMANCE EVALUATION METRICS

Packet delivery fraction: It is the ratio of the net packet received at destination learning node to the net packet transmitted by the various source learning nodes. It also called the packet received ratio.

TABLE 8.1

Simulation Setup

Simulation Parameters	Values Taken
Network Terrain	1450MX350M
Total Learning Nodes	50
Model Used for Mobility	RWP
Source Numbers	10,20,30
Top Speed	20M/S
Span of Simulation	15M
Maximum Range of Transmission	250M
MAC Protocol Used	802.11
Protocol Used for Routing	DSR
Size of the Packet	512
Data Rate	2MBPS
Traffic Type	CBR

Normalized routing load: Normalized routing load is the ratio of net routing control packets broadcasted by all learning nodes in the network to the net packets received by all destination learning nodes. It is also known as routing load.

8.4 ANALYSIS OF SIMULATION RESULTS

In this section, we show the simulation results for the DSR protocol, along with a detailed analysis of its performance. Analysis is done by varying learning node's pause time for different transmission sources like 10, 20 and 30.

8.4.1 CHANGING LEARNING NODE MOBILITY

Pause time is time of halt of a learning node at an intermediate point before moving to next random point [10]. A short pause period indicates high mobility, while a long pause time indicates low mobility. The plots in this paper depict various values of performance indicators as mentioned in the previous section, with pause times ranging from 0 to 900s. Figure. 8.1(a) indicates the plot between packet delivery fraction and pause time for 10, 20 and 30 values of transmitting sources.

It is observed from the plot that with 10 sources and 0s pause period, the packet received ratio is 0.39 high in comparison to 30 sources. It indicates when network traffic or the number of online learning subscribers increases the packet received ratio decreases. The increase in network traffic also increases the routing load and hence increases the unavailability of the route from source to destination. It is very clear from plot that with increase in pause period, the packet received ratio of DSR protocol increases. As the pause period increases, the number of link failure reduces; therefore, the congestion of network increases. We know that the DSR protocol keeps

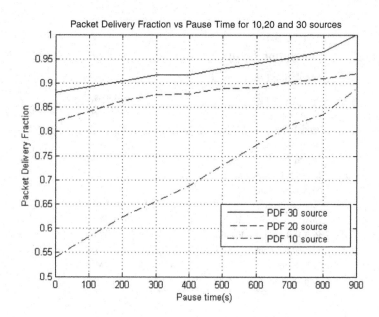

FIGURE 8.1(A)   Packet delivery Fraction vs. Pause time for a MANET of 50 learning nodes with 10, 20 and 30 sources.

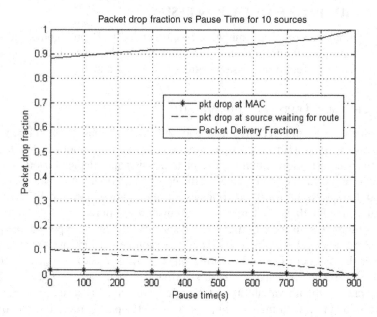

FIGURE 8.1(B)   Packet Drop vs. Pause time in a MANET of 50 learning nodes and 10 sources.

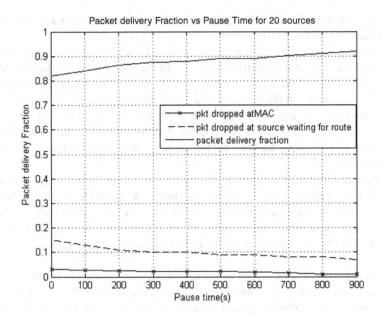

FIGURE 8.1(C) Packet Drop vs. Pause time in a MANET of 50 learning nodes and 20 sources.

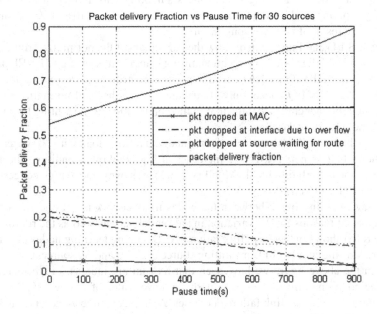

FIGURE 8.1(D) Packet Drop vs. Pause time in a MANET of learning 50 nodes and 30 sources.

many alternative paths for a destination, so the packet received ratio increases so online learning performance improves.

Figure 8.1(b) provides an unambiguous plot of packet drop ratio with 50 learning nodes having 10 transmitting sources. In high mobility, the packet drop at MAC layer is higher; as mobility decreases, the packet drop decreases as the link break decreases. When the pause period is low, the packet drop at the source waiting for the route is more; this is because high mobility link failure is also more; hence, routes are not available toward the destination. As mobility reduces, the link break also reduces and the packet drop reduces with a raise in the packet received ratio.

The plots in Figures 8.1(c) and 8.1(b) show that at low network load, the maximum number of packets dropped at the transmitting learning node due to the unavailability of path. As the pause period improves, the drop ratio also raises slowly. It is observed that many of the packets are lost at MAC layer because of the busy status of the channel as given in the figure is a tiny ratio, and it reduces with a raise in the pause period.

In Figure 8.1(d) it can be seen with a higher network traffic, the packet drop ratio is due to a busy route; packet spillover at the interface is above 20% at a lower value of the pause period. When the pause period increases, the packet drop ratio, because of the busy route and inaccessible node, reduces slowly. The packet drop ratio at the node interface reduces because of increase in pause time.

From Figure 8.1(e) it is seen that for 30 sources, the normalized routing load increases to 45% from 10 sources and 40% compared to 20 sources at high mobility condition; as the pause period increases from 0s to 900s, the link failure reduces, so routing load reduces. Routing load reduces smoothly with reduction in the node's mobility. Routing load is high for 30 sources in comparison to 10 and 20 transmitting sources as a result of network congestion.

Figure 8.1(f) and Figure 8.1(b) show the particulars of the normalized routing load (NRL) of a MANET with varying transmitting sources. It is seen that RREP packets contribute around 80% of NRL. RREP packets contribute more routing load than RREP packets. RREQ packet only contribute 20% of the total normalized routing load. The figure concludes that the maximum contribution of the routing load is from RREP and RERR packets.

Fig 8.1(h) shows the particulars of a normalized routing load with 30 sources. The plot shows that as network traffic increases at high mobility condition, the RREP increases due to high link break. Mobility decreases slowly due to high congestion in the network for high traffic.

The average link break between the nodes in a network is considered as one of the important reasons for the variation in packet delivery as well as the routing load. Figure 8.1(i) shows the average link failure (ALB) among learning nodes in a mobile network varying number of transmitting sources (10, 20 and 30 sources).

From the above figure we have seen that link failure increases with increase in learning node's mobility. We have seen that at lower value of sources (10, 20), as the pause period increases, link failure decreases. At higher source values, i.e., at 30, the link failures are observed to be higher in comparison to lower source values at higher learning node mobility. The link failure reduces with a raise in the pause period up

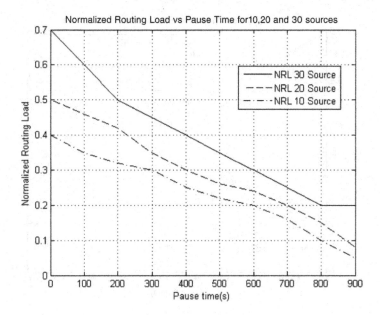

FIGURE 8.1(E) Routing Load vs. Pause time with 10, 20 and 30 source learning nodes.

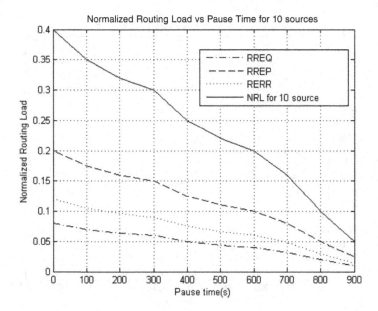

FIGURE 8.1(F) Routing Load vs. Pause time with 50 learning nodes and 10 sources.

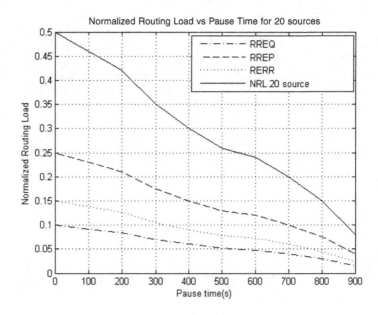

FIGURE 8.1(G)   Routing Load vs. Pause time with 50 learning nodes and 20 sources.

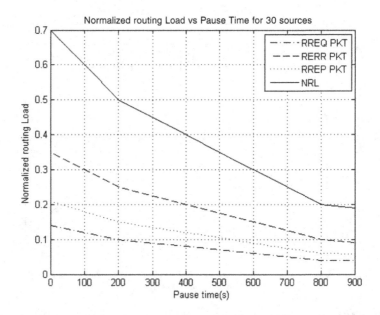

FIGURE 8.1(H)   Routing Load vs. Pause time with 50 learning nodes and 30 sources.

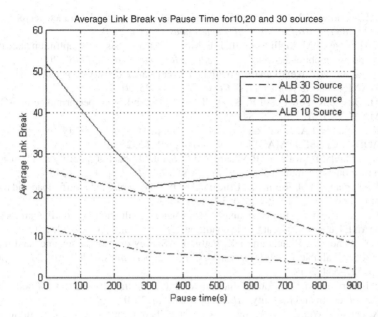

FIGURE 8.1(I)   Average link Failure vs. Pause time with different sources.

to it the value of 300s; after that there is a slow raise in link break due to network congestion.

8.5   CONCLUSIONS

This paper describes the impact of DSR routing protocol in a MANET-based online learning system briefly and analyzes the performance variation with changes in online learning nodes' mobility. The analysis outcome indicates that the DSR routing protocol of the MANET-based online learning system performs better when the number of sources is less and mobility is low. The performance of the MANET-based online learning system decreases when the mobility and number of online learning subscribers in a network increases.

8.6   REFERENCES

[1]   C.E. Perkins, "Ad-hoc Networking", *Text Book*, Addison-Wesley, 2001.
[2]   L. Bajaj, M. Takai, R. Ahuja, K. Tang, R. Bargodia and M. Gerla, "GlomoSim: A scalable network simulation environment", *CSD Technical Report*, University of California at Los Angles, 1997.
[3]   Josh Broch, David A. Maltz, David B. Johnson, Yih-Chun Hu and Jorjeta Jetcheva, "A Performance Compassion of Multihop Wireless Ad-hoc Network Routing Protocols", *MOBICOM'98*, pp. 85–97, October 1998.
[4]   C.E. Perkins, E.M. Royer, S.R. Das and M.K. Marina, "Performance comparison of two on demand routing protocols for Ad-hoc networks", *IEEE Personal Communications*, pp. 16–28, 2000.

[5] C.E. Perkins, E.M. Royer and S.R. Das, "Ad hoc on demand distance vector routing", IETF *internet draft(draft—ietf- manet- aodv-06.txt)*, 2000.

[6] E.M. Royer, P.M. Melliar-Smith, L.E. Moser, "An analysis of the optimum node density for ad hoc mobile networks", *Proceedings ICC*, vol. 3, pp. 857–861, 2001.

[7] N. Adam, M.Y. Ismail and J. Abdulla, "Effect of node density on performance of three MANET routing protocols", *ICEDSA*, pp. 321–325, 2010.

[8] M. Das, B.K. Panda and B. Sahu, "Impact of mobility on performance of AODV in MANET", *ICICA*, pp. 79–84, 2011.

[9] K. Amjad and A. J. Stocker, "Impact of node density and mobility on performance of AODV and DSR in MANET", *CSNDSP*, pp. 61–65, 2010.

[10] B.K. Panda, J. Swain, D. P. Mishra and B. Sahu, "Impact of mobility and transmission power on performance of AODV in MANET", *WOCN*, pp. 1–7, 2014.

[11] I. Ahamad and M. Rahman, "Efficient AODV routing based on traffic load and mobility of node in MANET", *ICET*, pp. 370–375, 2010.

[12] V. Arora and C. Ramakrishna, "Performance evaluation of routing protocols for MANET under different traffic condition", *ICCET*, vol. 6, pp. 79–84, 2012.

[13] B.K. Panda, U. Bhanja and P.K. Pattnaik, "Survey on routing schemes and mobility models available for real Terrain MANET", *Proceedings of ICMLIP 2019*, Springer, pp. 523–534, 2019.

[14] N.I. Sarkar and W.G. Lol, "Study of MANET routing protocols: Joint node density, Packet length and Mobility", *IEEE*, pp. 515–520, 2010.

[15] X. Hu, J.K. Wong, C.R. Wong and C. Wong, "Is mobility is always harmful to routing protocol performance of MANETs", *ICCEDCKD*, pp. 108–112, 2010.

[16] B.K. Panda, U. Bhanja and P.K. Pattnaik, "Impact of presence of obstacles in Terrain on performance of some reactive protocols in mobile adhoc network", *Proceedings of ICMLIP*, Springer, pp. 585–597, 2020.

9 Comparison between TRANSPOSE and MTF Algorithm with Closure Property

Tapaswini Dash[1], Alina Swain[1],
Pradyumna Kumar Mohapatra[1]
and Banoj Kumar Panda[2]
1 Vedang Institute of Technology (VIT), Odisha, India
2 Gandhi Institute for Education and
Technology, Odisha, India

CONTENTS

9.1 INTRODUCTION

As well as helping us achieve our academic goals, online learning can also help us gain new skills that are beneficial when starting a new career. LAP is a well-read research problem, in which is given a set of probe/elements in a list where the cost of an retrieving an item is proportional to its distance from the head of the list. LAP changes the list while processing the entire request sequence on the list and reduces the access cost. List accessing algorithms have MTF, TRANSPOSE and FC (frequency count) algorithm. As we already know that the request sequence is accessed

DOI: 10.1201/9781003272823-9

by the list accessing algorithm. The process of accessing the request sequence in the list based on the past and future request sequence is called list accessing algorithm. Any accessed data or element needs some cost to access the unsorted list using cost models, which is already defined in previous related papers. In list accessing algorithm we can take a list of elements and request sequence then search the request elements one by one; while we search the requested element one by one, we get access cost. Here we compare between MTF algorithm and TRANSPOSE algorithm on which algorithm reduces the access cost, then we show that TRANSPOSE algorithm reduces the access cost compared to the MTF algorithm.

9.2   PROBLEM STATEMENT

Many list accessing algorithms have been developed. MTF and TRANSPOSE algorithms are among them. In MTF when we search a request element in list, the probe/element is moved straight to the front of the list without hampering on the other element order of the list. In TRANSPOSE after accessing the request element in the list, the element is shifted one place left of the list. We show that MTF algorithm gives more access cost in some classes of request sequence. Our purpose is to reduce the access cost of those classes of request sequence using TRANSPOSE algorithm.

9.3   LITERATURE REVIEW

In our study, list accessing techniques were begun on the starting work of McCabe in 1965 [1]. He was the first person who operationally researched on serial files and developed 2 algorithms called Move-To-Front (MTF) and TRANSPOSE. In 1984 J.H. Hester and D.S. Hirschberg started surveying all the previously search papers, then they created the algorithm that modifies the order of linear search lists [2]. In 1985 D.D. Sleator and R.E. Tarjon searched about the amortized efficiency of the Move-to-Front algorithm and similar rules for dynamically maintaining a linear list [3]. In the year 2012 Rakesh Mohanty, Sangita Patel, Shiba Prasad dash and Burle Sharma observed that TRANS outperforms MTF for two special types of request sequence without locality of reference [4]. In 2018 Sasmita Tripathy et al. published a new method, MTHT algorithm, with look-ahead for the list accessing problem [5]. In the same year, 2018, Pratyasha Tripathy and Richismita Rout published a characterized request sequence; in that paper the cost is deliberate by calculating the total cost using a formula instead of calculating manually [6]. After that, in the year 2019 Shiba Prasad Dash and Puja Rani Nanda proposed an MTF algorithm using hash function [7].

LIST ACCESSING PROBLEM

There are mostly three basic algorithms developed; also, there are many such algorithms that were developed to date, but mostly three algorithms are used:

    i.   MTF (Move-to-Front) algorithm
   ii.   TRANSPOSE algorithm
  iii.   FC (Frequency Count) algorithm

I.   **MTF (Move-To-Front) algorithm:** In MTF algorithm there will be a known list and a request sequence. Each time we search an element or probe in sequence list, the element or probe is moved straight to the front of the list without changing the order of the list sequence. Then we find the access cost.

II. **TRANSPOSE algorithm:** Another list accessing algorithm is TRANS-POSE algorithm. In this algorithm we know the list but we don't know the request sequence. We have to take a random request sequence. Here each time we search an element in the list, the searched element will exchange with the left side of that element and move to the left side in the list.

III. **FC (Frequency Count) algorithm:** Another list accessing algorithm is Frequency Count (FC). This algorithm maintains the frequency count of the element in the list. Each time we access an element in the list, the frequency count increase to 1. Then the list of the element is rearranged to the non-increasing order. The following is an example for better understanding:

Where, List is 123 and Request Sequence is 132.

9.4   OUR CONTRIBUTION

List accessing problem is a vast area to research where many researchers research about more things like how to reduce access cost. They found that between MTF, TRANSPOSE and FC, MTF gives better results in the case of reducing access cost.

In this paper, we discuss MTF and TRANSPOSE list accessing algorithms. We have shown that TRANSPOSE gives a better result compared to MTF algorithm in the case of various request sequences. If we take a request sequence which is the closure of list and take a request sequence which is the closure of the reverse of the list, in those cases, TRANSPOSE gives less access cost compared to MTF algorithm. That we discuss in this paper deeply with theoretical and experimental analysis.

9.5   EXPERIMENTAL ANALYSIS OF TRANSPOSE

As we all know, in list accessing algorithm, after accessing an element in the list, an access cost occurs. As previous studied, MTF algorithm gives a better result compared to TRANSPOSE algorithm. Our purpose is to reduce the access cost. So, we compare between MTF and TRANSPOSE algorithms in various classes of request sequence. At the end we found that TRANSPOSE algorithm gives a better result than MTF algorithm in the case of (123)* and (321)* for which the list is 1234. With closure property we examine same dataset with a full cost model and a partial cost model.

9.5.1   EXPLANATION OF TRANSPOSE USING FULL COST MODEL

9.5.1.1   MTF (Move-to-Front) Algorithm

Here in MTF algorithm we take list 1234, request sequence (123)* which is 123123 and another one is (321)* which is 321321. Then we found the total access cost for (123)* is 15 and for (321)* is 18. As we all know, in MTF algorithm, after accessing an element in the list, the element is moved directly to the front of the list. Then we found the access cost. Here are a total 6 steps. All the steps are processing in this way. Afterward, we found the total access cost.

9.5.1.2 TRANSPOSE Algorithm

TRANSPOSE gives less access cost, which means it gives better results in both cases compared to MTF algorithm. In transpose algorithm, each time we searched an element in the list, the searched element will exchange with exact left side of that element and move to the left side in the list. After that, we found the total access cost. TRANSPOSE Algorithm with Closure Property can be found in Table 9.1 and Table 9.2.

9.5.2 EXPLANATION OF TRANSPOSE USING PARTIAL COST MODEL

Partial cost: In the partial cost model, the access cost of a probe is the number of the comparison requested for accessing the requested probe from the list of sequence; for example, if the access cost of a particular element, let's say x, and the position is of x is in i^{th}, then the cost accessing that element is i-1.

TABLE 9.1
TRANSPOSE Algorithm with Closure Property

Steps	R.S (123)*	R.S (321)*	L.C for (123)*	L.C for (321)*	A.C for (123)*	A.C for (321)*
1	1	3	1 2 3 4	1 2 3 4	1	3
2	2	2	1 2 3 4	1 3 2 4	3	6
3	3	1	2 1 3 4	1 2 3 4	6	7
4	1	3	2 3 1 4	1 2 3 4	9	10
5	2	2	2 1 3 4	1 3 2 4	10	13
6	3	1	2 1 3 4	1 2 3 4	13	14
	Total access cost for (123)* = 13			Total access cost for (321)* = 14		

TABLE 9.2
TRANSPOSE Algorithms with Closure Property

Steps	R.S (123)*	R.S (321)*	L.C for (123)*	L.C for (321)*	A.C for (123)*	A.C for (321)*
1	1	3	1 2 3 4	1 2 3 4	1	5
2	2	2	1 2 3 4	1 3 2 4	2	7
3	3	1	2 1 3 4	1 2 3 4	4	7
4	1	3	2 3 1 4	1 2 3 4	6	9
5	2	2	2 1 3 4	1 3 2 4	6	11
6	3	1	2 1 3 4	1 2 3 4	8	11
	Total access cost for (123)* = 8			Total access cost for (321)* = 11		

Using partial cost, the next table is calculated taking the same example which is taken in full cost TRANSPOSE algorithm. After finding an element from the list each time, access cost is calculated by i-1.

9.5.2.1 Comparing TRANSPOSE and MTF Algorithm in Each Case

Comparing TRANSPOSE algorithm, which is calculated using full cost model and partial cost model, with normalized MTF algorithm to find out whether the result or access cost of both is less than MTF or not, in the next Table 9.3, we can clearly see difference between access cost of MTF and TRANSPOSE (Figure 9.1).

PROOF 1

MTF algorithm

List = 1234
Request sequence = (1234)* = 123412341234
Step 1
Access 1

1	2	3	4

1 is already in the front of the list, no need to change.
Access cost = 1
Step 2
Access 2

2	1	3	4

2 moves to front of the list.
Access cost = 2
Step 3
Access cost 3

3	2	1	4

Move 3 to the front of the list.
Access cost = 3
Step 4
Access 4

4	3	2	1

Move 4 to the front of the list.
Access cost = 4
Step 5
Access 1

1	4	3	2

Move 1 to front of the list.
Access cost = 4
Step 6
Access 2

| 2 | 1 | 4 | 3 |

Move 2 to front of the list.
Access cost = 4
Step 7
Access 3

| 3 | 2 | 1 | 4 |

Move 3 to front of the list.
Access cost = 4
Step 8
Access 4

| 4 | 3 | 2 | 1 |

Move 4 to front of the list.
Access cost = 4
Step 9
Access 1

| 1 | 4 | 3 | 2 |

1 moves to the front of the list.
Access cost = 4
Step 10
Access 2

| 2 | 1 | 4 | 3 |

Move 2 to front of the list.
Access cost = 4
Step 11
Access 3

| 3 | 2 | 1 | 4 |

Move 3 to front of the list.
Access cost = 4
Step 12
Access 4

| 4 | 3 | 2 | 1 |

Move 4 to the front of list.
Access cost = 4
Total access cost of MTF algorithm = 1 + 2 + 3 + 4 + 4 + 4 + 4 + 4 + 4 + 4 + 4 + 4 = 42

TRANSPOSE Algorithm

List = 1234
Request sequence = (1234)* = 123412341234
Step 1
Access 1

| 1 | 2 | 3 | 4 |

1 is already in the leftmost side of the list, no need to change it.
Access cost = 1
Step 2
Access 2

| 2 | 1 | 3 | 4 |

Exchange 2 with exact left side of the element and change its place.
Access cost = 2
Step 3
Access 3

| 2 | 3 | 1 | 4 |

Exchange 3 with left side of the element.
Access cost = 3
Step 4
Access 4

| 2 | 3 | 4 | 1 |

Exchange 4 with left side of the element.
Access cost = 4
Step 5
Access 1

| 2 | 3 | 1 | 4 |

Swap 1 with exact left side of the element.
Access cost = 4
Step 6
Access 2

| 2 | 3 | 1 | 4 |

2 is already in the leftmost side of the list.

Access cost = 1

Step 7

Access 3

3	2	1	4

Exchange 3 with left side of the element.

Access cost = 2

Step 8

Access 4

3	2	4	1

Exchange 4 with exact left side of the element.

Access cost = 4

Step 9

Access 1

3	2	1	4

Swap 1 with left side of the element and change its place.

Access cost = 4

Step 10

Access 2

2	3	1	4

Swap 2 with the left side of the element.

Access cost = 2 .

Step 11

Access 3

3	2	1	4

Swap 3 with exact left side of the element.

Access cost = 2

Step 12

Access 4

2	3	4	1

Exchange 4 with left side of the element.

Access cost = 4

Total access cost of TRANSPOSE algorithm = 1 + 2 + 3 + 4 + 4 + 1 + 2 + 4 + 4 +
2 + 2 + 4 = 33

Here we show that TRANSPOSE algorithm gives a better result compared to
MTF algorithm in case of closure.

PROOF 2

MTF Algorithm

List = 1234
Request sequence = (4321)* = 432143214321
Step 1
Access 4

4	1	2	3

Move 4 to the front of the list.
Access cost = 4
Step 2
Access 3

3	4	1	2

Move 3 to the front of the list.
Access cost = 4
Step 3
Access 2

2	3	4	1

Move 2 to the front of the list.
Access cost = 4
Step 4
Access 1

1	2	3	4

Move 1 to the front of the list.
Access cost = 4
Step 5
Access 4

4	1	2	3

Move 4 to the front of the list.
Access cost = 4
Step 6
Access 3

3	4	1	2

Move 3 to the front of the list.
Access cost = 4

Step 7
Access 2

2	3	4	1

Move 2 to the front of the list.
Access cost = 4
Step 8
Access 1

1	2	3	4

Move 1 to the front of the list.
Access cost = 4
Step 9
Access 4

4	1	2	3

Move 4 to the front of the list.
Access cost = 4
Step 10
Access 3

3	4	1	2

Move 3 to the front of the list.
Access cost = 4
Step 11
Access 2

2	3	4	1

Move 2 to the front of the list.
Access cost = 4
Step 12
Access 1

1	2	3	4

Move 1 to the front of the list.
Access cost = 4
Total access cost of MTF algorithm = 4+4+4+4+4+4+4+4+4+4+4+4 = 48

TRANSPOSE Algorithm

List = 1234
Request sequence = (4321)* = 432143214321

Step 1
Access 4

1	2	4	3

Swap 4 with exact left side of the element.
Access cost = 4
Step 2
Access 3

1	2	3	4

Exchange 3 with left side of the element.
Access cost = 4
Step 3
Access 2

2	1	3	4

Exchange 2 with left side of the element.
Access cost = 2
Step 4
Access 1

1	2	3	4

Swap 1 with left side of the element.
Access cost = 2
Step 5
Access 4

1	2	4	3

Exchange 4 with left side of the element.
Access cost = 4
Step 6
Access 3

1	2	3	4

Exchange 3 with exact left side of the element.
Access cost = 4
Step 7
Access 2

2	1	3	4

Exchange 2 with exact left side if the element.
Access cost = 2

Step 8
Access 1

1	2	3	4

Swap 1 with the left side of the element.
Access cost = 2
Step 9
Access 4

1	2	4	3

Exchange 4 with exact left side of the element.
Access cost = 4
Step 10
Access 3

1	2	3	4

Exchange 3 with left side of the element.
Access cost = 4
Step 11
Access 2

2	1	3	4

Exchange 2 with exact left side of the element.
Access cost = 2
Step 12
Access 1

1	2	3	4

Exchange 1 with left side of the element.
Access cost = 2

TABLE 9.3
Comparison between TRANSPOSE Algorithm and MTF

Sl-no	TRANSPOSE A_c (123)* Using Full Cost Model	TRANSPOSE A_c (321)* Using Full Cost Model	TRANSPOSE A_c (123)* Partial Cost Model	TRANSPOSE A_c (321)* Partial Cost	MTF A_c (123)* Full Cost Model	MTF A_c (321)* Full Cost Model	MTF A_c (123)* Partial Cost	MTF A_c (321)* Partial Cost
1	1	3	1	5	1	3	1	5
2	3	6	2	7	3	6	2	7
3	6	7	4	7	6	9	4	9
4	9	10	6	9	9	12	6	11
5	10	13	6	11	12	15	8	13
6	13	14	8	11	15	18	10	15

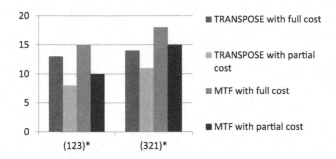

FIGURE 9.1 Graphical representation of MTF and TRANSPOSE algorithm.

Total access cost of TRANSPOSE algorithm = 4 + 4 + 2 + 2 + 4 + 4 + 2 + 2 + 4 + 4 + 2 + 2 = 36
Here in this case, we also show that TRANSPOSE algorithm gives a better result than MTF algorithm.

Graphical representation of the comparison between MTF and Transpose with full cost and partial cost.

9.6 CONCLUSION

In order to successfully complete our online coursework, we will need to become familiar with a variety of digital learning tools, content management systems, collaboration tools and basic technical assistance. In this paper, we conclude that MTF has given better results almost every time, but in some cases, TRANSPOSE gives better results than MTF; hence, we conclude that the TRANSPOSE is closed under closure property and MTF is not.

9.7 REFERENCES

[1] J. McCabe, "On serial files with relocatable records," *Operations Research*, vol. 12, pp. 609–618, 1965.
[2] J. H. Hester, and D. S. Hirschberg, "Self –organizing linear search," vol. 17, pp. 295–312, 1984.
[3] D. D. Sleator, and R. E. Tarjan, "Amortized efficiency of list update and paging rules," *Communications of the ACM*, vol. 28, no. 2, pp. 202–208, 1985.
[4] R. Mohanty, S. P. Dash, B. Sharma, and S. Patel, "Performance evaluation of a proposed variant of frequency count (VFC)," *International Journal of System, Algorithms and Applications*, vol. 2, pp. 2277–2677, 2012.
[5] Tripathy, Sasmita, et al. "Move-to-head-or-tail (MTHT) algorithm for the list accessing problem," *IUP Journal of Information Technology*, vol. 14, no. 2, pp. 90–98, 2018.
[6] Satapathy, Pratyashi, and Richismita Rout. "Characterization and performance evaluation of request sequence for moveto-front algorithm." 2018 Second International Conference on Green Computing and Internet of Things (ICGCIoT). IEEE, 2018.
[7] An Approach to Improve the Performance of MTF Algorithm in List Accessing Problem International Journal of Scientific Research in Computer Science and Engineering, vol. 8, no. 4, pp. 32–36, August 2020. E-ISSN: 2320-7639.K.

10 An Advanced Transpose Algorithm Using the Hash Function with Partial Cost Model

Tapaswini Dash[1], Pradyumna Kumar Mohapatra[1]
and Banoj Kumar Panda[2]
1 Vedang Institute of Technology (VIT), Odisha, India
2 Gandhi Institute for Education and
Technology, Odisha, India

CONTENTS

10.1 INTRODUCTION

Online learning in higher education is generally carried out through a learning management system (LMS), such as asynchronous learning (where students do not have to be online at the same time and use discussion boards and e-mails to complete coursework) or synchronous learning (where all students must be online). In this era of fast and forward, we always want to speed up our day-to-day life with some extra life hacks. The motto is to speed up the time required for doing any work. As well as in data structure, we are optimizing the existing algorithm to speed up the cost. An unorganized linear list in data structure is one of the simplest data structures which is used to access the data and sort the elements. If we want to carry out an access operation, the list has to be traversed (which means searching operation) linearly until the requested item is found. The performance of the accessing of data can be increased by self-organizing techniques [1]. Generally, what we do using unarranged data is we just swap or move the element and reorder. An algorithm which updates the list rooted on the current and last requests is called a list accessing algorithm [1]. These algorithms are called online since they do not know what the forthcoming requests will be and are called offline if entire requests are known. If the present request sequence which is going to be served is known by the algorithm, not only the present but the future request sequence is known and is called as the look-ahead. This type of issue usually arises in our real-life situations. Practically, in an application, requests do not arrive one by one; they come in blocks, possibly in a variety of sizes. In addition, the request generates faster than it can be processed by a list accessing algorithm. Some request sequence usually is waiting online, which is processed by an algorithm further. In some applications, it may also be possible to delay the service of requests to wait for some incoming requests. To access a requested element in a linear unsorted list that bears some cost, that cost is known as access cost [2]. It also bears some cost for reorganizing the elements in the linear unsorted list; this cost is known as exchange cost. A cost is defined by the cost models, how cost is assigned to an element when it is retrieved in the linear unsorted list [3].

- **Cost Models**

There are some cost models defined to calculate the cost of the request access time. Various cost models in the list accessing problem are as follows:

1. Full cost model: Sleator and Tarjon developed the full cost model, which is considered as the base of all cost models of LAP. In the full cost model, the access cost is equal to the requested element position, for example, accessing an element 'n' at the position 'i', the ith is the access cost [3].
2. Partial cost model: Partial cost model defines that the access cost of a probe/element is the number of comparisons requested for accessing the requested probe from the list of sequence; for example, if the access cost of a particular element, let's say 'n', and the position is of the n is in i^{th}, then the cost accessing that element is i-1.
3. P^d cost model: The P^d cost model was developed by Manasse et al. [3] and Rheingold et al. [3]. In the P^d cost model, there is no free exchange between the desired element, and each element has a paid exchange cost 'd'.
4. Centralized cost model: Rakesh Mohanty et al. [3] developed this cost model, which used a doubly linked list. According to Rakesh Mohanty et al. [3], the cost for accessing an element is equal to the distance from the central element of the list. Free exchange is the move to the currently accessed

element to any position of the list either forwarded or backwarded in the center of the list having no cost. Paid exchange means that the exchange is considered when the requested element must be paid for to access it other than the free cost movement. The cost transacted between the two elements is going to be traversed in the paid movement.

5. Buffering look-ahead cost model: This cost model list is called the visited list and makes a visitor point to the elements. If matched, the element from the visited list to the request sequence then is stored in the buffer list. In this model, buffer is a temporary memory to store the elements. If there is any repeated element present in the requested sequence, the list is marked as flagged so that it will be marked that this element is already stored in the buffer list.

A list accessing problem is nothing but the self-organizing algorithm. It is a wide research problem in the context of perceptible probe/elements with a request sequence. The MTF algorithm has always manifested to be the best execute LA online algorithm to date in the literature of linear searching techniques. In 1965, McCabe [1] was the first person to investigate this problem and handed us two algorithms that are used to date. We will know about all proposed algorithms in the literature section (2). The list accessing problem is also called multiple linear searches; in multiple linear searches consist of the list sequence and request sequence, and we must find out the cost in terms of searching time. Why should we do a linear search? Suppose we probe for a particular request sequence from a list; it will cost some time to search and find the record. The place where the record is available is called cost; we can say that the cost is the search (Table 10.1).

10.2   BACKGROUND

In computer science, linear search is one of the elementary search algorithms to find a particular record/element from the list. In linear search, a record is searched sequentially one by one within a fixed rule in the fixed-size linear list from the start of the list to the end of the list. The performance of this data structure can be amplified using self-organizing techniques. After accessing the probe element, we reorganize the list by exchanging the adjacent record so that the frequently requested record is moved closer to the front of the list so that the cost is reduced.

In an online list accessing problem algorithm, sequential searches are performed. A search where a list of the unordered record is performed is known as a sequential search. To analyze online algorithms, a method was invented called competitive analysis. In competitive analysis, the performance of an algorithm is compared to an optimal offline algorithm. An algorithm is called competitive if the competitive ratio is the ratio between the performance of an algorithm and an optimal offline algorithm is bounded.

The list update problem has been a highly interesting topic for the last four decades because it is extensively used in problem-solving in various application areas. One of the most used applications is data compression.

10.2.1 Types of Lists Accessing Problem

However, much work related to linear search has been followed, consisting of various new hybrid algorithms, but primarily, measures are followed within the existing algorithms.

- **Move-to-front:** In this technique, an algorithm is used in the foregoing example of the effects of the locality. Let's understand by an example. Suppose there exist a list sequence which is known to the algorithm and request sequence; hence, we are using an online algorithm request sequence that is unknown. When the record of the request sequence is accessed and searched, if the element/probe is found in the list, then it is moved to front of the list. If the cost of the previous requested record is high, then there will be no change, or else it moves to the front of the list. MTF is an algorithm prone to coincide quickly but has a big asymptotic cost. In J.H. Hester and D.S. Hirschberg's [4] paper, they have claimed that every time a record with low access probability is accessed, it is moved to the front, which increases the cost of the future accesses to many other records. The following is an example of MTF algorithm works: Here the list sequence<123> request list is <23312> is continued in next page.
- **Transpose:** In this algorithm, the accessed record is not moved to the front of the list but instead is swapped up to exactly one position by changing the place with the record present previously. Understand that using a suitable example, suppose there is a list sequence and randomly we will take some request sequence as the request sequence is unknown in the deterministic algorithm. McCabe was the first person to work on Transpose. This paper is based on the Transpose algorithm using the hash function. For example, list sequence <123> request list is <23312>.
- **Frequency count:** In frequency count, the record or element is kept in an extra field of memory, in which a count of access is maintained. In the frequency count algorithm, the array of the list is updated in every count when an element is searched in the frequency count algorithm. In the frequency count, the list is taken, and after each access of an element in the request list, the frequency count array is incremented plus one. If the frequency count of an element is greater than another element present in the list, then we have to swap the element. For example, the list sequence <123> request list is <23312>.
- **Offline algorithm:** In an offline algorithm, the entire sequence is known and bequeaths a complete strategy before serving the first request sequence. Here, the online algorithm is further divided into deterministic and randomized. Move-to-front and frequency count are always considered as the best-performing algorithm for most of the online algorithms and Transpose is considered as the worst-performing algorithm based on their worst-case analysis. Here Transpose is used to give a better result if we compare move-to-front with the hashing function. In this thesis, we try to minimize the access cost by calculating the hash function using a partial cost.

10.2.1.1 Literature Review

In 1965 McCabe [1] was the first person to work on two algorithms consisting of MTF and Transpose. In between 1965 and 1985 all linear search was based on probability and permutation. After the great success of this paper in 1985, J.H. Hester and D.S. Hirschberg [2] started a survey on the algorithms that can help modify the order of linear search. He started computing the algorithm practically.

After that, in 1996, Westbrook & Reingold [3] started a detailed study of an online algorithm for the LUP. After 2 years, in 1998 Susanne Albers [5] proposed a competitive analysis of the LUP with a look-ahead algorithm. In the same year, Susanne Albers [5] introduced an algorithm combining two randomized algorithms called BIT and TIMESTAMP and developed one called COMB. In this paper, two models of look-ahead have been introduced whereas both are different, and by using these models, the list update problem developed lower bounds on competitiveness that can be achieved by deterministic online algorithm look-ahead as well present online algorithms with look-ahead that is competitive against the static offline algorithm. Rakesh Mohanty and Sasmita Tripathy [4, 6] published a complete study of the MTF algorithm and proposed an Improved MTF (IMTF).

In 2011, again Mohanty et al. [7] described the characteristics of request sequence in the list accessing problem. Tripathy et al. [8] in 2018 showed a new method, the MTHT algorithm, with a look-ahead for the LAP. Pratayash Sathpathy and Richismita Rout [9] in 2018 published a characterized request sequence, in which the total cost of a request sequence from the list sequence was calculated directly using a formula instead of calculating manually. There are various online algorithms in the literature. In 1979, Bitner and Gonnet et al. [10] provided a brief survey on the most common algorithms and their analyses.

Hashing: Hashing is an approach that is used in sorting and retrieving data from the database. This information is associated with key properties and makes use of individual characters and numbers in the key itself. Hashing is a technique for implementation in keyed tables. In hashing, the transformation of a string of characters into a frequently shorter fixed-length value or key that represents the original string is done.

10.3   PROPOSED ALGORITHM

In our proposed algorithm, we organize the list having less access cost in the list accessing algorithm [11–14]. The inputs of the list accessing algorithm are a combination of perceptible elements/probes and a sequence of requests. A *request* is accessed through the operation on an element/probe in the list that is to be performed, and a request sequence is a series of requests in a specific order. A request sequence is said to be served when every element in the sequence is accessed in the list by traversing the list and by incurring some access cost.

Our purpose is to subdue this access cost by reorganizing the list. A sort of sequential search [15] in an unsorted linear list can be enhanced by using a hash function in the Transpose algorithm list accessing problem. Hence, MTF always performs better than Transpose, but in *closure,* the Transpose algorithm performs better than MTF when the list has a high degree of locality of reference.

TABLE 10.1

Example of MTF Algorithm Using Closure Property

No. of Observation	Request Sequence of Size 3	Total Access Cost of MTF
1	2 1 3 4	1
2	2 3 1 4	2
3	2 3 4 1	3
4	2 3 1 4	4
5	2 3 1 4	4
6	3 2 1 4	1
7	3 2 1 4	2
8	3 2 4 1	3
	Total cost	24

We calculate the total access cost for all request sequences of size 8 and list size 4 using transpose algorithms. Let the configuration be <1 2 3 4 1 2 3 4>.

10.3.1 Work and Contribution

The list access problem or list update problem is actively in demand for the last 4 to 5 decades. So many publishers have published on this topic. As we already know, all successful algorithms are written to reduce or minimize the access cost of an unsorted list when a request sequence is given. In this paper, we proposed a new way of optimizing the access cost. As we have known, Transpose gives us the worst performance rather than the MTF algorithm. So, here we will discuss that if we give a request sequence with closure of the list, it will provide better performance compared to the MTF algorithm.

In this paper, we study deeply both MTF and transpose algorithms. Our goal is to increase the performance and decrease the access cost. The proposed algorithm is based on the concept of a transpose list accessing [16–21] and separate chaining using the method of a hash function for searching.

Here, a given list sequence is stored in a hash table. To find out the position of each element in the hash table, we are using single hashing for each of the elements proportional to the size of the hash table. After hashing, all the elements are stored in the hash table. Now, the request sequence is accessed through that hash table.

10.3.1.1 Experiment Performed

In this experiment, we decided to implement Transpose algorithm with the help of the hash function using partial cost. The fact is that if we use Transpose algorithm, it is known as the worst algorithm till date. Our motive is to reduce the access cost of Transpose algorithm. After calculating we get to know that if we use the hash function in TUHIP, it will give us the best result compared to the previous Transpose algorithm.

So, what we did is we use the hash table to store maximum data/input to a list using a hash pointer. After using the hash function, we got to know that we can store more data comparatively. Using the hash function automatically reduces the search time but not the access time. So to reduce the access cost, we apply the partial cost model rather than the full cost model. In this new hybrid algorithm (TUHIP), the data is stored in the hash table, and when we request an element/probe to search in a linked list, it is called a requested list.

This can be done by using two loops—outer loops for the request sequence and inner loop for the input list. Suppose the position of the requested element in the input linear list. After accessing the requested probe, search the requested probe in the next(i-1) probe in the request list from the current request element by traversing the (i-1) node from the requested node in a linked list generated. If the requested element is present in the (i-1) element of the request sequence, then shift the access element to the exact right of the (i-1) list. Otherwise, exit from the block. This process will continue at the end of the outer loop of the list [22]. The outer loop will display the total access cost for all the probes. The complete process is depicted through Figure 10.1.

PSEUDOCODE FOR TRANSPOSE ALGORITHM USING THE HASH FUNCTION WITH THE PARTIAL COST MODEL

Inputs:- Here given List is L: - L_0, L_1, L_2, L_3 . . . . . . L_i; Request Sequence is
R: - R_1, R_2, R_3, ... R_p; Partial cost: - p-1;
Output:- Access Cost = Cost of Transpose Algorithm using hash function = $(p_i$-1);
Notations: L_i—ith scanned item in the list where $1 \leq i \leq L$; R_p—ith position of the request sequence where $1 \leq p \leq R$; A_c—Access cost of R_p in list; P_i—position if the ith item in the list; L_j—jth scanned items in the list. P_c—Partial Cost

ALGORITHM

⇨ *Initialize an array of a linked list with the hash table of the given size;*
⇨ *Scan each element of L_i;*
⇨ *Find the index = L_i % size of Table $(L_{i =} K_j)$;*
⇨ *If index == NULL;*
⇨ *Call add key points (1, 2, 3, 4) to the index node (L_i);*
⇨ *Else;*
⇨ *Insert the key at the end of the Index (L_j);*
⇨ *Read the Requested element to be searched;*
⇨ *Scan R_p in the L_i;*
⇨ *Let P_i be the position of R_n in L_j;*
⇨ *Computer Hash key;*
⇨ *Go to match the address;*
⇨ *$A_c = A_c + (P_i—1)$;*
⇨ *Do Transpose;*
⇨ *Else;*
⇨ *Return;*

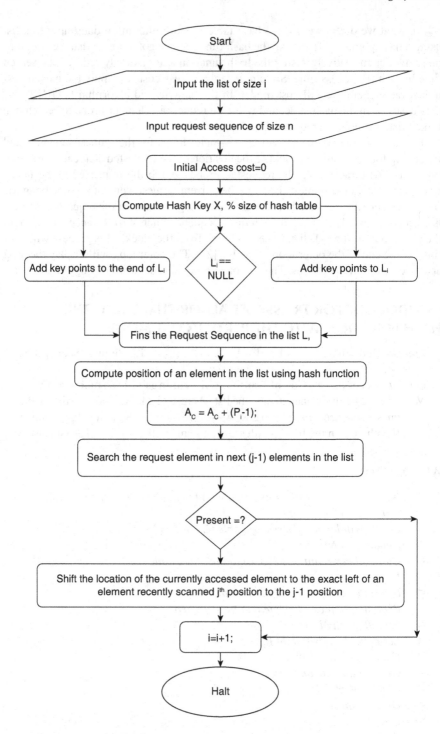

FIGURE 10.1   Flowchart for transpose using a hash function with partial cost.

10.3.2 THEORETICAL ANALYSIS

In our algorithm we use partial cost to calculate the access cost. Here we have to insert n number of elements (L_i). Here we are assuming some random list that comes under closure property. After inserting the entire element into the hash table using the hash function, if there is already an element present in the linked list, then store the new element at the end of the L_j. Now, we have to insert the request sequence, which is going to be scanned. Each element is read one by one and scanned in the list. If the element is present in the list, then check the position of the element P_i. Calculate the partial access cost (P_i -1). Now, shift the exact left of the element which is scanned; here access cost is calculated based on the position of the element before transposing.

ANALYSIS OF TUHWAP ALGORITHM

Explanation:
Here we have assumed 1 2 3 4 as the list and 12341234 as the request sequence
for our delineation:
Configuration {1, 2, 3, 4} and Request Sequence as {12341234}
Access 1

1	2	3	4

As it is already in the first position, no need to do transpose.
Access cost = 1, Total cost =1+(1–1)=1;
Access 2

2	1	3	4

Here 2 is in the 2nd position; transpose to the exact left of the accessed element.
Access cost = 2, total cost = 1+ (1 – 1) = 1;
Access 3

2	3	1	4

(Transpose 3 to the exact left of the element which is 2nd position.)
Access cost = 3, Total cost = 1 + (2 – 1) = 2;
Access 4

2	3	4	1

(Transpose 4 to the 3rd position.)
Access cost = 4, Total cost = 2 + (3 – 1) = 4;
Access 1

2	3	1	4

(Swap to the 3rd position.)
Access cost = 4, total cost = 4 + (3 – 1) = 6;

Access 2

| 2 | 3 | 1 | 4 |

(No need to swap.)
Access cost = 1, total cost = 6 + (1 − 1) = 6;
Access 3

| 3 | 2 | 1 | 4 |

(Swap 3 and 2.)
Access cost = 2, total cost = 6 + (1 − 1) = 6;
Access 4

| 3 | 2 | 4 | 1 |

(Swap 4 and 1.)
Access cost = 3, total cost = 6 + (3 − 1) = 8.

10.3.2.1 Analysis of Transpose Algorithm with Hash Function

Let us take an example considering the list as 1 2 3 and request sequence as 123123.

With configuration [1–3] Request Sequence [123123], we take that the hash table size is 5; initialize each index to NULL. This is explained in Figures 10.2 and 10.3.

Step 1   Insert 1
   In index [1] as a first key element to the node.
Step 2   Insert 2
   In index [2] as the second key element to the node.

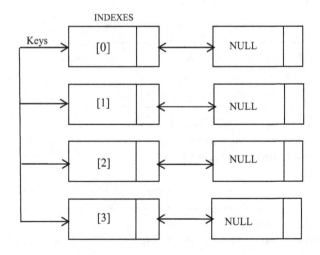

FIGURE 10.2   Detailed explanation of hash table in trans.

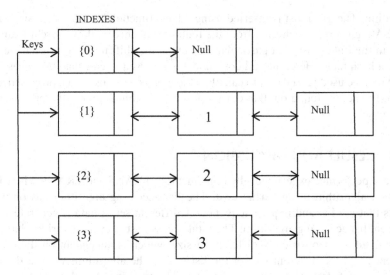

FIGURE 10.3   After inserting data set in a hash table.

Step 3   Insert 3
   In index [3] as the third key element to the node.

Calculation of Access Cost
When request 1 is available at the principal position in the list, considering
   the position as 1, the access cost is 1, but here we are using the partial cost
   (position of the element -1), which is $(1 - 1) = 0$.
The total access cost is 0.
As the next request is available at the principal position in the list, the access
   cost is 2 since 2 is the position and we are using partial cost model $2 - 1 = 1$.
   The total access cost is $0 + 1 = 1$. As the next request is available at the principal position in the list, the access cost is 3 since 3 is the position and we
   are using a partial cost model $(3 - 1) = 2$. Total access cost is $2 + 1 = 3$ and
   so on.

10.3.3 EXPERIMENTAL ANALYSIS

In this proposed algorithm, we have carried out Trans and TUHWAP with hash
function algorithm. In our code, we just use a predefined class called linked list class
which stores the distinct character of the list. In Trans, the given request sequence
and the given list are used to calculate the access cost with the full cost model.
Hence, the total access cost is carried out using the Transpose algorithm. From the
request sequence, data is read each time and by shifting the element by the exact left
of the scanning element in the list.

   In TUHWAP (Transpose using Hash Function Algorithm with Partial Cost), for
a given request sequence and the list, the total access cost is calculated by using an

algorithm. The given list is inserted using a hash function having the % size of the table. A data is read each time from the request sequence, and by searching an element in the linked list, that particular element is the shift to the left of the element using a hash table. Here, the full cost model is not used to calculate the access cost of TAHF; we used partial cost to calculate the total access cost of the proposed algorithm. Hence, we found out that our proposed algorithm is giving the best result in some cases.

10.4 RESULT AND DISCUSSION

We have performed experiments by implementing TRANS and TRANS with a hash function algorithm using partial cost. The list accessing algorithm has only two inputs that are list and request sequence. A different set of data is generated for a different list accessing algorithm. The total access cost of every algorithm has been determined as inconsistently different in size, which is dependent on the request sequence and the different size of the list size in the algorithm. We use the hash table size of 5 for calculating access cost. The working model can be found in Figure 10.4 and Figure 10.5.

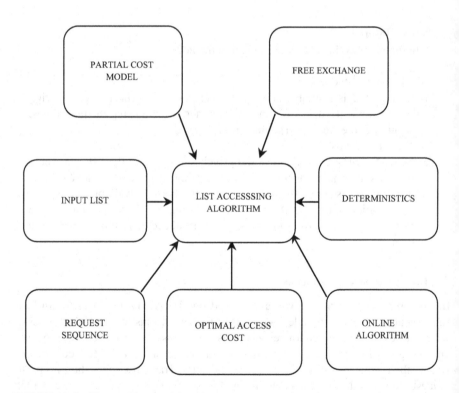

FIGURE 10.4   The working model.

TABLE 10.2

Experiment Using Different Data Set Using Full Cost Model without Hashing and Partial Cost Model with Hashing

Sl_no	Data Set for Request Sequence	Total Access Cost of Basic Transpose Algorithm	Total Access Cost of Transpose Algorithm with Hashing Using Partial Cost model(p-1)	Gain = (Trans-THFAP)*100/Trans
1	12341234	21	8	66.6%
2	43214321	24	8	66.6%
3	43332211	23	7	69.5%
4	32143214	23	7	69.5%
5	43111134	19	3	84.2%
6	32411423	22	6	72.7%
7	23422342	18	4	77.7%
8	11223344	17	1	94.1%
9	33444433	18	1	94.4%
10	12344321	21	5	76.19%

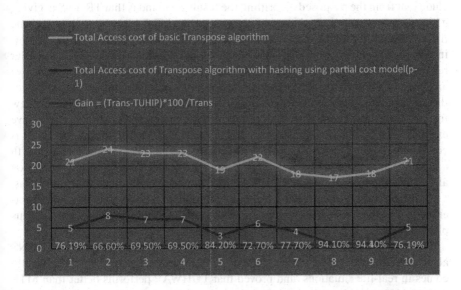

FIGURE 10.5 Line chart of TRANS and TRANS using hash function with partial cost model.

Calculating Gain

Let L = list and R is the request sequence;

Let THFAP = total access cost of Transpose with hash function algorithm =
    Access cost = A_c;

Gain = G;

To calculate the gain percentage of an access cost as follows:

$$G = \frac{(TRANS - THFAP) \times 100}{TRANS}$$

As we have only considered 8 different data set as request sequences, in future we will be considering a large data set to be searched or scanned with minimal access cost and faster than other algorithms. As we mentioned, we used the hash table to insert the list for ease access; here the hash table is manually calculated and the elements inserted; hence, we found out that element 1 is inserted in 1st position of 1 when calculated as a hash function. So, for programming we have not shown the hashing in Table 10.2. In future we may calculate a more refined algorithm to overcome the disadvantages of other algorithms.

10.5 CONCLUSION

Unending flexibility is a major benefit of using online resources. Online learning providers face a major challenge in replicating the in-person interactions and discussions that a traditional on-campus institution can easily provide. Here we conclude that from the proposed algorithm, the result we found is that TRANS is giving a high access cost compared to other algorithms like MTF. Here we try to overcome the condition of TRANS and developed a new algorithm called TUHWAP. Now in this proposed algorithm, we found out that a particular data set gives us better results compared to MTF and TRANS itself. Because of this research work, we analyze the TRANS algorithm, which has been uncommon from an algorithm for the list accessing problem to date in the literature. Here we have a present new form of Trans algorithm with hash function using the partial cost model. We have executed experiments by considering MTF, Trans and Thfap. Total access cost is computed of each algorithm for different request sequences of the same size with a common list. Here we have compared both MTF and Trans with our proposed algorithm, and I conclude that TUHWAP is performing better than MTF and Trans.

In the future, I will consider a large amount of data with various lists and different request sequences. I will further implement this algorithm in the Calgary corpus platform.

Here we compare the access cost incurred by the MTF algorithm and TRANS algorithm with TUHWAP for a specific type of request sequence, which frequently comes in real-life situations, and proved that TUHWAP performs better than MTF and TRANS algorithms by generating formula.

The next challenging research issue for us is to develop an improved online algorithm for the list accessing problem with a look-ahead. In the next work, a new online version can be designed.

10.6   REFERENCES

[1]   J. McCabe, "On Serial Files with Relocatable Records." *Operations Research*, vol. 12, pp. 609–618, 1965.

[2]   J. H. Hester, and D. S. Hirschberg, "Self –Organizing Linear Search," *CACM*, vol. 17, pp. 295–312, 1985.

[3]   Rakesh Mohanty, Seetaya Bhoi, and Sasmita Tripathy, "A New Proposed Cost Model for List Accessing Problem Using Buffering." *arXiv preprint arXiv:1109.2232*, 2011.

[4]   Pujarani Nanda and Shiba Prasad Dash, "An Approach to Improve the Performance of MTF Algorithm in List Accessing Problem." *International Journal of Scientific Research in Computer Science and Engineering*, vol. 8, no. 4, pp. 32–36, August 2020. E-ISSN: 2320-7639.

[5]   Susanne Albers, "A Competitive Analysis of the List Update Problem with Lookahead." *Theoretical Computer Science*, vol. 197, no. 1–2, pp. 95–109, 1998.

[6]   R. Mohanty, and S. Tripathy, "An Improved Move-to-Front (IMTF) Off-line Algorithm for the List Accessing Problem." *International Journal of Advanced Computing and Communications*, vol. 3, no. 1, pp. 19–23, 2011.

[7]   R. Mohanty, B. Sharma, and S. Tripathy, "Characterization of Request Sequences for List Accessing Problem and New Theoretical Results for MTF Algorithm." *International Journal of Computer Applications*, vol. 22, pp. 0975–8887, 2011.

[8]   Sasmita Tripathy, et al. "Move-To-Head-or-Tail (MTHT) Algorithm for the List Accessing Problem." *IUP Journal of Information Technology*, vol. 14, no. 2, pp. 90–98, 2018.

[9]   Pratyashi Satapathy, and Richismita Rout, "Characterization and Performance Evaluation of Request Sequence for Move-To-Front Algorithm." *2018 Second International Conference on Green Computing and Internet of Things (ICGCIoT).* IEEE, 2018.

[10]   G. H. Gonnet, J. I. Munro, and H. Suwanda, "Towards Self-Organizing Linear Search." *IEEE*, pp. 169–174, 1979.

[11]   Daniel D. Sleator, and Robert E. Tarjan, "Amortized Efficiency of List Update and Paging Rules." *Communications of the ACM*, vol. 28, no. 2, pp. 202–208, 1985.

[12]   Allan Borodin, Nathan Linial, and Michael E. Saks, "An Optimal On-line Algorithm for Metrical Task System." *Journal of the ACM (JACM)*, vol. 39, no. 4, pp. 745–763, 1992.

[13]   Rakesh Mohanty, Burle Sharma, and Sasmita Tripathy, "Characterization of Request Sequences for List Accessing Problem and New Theoretical Results for MTF Algorithm." *arXiv preprint arXiv:1109.2231*, 2011.

[14]   Debashish Rout, "Experimental Analysis of Hybrid MTF-TRANS-FC (HMTFC) Algorithm." *International Journal of Research in Advent Technology*, vol. 1, no. 5, 2013.

[15]   Jon L. Bentley, and Catherine C. McGeoch, "Amortized Analyses of Self-Organizing Sequential Search Heuristics." *Communications of the ACM*, vol. 28, no. 4, pp. 404–411, 1985.

[16]   A. Mishra, "A Study of Some List Accessing Algorithm and Novel Analytical Results." *International Journal of Computer Trends and Technology*, vol. 4, no. 6, pp. 1641–1649, 2013.

[17]   Sanjaya Kumar Panda, "A Novel Algorithm for List Accessing Problem." *2014 Seventh International Conference on Contemporary Computing (IC3).* IEEE, 2014.

[18]   Ran Bachrach, Ran El-Yaniv, and M. Reinstadtler, "On the Competitive Theory and Practice of Online List Accessing Algorithms." *Algorithmica*, vol. 32, no. 2, pp. 201–245, 2002.

[19] Rakesh Mohanty, Shiba Prasad Dash, Burle Sharma, Sangita Patel. "Performance Evaluation of A Proposed Variant of Frequency Count (VFC) List Accessing Algorithm." *arXiv preprint arXiv:1206.6185*, 2012.

[20] Ronald Rivest, "On Self-Organizing Sequential Search Heuristics." *Communications of the ACM*, vol. 19, no. 2, pp. 63–67, 1976.

[21] Banhisikha Samanta, and Shiba Prasad Dash, "A Novel Hybrid Approach to List Accessing Problem Using BIT Algorithm." *2015 International Conference on Man and Machine Interfacing (MAMI)*. IEEE, 2015.

[22] Reza Dorrigiv, and Alejandro López-Ortiz, "List Update with Probabilistic Locality of Reference." *Information Processing Letters*, vol. 112, no. 13, 540–543, 2012.

11 Study on Provisions for Continuity with Online Education

Jyoti Deshmukh, Sunil Wankhade, Pranali Khuspe and Akshay Kedar

Rajiv Gandhi Institute of Technology, Andheri (W), Mumbai

CONTENTS

11.1 INTRODUCTION

Several world equations have shifted in the last few months as the pandemic has wreaked devastation on the planet. The practice of separating oneself from

DOI: 10.1201/9781003272823-11

another person has become the new standard. Visitors are no longer welcome in many buildings. Adults and children are no longer compelled to attend school or work. Rather than postponing activities forever, people are looking for alternate ways to complete them. Education, for example, can be discontinued temporarily but not permanently. This is why, rather than conducting training and lessons face-to-face, schools, colleges, universities, and businesses have turned to digital methods.

Defining learning is essential as it completes our lives. Though professionals have defined learning from time to time, it is impossible to describe learning precisely in light of continual change [1]. Education has relied on classroom methods for centuries, but technology-enhanced learning has the potential to revolutionize learning by making high-quality, cost-effective education available to a wider audience.

Due to the severe global pandemic Covid-19, education has altered tremendously, with the remarkable expansion of e-learning, where teaching is done remotely and on digital platforms. E-learning is transforming education systems since it is the only choice available during the current crisis and has enormous potential for completing instructional plans and protecting students' learning rights. The core benefits of e-learning include accessibility to learning at any time and from any location, cost savings, the potential to reach a broader market, more effective learning with individualized instructions, and flexibility [2].

However, in order to reach the full potential of e-learning, content, services, and systems from many vendors must all function together. As the need for online learning is increasing, various online learning platforms have come up with their innovative ideas and teaching styles. In this application development race for online teaching, there is a need to evaluate which platform is better and how one can select an e-learning platform that will fulfill all their needs and expectations.

11.2 TRADITIONAL VERSUS MODERN TEACHING AND LEARNING

The Covid-19 epidemic ushered about a sea change in the global education system. Due to the imposition of lockdown, physical classrooms were closed, and online education became the new standard. Despite the fact that online learning has kept education alive in these difficult times, it cannot totally replace it. After many articles and informational websites, it has become clear that traditional and current teaching and learning approaches are vastly different. In summarizing the old approach to teaching and learning, traditional education assumes that students will learn because they are instructed to do so. It is more concerned with context, behavior, and motivation than with new and developing technologies.

Traditional teaching methods such as 'chalk and talk' have been in use for hundreds of years; however, they no longer suit modern practice. In today's classrooms, students require new and modern teaching approaches. The previous method of delivering education was through recitation and memorization techniques, whereas the new method employs interactive methods.

BENEFITS OF TRADITIONAL LEARNING:

- Traditional classroom teaching methods emphasize student engagement and provide an appropriate atmosphere for students to learn from one another.
- One-on-one or in-person teaching is beneficial and exhibits greater levels of student engagement with teachers.
- A conventional school's social atmosphere is ideal for the development of a child's character and individuality.
- In a typical learning environment, teachers play a vital role in imparting discipline and giving a sense of guidance to students.

Many of the educational methods used at the time included extremely repetitive (drill) assignments that emphasized memorization (rote learning) while undermining critical thinking, problem-solving, and metacognitive and social abilities. Students spoke little, the teacher spoke a lot, and discipline was often harsh, even by today's standards. Instead of assuming that all pupils are not at the same level of comprehension, modern educational approaches play a greater emphasis on the specific requirements of each student. Questioning, explaining, demonstrating, and collaborative strategies are used increasingly frequently in modern teaching.

Modern methods in use in education are as follows:

- Technology-driven classrooms
- Continuous comprehensive evaluation
- Focus on conceptual understanding
- Relating academics to life
- Focus on skill building, life skills, and values
- Collaborative learning
- 3D modeling and virtual reality
- Differential learning
- Activity-based learning and learning labs
- Gamification
- Integrative and social responsibility and civic engagement
- Problem-based learning
- Flipped classroom
- Social media training
- Mobile and micro learning
- Digitization in teaching, learning assessment, and feedback

11.3   e-LEARNING

11.3.1 DEFINITION

E-learning refers to the employment of information and communication technologies to support the development and delivery of learning in academic and professional development institutions. E-learning is used widely with other terms such as online learning, technology-mediated learning, web-based learning, computer-based learning, etc.

Clark and Mayer defined e-learning as instructions delivered through digital devices with the intent of supporting learning in their research paper [3]. Ruiz, Mintzer, and Leipzig defined e-learning as the use of internet technology for enhancing performance and knowledge in their research paper [3]. Moving on to internet resources, eLearningNC.gov has defined e-learning as learning by utilizing electronic technologies for accessing educational curriculums outside of traditional classrooms [3].

The *Economic Times* newspaper says that a learning system based on formalized teaching but with the help of electronic resources is known as e-learning [4]. E-learning can also be termed as a network-enabled transfer of skills and knowledge, and the delivery of education is made to a large number of recipients at the same or different times.

11.3.2 FEATURES OF e-LEARNING

Figure 11.1 shows the features of e-learning. The internet provides new and interesting opportunities for learning, supported by the use of interconnected multimedia devices. Now, as seen, e-learning is clearly taking the lead in the global educational sector given its distinct advantages. For this reason, governments and people across the world are rapidly adopting e-learning to such an extent that it stands a chance of emerging as the preferred mode of education in the years to come.

11.3.3 ADVANTAGES OF e-LEARNING

11.3.3.1 Flexibility

Learning content is usually made available in short modules and can be paused at any time. The instructional material may easily be integrated into your everyday routine, whether you log on while commuting at work or during your free time. Even if you can't attend a live online workshop, you can usually receive written summaries or a video of the event. People who work or are in education or simply wish to learn more about their favorite hobbies or interests, will benefit from e-learning [5].

11.3.3.2 Availability

Anyone with internet access can access learning opportunities at the same time without any physical boundaries—as long as the servers are robust enough to bear the load. Learning materials are available 24/7, and assessments can be completed at our leisure.

11.3.3.3 Efficiency

The time it takes to finish a course is greatly shortened since e-learning packages adapt to the individual student. A single person, on the other hand, rarely requires everything that the group has to offer. There's no need to travel to the course either. Teachers can become more efficient educators by expanding the lesson plan beyond traditional textbooks to include online resources [5].

FIGURE 11.1   Features of e-Learning.

11.3.3.4 Affordability

A user can re-use an e-learning package as many times as they want without incurring additional costs. There are also numerous free course offers and "free-mium access" choices available. E-learning is often less expensive than traditional learning offerings because it allows for more course participants at the same time.

11.3.4 DISADVANTAGES OF e-LEARNING

11.3.4.1 Internet Connection

The most evident issue is a lack of internet connectivity, which affects more than 40% of the global population. There could be issues with high-speed internet, insufficient data volume, or connection issues that are not immediately resolved. As a result, e-learning is not accessible from home for more than half of the world's population.

11.3.4.2 Practical Knowledge

While teaching theoretical knowledge online is feasible, many people still feel the training of actual skills to be inadequate. In a virtual classroom, hands-on or lab activity is impossible to replicate [5].

11.3.4.3 Lack of Communication Skill Development

E-learning methods are proven to be highly effective at improving the academic knowledge of the students. Developing students' communication skills, on the other hand, is an area that is sometimes overlooked during online sessions. Neglecting students' communication skills would undoubtedly result in a large number of graduates who excel in theoretical knowledge but struggle to transfer that information to others [6].

11.3.4.4 Student-Teacher Communication

Eye contact and body language are crucial aspects of human communication while communicating face-to-face, but as one can't fully maintain eye contact or use body language in online learning, it might be difficult to understand what the other person is saying. It causes a communication gap between professors and students because e-learning struggles with student feedback [6].

A SWOC analysis is performed to get a better understanding about various pros and cons of e-learning systems. Figure 11.2 shows the SWOC analysis of e-learning [7].

11.3.5 Health and Environmental Effect of e-Learning

- E-learning not only decreases the quantity of trees chopped down for paper manufacture, but it also has the ability to minimize carbon emissions, lowering students' and staff's travel and environmental impact and effect.
- Excessive usage of e-learning may result in social isolation, which can lead to depression. Due to the deadlines for assignment submissions, e-learning is also responsible for sleep deprivation.

Strengths	Weaknesses
1. Time flexibility, location flexibility	1. Technical difficulties
2. Catering to wide audience	2. Learners' capability and confidence level
3. Wide availability of courses and content	3. Time management
4. Immediate feedback	4. Distraction, frustration, anxiety, and confusion
	5. Lack of personal/physical attention

Opportunities	Challenges
1. Scope for innovations and digital development	1. Unequal distribution of ICT infrastructure
2. Designing flexible programs	2. Quality of education
3. Strengthen skills: problem-solving, critical thinking, and adaptability	3. Digital illiteracy
4. User can be of any age	4. Digital divide
5. An innovation pedagogical approach	5. Technology cost & obsolescence

FIGURE 11.2 SWOC analysis.

- Virtual learners do not need to attend classes in person. As a result, electrical devices in unoccupied rooms are switched off. This implies that schools will use less energy for lighting, heating, and cooling, which is healthier for the environment.
- Because students spend so much time in a sedentary position, generally inside, e-learning has been associated with weight gain and dissatisfaction. Increased screen time has also been linked to anxiety and headaches.
- Overuse of computers has the potential to cause eyestrain and muscle problems. Excessive usage of electronic devices is linked to an increased risk of death from sitting too long in front of a screen.

11.4 PROVISIONS FOR CONTINUITY WITH ONLINE EDUCATION

According to UNESCO, 1.37 billion students in 138 countries have been affected by the closure of schools and colleges since the outbreak of Covid-19 began. In the United States, over 60.2 million instructors and university professors are no longer engaged in the classroom.

Since the entire country is on lockdown, e-education is the best and only option left. University teaching personnel are making accounts on online videoconferencing platforms such as Zoom, Skype, Google Classroom, and Meet, among others, in order to engage with students. Although this new medium promises on-demand access to material at any time and on any digital device, it proves challenging for both administrators and students to implement. Presently, e-learning combines conventional learning techniques such as books and notebooks with digital applications such as e-books and pdfs. The following Table 11.1 represents the table of leading online learning platforms [8].

With the rising use of the internet and new technology, it is now feasible to obtain high-quality education online with a computer and a web connection. It is a technology era in which e-learning in education is fairly prevalent as well as a novel notion. Online education is a wise decision that has shown to be beneficial to the majority of students. Whether one is a youngster or an adult, e-learning in education may always help refine their abilities and eventually advance in their career.

Following are the provisions with continuity with online learning, which facilitates satisfaction and joy in various student's learning process:

1. *More adaptable*
   Online education allows students to set up their own learning space. There is some freedom in determining their timetable based on the needs that meet their agenda. As a result, one may better balance their academics while maintaining their present routine. One will also learn how to efficiently manage their time and multitask. Learning new things may give an individual's career a push and finally start developing [9].

   When the pandemic is over and people return to classroom-based education, the lectures should be videotaped and uploaded online somewhere so that if a student is unable to attend the lecture physically, he or she can

TABLE 11.1

Leading Online Learning Platforms in India

E-Learning Platforms	Description	Subject and Grades	Cost
Khan Academy www.khanacademy.org/	Khan Academy provides class work, instructional videos, and an individualized learning dashboard, allowing students to study with their own speed. Every day, millions of students from all over the globe, each with their own distinct background, learn at their own leisure at Khan Academy.	Math, science, computing, history, art, history, economics, and more, including K–14 and test preparation (SAT, Praxis, LSAT) content.	Free
Coursera www.coursera.org	Coursera collaborates with over 200 premier institutions and corporations to provide individuals and organizations with flexible, reasonable, employment online learning. It is a platform that provides online courses and degrees from world-class institutions and businesses to anybody, anywhere.	Specializations, job-ready professional certifications, university-issued certificate, and master's/bachelor's degrees.	Learn with affordable prices as well as financial aid available for most courses.
Byju.s https://byjus.com	Byju's offers highly personalized and effective learning programs. The app integrates these well-crafted lessons from our teachers and assessments along with analysis and recommendations, personalized to suit each student's learning style.	Math, Physics, Chemistry and Biology for CBSE and ISC (Classes 1–12) Competitive Exams- JEE, NEET, IAS preparation courses	It charges around 3,000 per month for class 1–12 and around 91,000 for civil service and entrance classes.
Great Learning https://www.mygreatlearning.com/	Great Learning is a prominent worldwide edtech firm for corporate and higher education, providing industry-relevant curriculum in hybrid classroom and entirely online formats spanning technology, data, and business disciplines.	PG programs, undergraduate courses, specialization courses such as cloud computing, machine learning, AI, etc.	It is a paid platform to study, but many beginner level courses are free.

watch it according to their leisure and also later during examination period, ensuring that no one is left behind in terms of knowledge.

2. *Wider choices*

Nowadays, in the contemporary world, there are an endless number of disciplines to master, and one may choose whatever one best matches their interests and background. For example, if someone has a background in IT, he/she may pursue training in a new area such as Salesforce, Tableau, AI, and others. When more and more courses appear on the scene, you should make an informed selection that will help you progress your profession. He/she can choose between board-pen based learning and presentation-based learning for better visualization [9].

A student can study the courses that are specified under his or her specialized department in the current educational system. For example, a mechanical engineering student may be interested in coding, but their department does not offer a coding-related course. To overcome this limitation, faculty-based and course-based recorded video lectures should be made available online so that students can study subjects other than departmental subjects and broaden their knowledge rather than limiting themselves to departmental course subjects.

3. *Valued certifications*

There is an opportunity to obtain certification or a recognized certificate in the relevant courses. You are not required to attend universities or campuses for four years, but you may select a subject of interest and continue your education. It is appropriate for all students, from pre-college through high school. Many companies are now accepting the certificates as proof of knowledge for hiring purposes.

A student can learn a course outside his domain but still won't have any certifications which would signify his/her knowledge in that course. To overcome this limitation, a college can conduct examinations once a month for the students taking courses outside their domain and thus grade them. This would help the student greatly as a certification from a college looks more promising and truer than a third-party website.

4. *Innovative teaching methodology*

Some platforms are now providing two teacher benefits. One professional instructor employs great visuals and narrative to explain topics in depth to ensure deeper understanding, while the second teacher removes instant doubts, pays personal attention, and makes the sessions interactive and interesting.

Along with classroom learning, live teaching should be implemented, allowing students who are unable to physically attend the lecture to participate remotely. This will keep students up to date with classroom instruction while also allowing them to save time the other day by watching the recorded segments [10].

5. *Low-cost loan options*

Online learning is typically less costly and more economical when compared to classroom instruction. In addition, there are other payment alternatives available, including payments in installment. One may now get student loans that do not need them to pay any interest or additional fees on the monthly payments. There is no need to buy books or other study materials while learning online. Overall, it is less costly and yields better results [5].

6. *Integrated learning resources*
Online education is available in a variety of formats. People can choose to learn in a group setting or request personalized classes in which the course content is specifically tailored according to their needs. There is greater interaction in live instructor-led classes than in self-paced online learning. Mentors pay more attention to the challenges and particular interests. Online-learning platforms typically give study materials in a variety of formats, including PowerPoint presentations, assignments, MCQs, blogs, articles, whitepapers, e-books, video content, presentations, or complete tutorial PDFs, etc. He/she doesn't need to travel anywhere to learn everything from the beginning to the high level [9].

7. *Competitions and placement opportunities*
Various institutes organize competitions, so to take part in it, students from various colleges need to visit the institute where the competition is arranged. This consumes time as well as travel expenses. If these competitions are being conducted online, then it will be very useful to students as well as to the institute as online data is easy and safe to handle. Institutes can tie up with these e-learning platforms and can conduct internal and external assessment and also various competitions and hack-a-thons wherein students can compete among themselves and get a better understanding of what their true potential is. Many companies should also be invited to these challenges and competitions, wherein they can observe the students who perform well and based on their performances provide them placement offers.

11.4.1 COMPUTER TECHNOLOGY AND ONLINE LEARNING PROVISIONS

As the world is emerging so fast, technology is becoming more advanced. In the 21st century, machines and technology are becoming the basic need of every individual. Computers and their applications are playing a major role in developing the future of education. Artificial intelligence, machine learning, IOT, and cloud computing are some of the developing technologies without which one cannot leave. Today WhatsApp as well as Instagram which is being used is basically built with the help of these technologies.

Artificial intelligence (AI) systems can help with online learning and teaching by personalized learning for students, automating routine tasks for instructors, and enabling adaptive assessments. For global corporations facing the issue of providing meaningful material for branches in several countries or for the increasingly prevalent circumstance of companies working with remote staff that speak different languages, AI has made it feasible to generate multi-language content.

Virtual assistants can be used to make the online education process more fruitful. Helpers in the virtual world, such as chatbots, can aid both students and instructors by addressing inquiries that would otherwise be sent to the instructor or by assisting students in navigating course material in a more friendly manner.

Because students are now learning online, many of the practical sessions that they used to attend during their offline college days are no longer functioning properly. Virtual labs are now available online, where students can develop practical skills in technical subjects. This would aid students' comprehension of the subject. However, these laboratories aren't up to par. If these labs can be designed with proper required things and material, then it will be very useful for students to study online with the offline learnings.

11.5 FUTURE WORK

11.5.1 TECHNOLOGY DEVELOPMENT IN RURAL AREAS

Long before the current pandemic, rural populations lacked access to quality education. A shortage of qualified teachers and staff, a lack of access to basic technologies, data, and gadgets, gender inequality, concerns about girl safety, and so on. Consideration and action on the following points may aid in the development of rural areas. Online education can aid in the elimination of gender inequality as well as the acquisition and enhancement of teachers' knowledge and skills. This will also help students learn more enthusiastically. Infrastructure facilities are also lacking in rural areas. Online education does not necessitate any infrastructure; all that is required is a laptop and perhaps a mobile device with access to the internet.

Many parents in rural areas do not want to send their children to educational institutions in order to increase their family's earning power by engaging their children in household and outdoor chores, resulting in lower school attendance. If the government or the leaders of rural areas provide adequate technological assistance, financially immigrant children may be able to acquire insight. If proper internet facilities are provided to rural areas at a low cost, it will help parents to let their children pursue education.

11.5.2 LINGUISTIC PROBLEM

In India, nearly 85% of the population does not speak English. The lack of standardized content in Hindi and other regional languages stifles the uptake of new online courses. Not everyone understands English, and as a result, they do not attend lectures. A solution to this problem may aid in increasing the number of educated people in India. Knowledge is something that is always beneficial to gain in any language. We can provide video content in various languages that students can understand [11].

11.6 CONCLUSION

From the above study, it has been observed that offline study is the foundation of education. In this Covid-19 pandemic period, online education has essentially become the sole option for pursuing one's education. Offline learning has its own set of advantages that e-learning cannot match. However, to exist in today's technologically evolved society, one must be able to deal with technology and possess a basic understanding of it. Things changed dramatically during the crisis, and many people were obliged to work online. People struggled, but most importantly, they made it through.

Humans will surely benefit in the next 20 years if the previously mentioned provisions are put into force today and everyone seeks to cooperate with them. Although e-learning may appear to be challenging or only a temporary solution until the epidemic is over, it offers several advantages. Combining online and offline schooling will surely be the most effective way to learn in the next few years. As a result of technology improvements, learning will become more accessible, inclusive, and focused on some of the most essential themes.

When the pandemic is over, one must guarantee that they have learned from their mistakes and implement reforms that will lead to a better and brighter future. One must ensure that any digital transformation is not solely driven by tech companies but that teachers, students, governments, civil society leaders, and privacy advocates are all involved in shaping these changes.

11.7   REFERENCES

[1]   P. Toan, T. Dang, and L. Hong, "E-Learning Platform Assessment and Selection Using Two-Stage Multi-Criteria Decision-Making Approach with Grey Theory: A Case Study in Vietnam". in Proceedings of RePEc Biblio, 2021.

[2]   J. Kolodinsky, and S.J. Goetz, "Theme Overview: Rural Development Implications One Year After COVID-19", *Choices Quarter* 3, https://www.choicesmagazine.org/choices-magazine/theme-articles/rural-development-implications-one-year-after-covid-19/ th eme-overview-rural-development-implications-one-year-after-covid-19 (Accessed: 2021).

[3]   S. Tamm, "What Is the Definition of e-Learning", https://e-student.org/what-is-e-learning/ (Accessed: 2020, December 21).

[4]   Talent Garden, "Online Learning: The Advantages and Disadvantages of E-Learning", https://talentgarden.org/en/digital-transformation/online-learning-the-advantages-and-disadvantages-of-e-learning/ (Accessed: 2020, September 15).

[5]   S. Tamm, "10 Biggest Disadvantages of e-Learning", https://e-student.org/disadvantages-of-e-learning/ (Accessed: 2022, January 7).

[6]   P.Gupta,"10ReasonsWhyE-learningIstheFutureofEducation",January2021,https://edtechreview.in/e-learning/4456-10-reasons-why-e-learning-is-the-future-of-education.

[7]   S. Dhawan, "Online Learning: A Panacea in the Time of COVID-19 Crisis", *Journal of Educational Technology Systems*, Vol. 49, Sagepub, June 2020.

[8]   D. Belias, L. Sdrolias, M. Koutiva, and A. Koustelios, "Traditional Teaching Methods Vs. Teaching Through the Application of Information and Communication Technologies in the Accounting Field: Quo Vadis?", *European Scientific Journal*, Vol. 9, No. 28, pp. 73–101, 2013.

[9]   BYJU's, "Byju'S Classes Introduces One of Its Kind Two Teacher Model", https://byjus.com/press/byjus-classes-introduces-one-of-its-kind-two-teacher-model/ (Accessed: 2021, August 26).

[10] S. Roy, S. Bhattacharya, and P. Das, "Identification of e-Learning Quality Parameters in Indian Context to Make It More Effective and Acceptable", *PES Journal*, Vol. 2, No. 3, pp. 209–222, 2020.

[11] United Nations Educational, Scientific and Cultural Organization, "Education in a Post-COVID World: Nine Ideas for Public Action", in Proceedings of the International Commission on the Futures of Education, 2020.

[12] F. Reimers, A. Schleicher, J. Saavedra, and S.Tuominen, "Supporting the Continuation of Teaching and Learning During the COVID-19 Pandemic: Annotated Resources for Online Learning", in Proceedings of Organization for EconomicCo-operation and Development (OECD), 2020.

[13] Rimmi Anand, Sharad Saxena, and Shilpi Saxena, "E-Learning and Its Impact on Rural Areas", *International Journal of Modern Education and Computer Science*, Vol. 5, pp. 46–52, 2012.

[14] Dan Dixon, Hayden Thorne, Maria Armoudian, Lachlan McCarron, Kate Rivington, and Forkan Ali, "Academic Careers and the Covid-19 Pandemic", *Australasian Journal of American Studies*, Vol. 39, No. 1, pp. 225–240, December 2020.

[15] Barnett Berry, "Teaching, Learning, and Caring in the Post-COVID Era", *Proceedings of The Phi Delta Kappan*, Vol. 102, No. 1, pp. 14–17, September 2020.

[16] Simon Boxall, "A Viral Shift in Higher Education?" *Published in Oceanography*, Vol. 33, No. 3, pp. 78–79, September 2020.

12 Prediction of Selection of Communication Tools and Platforms to Support Education 4.0 in India

Rajkamal C. Sangole[1] and Darshana Desai[2]
1 Department of MCA, Pimpri Chinchwad
College of Engineering, Pune, India
2 Department of MCA, Indira College of
Engineering & Management, Pune, India

CONTENTS

DOI: 10.1201/9781003272823-12

12.1   INTRODUCTION

The way of teaching is being reimagined by Education 4.0. Education and teaching are getting redefined across the globe to adopt Education 4.0. Education 4.0 is moving in the right direction to make drastic changes in the current education system for the betterment of the learners. Education 4.0 represents the changes with respect to Industry 4.0. Industries that have adopted IR 4.0 demand well-trained candidates. The objective of education is to enable a person to have a successful life and make the best contributions to self and society. With the help of education, the true potential of the student can be relieved and recognized. Education is the most powerful tool or platform for any nation to transform. Day by day the demographic structure of India is changing. As per [1] digital competencies can be improved using implementing digital communication tools with the help of Education 4.0. Education 4.0 has the biggest impact on Industrial Revolution 4.0 with respect to growth in the education system for the betterment [2].

Digital Communication Tools (DCL) is an outcome-based practice in a teaching and learning activity that in turn improves the learning abilities of the learner. DCL can be achieved using different DCL tools for enhancing strategies in the education system. DCL provides flexibility in teaching at any possible time. DCL platforms and tools provide personalization, effectiveness, flexibility, understanding, user-friendliness, user experience, and pace of learning while using them. Because of this reason many lecturers and students are approaching DCL. During Covid-19 DCL evolved enormously. It enabled people from different locations and different domains to come together and learn common concepts together. DCL has enabled blended, personalized, and flipped learning for the effective engagement of learners. Due to DCL, students' learning ability has increased with a personalized experience. The more they explore, the more knowledge they can gain in that respective subject, and in case of doubts they can put it across to their colleagues for discussion purposes and can get the appropriate solution for the said problem. Thus, the objective of the paper is to identify which tools are being mostly used in India and why they are used. With the help of Education 4.0 digital communication tools, lecturers and students will be able to gain educational outcomes such as remembering, understanding, applying, analyzing, evaluating, and creating.

Researchers in this field have discussed various platforms and tools on. Different theories were put forward for using communication tools. However, different characteristics such as ease of use, better user experience, personalized experience, user-friendliness, and usefulness were not part of the research. This study aims to identify and analyze platforms and tools used by educational institutes and universities across India with an intention to use specific communication tools for teaching-learning processes in Covid-19 and post-Covid-19 situations using different selection characteristics. Research identifies different characteristics used in education tools used for digital learning.

12.2   RELATED WORK

Day by day, Industrial Revolution 4.0 is changing the world in terms of requirements in industries. It is very difficult for our education system to catch up with the pace and satisfy the demands of IR 4.0. Using Industrial Revolution 4.0, our education system needs to use a different approach to adapt to Education 4.0. It provides the competence in inculcating different skills such as problem-solving, self-determined learning, and cognitive ability [3–5] to the students. In the report of [5], it is an evolution of better learning techniques, which is beneficial for the overall development of students with respect to their lifelong learning skills. According to [2], education provides motivation for a self-learning attitude in students as per their availability.

With the help of Education 4.0 tools and platforms, lecturers can create their own innovative ideas and materials for providing better knowledge to the students related to their respective subjects. To hold up Education 4.0, different digital platforms and tools are available. Out of all the available tools and platforms, the choice has to be made by lecturers and students for the teaching and learning process. According to [6] the following list shows different digital learning tools and platforms used for communication purposes.

- Google Meet
- Microsoft Teams
- Webex
- Zoom
- Google Classroom
- A Web Whiteboard App

According to [7–10] personalization plays a very important role during the process of selection of any online tool. As per [7] personalization fascinates the users to a great extent. Also, it is used as an upcoming strategy for bringing down the overload of information and selecting the desired tool. [8] says that personalization is majorly used for addressing online tools and platforms to build customer relationships and retain them. According to [9] personalization provides information customization, presentation, and structure of a website according to the user's demands. [9] also says artificial intelligence and personalization work hand in hand to provide personalized solutions to the uses of different tools or websites. [10] says different stakeholders access information depending on recommendation systems that provide personalized information. According to [11] personalization is widely recognized as an important component in end-user applications such as electronic catalogues and corporate web portals. With the dramatic growth that has been experienced on the web, personalization technology (PT) captures enterprises' interest/attention.

The relationship between ease of use, usefulness, and personalized experience gives lifelong learning to the users. In the technology acceptance model, the dimension of ease of use is used as a predictor to perceive the usefulness [12]. User experience plays a vital role in the selection of tools. The platforms and tools need improvisations in user experience so that users will get attracted during their use [13].

12.3 HYPOTHESES

12.3.1 Users' Effective Tool Usage Is Highly Affected by Personalized Experience

Artificial intelligence gives a personalization experience to users to bring ease of use. Personalized experience gives a real-time analysis of data, and then artificial intelligence will generate consumer experience [7–9]. Ease of use in tools can be enhanced by users' personalized experience in support of self-confidence [12]. A personalized experience, created by the integration of intelligent analysis of user behavior and historical data of similar users, can improve the effectiveness of tool usage.

12.3.2 PERSONALIZED EXPERIENCE PLAYS A SIGNIFICANT ROLE IN SELECTING THE TOOLS BASED ON THE USER-FRIENDLINESS OF THE TOOL

During the usage of online shopping websites or platforms, the decisions of users are affected by the safety and user-friendliness of the websites or platforms [14]. Any website or tool which does not provide user-friendliness will definitely not be revisited or reused by users due to the lack of personalized experience in it.

12.3.3 PERSONALIZED EXPERIENCE HAS A VITAL ROLE IN THE SELECTION OF THE COMMUNICATION TOOL DEPENDING ON THE USEFULNESS OF THE TOOL

Whether the tool is useful or not can be decided depending on its usage, which is directly linked with the personalized experience of the user. The usefulness of the tool has a positive and significant effect on the repurchase [15]. If any tool does not provide a personalized experience that directly questions the usefulness of the platform or tool, it will reduce the chances of repurchasing the tools.

12.3.4 PERSONALIZED EXPERIENCE OF THE USER CAN BE USED TO SELECT COMMUNICATION TOOLS BASED ON THE USER'S EXPERIENCE WITH THE TOOL

Users' experience of tools can be built according to the personalized experience of the users [13]. There is a need for improvement in the user experience of the different tools. Relational improvement of the tool is very important with respect to the personalized experience of the tools and platforms so that easy access of information can be done between the users.

12.4   RESEARCH METHODOLOGY

12.4.1 DATA COLLECTION

A comprehensive study of eight e-learning communication platforms (Google Meet, Webex, Microsoft Teams, Zoom, TeachMint, Visme, Google Classroom, A Web Whiteboard App) was done to understand whether the platform provides personalization, effectiveness, flexibility, understanding, user-friendliness, user experience, and pace of learning to lecturers and students. This study was done to find the most chosen communication and learning platform and tool among students and lecturers. A survey-based approach was used to understand the perception of Indian students on the available e-learning tools. This study had questions based on demographic data of the respondents and their opening about different Education 4.0 digital learning tools and platforms. From this survey, we have got 350 respondents, out of which 57 were the faculty and 293 were students from different colleges.

In this study, a sample of 350 students and faculties was taken. Out of 350 responses, 102 (29.14%) females and 248 (70.85%) males from 32 different colleges across India were included. In these 32 colleges the following departments were considered: Bachelor of Business Administrator (BBA), Bachelor of Computer Application (BCA), Bachelor of Computer Science (BCS), Bachelor of Engg./Tech (BE/BTech), Bachelor of Science (BSc), Master of Business Administrator (MBA), Master of Computer Application (MCA), Master of Engg./Tech (ME/MTech), Master of Science (MSc), and others. This study was designed using quantitative methods through open-ended and closed-ended questions.

We have prepared a set of questionnaires to investigate which communication and learning tools and platforms are used for teaching and learning purposes according to the needs of the lecturers and students from colleges in India. As data shown in Table 12.1 indicates that the majority of the respondents have chosen the Google Meet (250 out of 350 respondents) platform as a communication platform over other available platforms. Udemy (120 respondents) and Coursera (105 respondents) have been chosen as the most preferred learning platforms. These are the platforms that are used day in and day out by the respondents (262). This proves that digital learning platforms and tools are chosen because of their effectiveness, providing a better understanding of the subject or the topic.

12.5   DATA ANALYSIS

Analysis was done to identify key factors and to predict which communication tools are selected depending on ease to use, user-friendliness, usefulness, better user experience, and personalized experience. This analysis will help to select appropriate communication tools for digital learning in support of Education 4.0. We have used a simple linear regression analysis model to study the variables and to determine the relation between the dependent variables (ease of use,

TABLE 12.1
Sample Demographics

Measure	Item	Frequency
Gender	Male Female Other	Male: 102
		Female: 248
		Other:0
Professional Status	Faculty Student	Faculty: 57
		Student: 293
Number of Institute	Across India	32
Number of Respondents	Across India	350

user-friendliness, usefulness, better user experience) and independent variables (personalized experience).

The proposed hypothesis is that the communication tool for digital learning to support Education 4.0 can be selected by the following factors, i.e., ease of use, user-friendliness, usefulness, better user experience, and personalized experience of the tools. To test this hypothesis, a simple linear regression analysis was used. The data analysis was done using the Microsoft Excel software to determine the impact of the independent variables on the dependent variables. The simple linear regression equation is $Y=f(X,)$, where Y represents the dependent variable, X represents the independent variables, and f represents the unknown parameter. The report generated by the regression model provides us with factors that are significant in selecting the communication tool for digital learning.

12.5.1 SIMPLE LINEAR REGRESSION ANALYSIS

At this stage for evaluating the collaborative role of the independent variable on the dependent variable, stepwise a simple linear regression analysis has been used. In this analysis, the 4 dependent variables (ease of use, user-friendliness, usefulness, user experience) were tested individually with 1 independent variable (personalized experience). After the execution of the simple linear regression analysis, the following results were generated:

a) **Ease of use (EU) and personalized experience (PE):** For analysis of variance two variables, personalized experience and ease of use were used, and the following results were obtained. As per the reports, the significance of F 0.0050 is observed, which indicates a strong relationship between the used variables. In observing the coefficients of personalized experience, it can be commented that the data available for personalized experience is associated with ease of use. Apart from ANOVA, other techniques can also be imposed to verify the relationship gradience between the variables.

Summary Output

Regression Statistics	
R Square	0.022344277
Adjusted R Square	0.019534921
Observations	350

ANOVA

	df	F	Significance F
Regression	1	7.953524101	0.00507441
Residual		348	
Total		349	

	Coefficients	P-value
Intercept	0.925531915	8.268E-166
Personalized Experience	0.058843085	0.00507441

b) **User-friendliness (UF) and personalized experience (PE):** For analysis of variance two variables, personalized experience and user-friendliness were used, and the following results were obtained. As per the reports, the significance of F 0.0078 is observed, which indicates a strong relationship between the used variables. By observing the coefficients of personalized experience, it can be commented that the data available for personalized experience is associated with ease of use. Apart from ANOVA, other techniques can also be imposed to verify the relationship gradience between the variables.

Summary Output

Regression Statistics	
R Square	0.020113032
Adjusted R Square	0.017297265
Observations	350

ANOVA

	df	F	Significance F
Regression	1	7.143003	0.00787999
Residual	348		
Total	349		

	Coefficients	P-value
Intercept	0.829787234	1.97E-87
Personalized Experience	0.095994016	0.00788

c) **Usefulness (USE) and personalized experience (PE):** For analysis of variance two variables, Personalized Experience and Usefulness are used and the following results were obtained. As per the reports, the Significance of F is 3.51E-10 observed, which indicates a strong relationship between the used variables. By observing the coefficients of Personalized Experience, it can be noted that the data available for Personalized Experience is associated with the Ease of Use. Apart from ANOVA, other techniques can also be imposed to verify the relationship gradience between the variables.

SUMMARY OUTPUT

Regression Statistics	
R Square	0.10711001
Adjusted R Square	0.104544234
Observations	350

ANOVA

	df	F	Significance F
Regression	1	41.74566165	3.51E-10
Residual	348		
Total	349		

	Coefficients	P-value
Intercept	0.723404255	5.83E-75

Personalized Experience	0.229720745	3.50731E-10

d) **Better User Experience/Satisfaction (SAT) and Personalized experience (PE):** For analysis of variance, two variables, personalized experience and usefulness, are used, and the following results were obtained. As per the reports, the Significance of F 1.06E-08 is observed, which indicates a strong relationship between the used variables. Looking at the personalized experience, it can be noted that the data available for personalized experience is associated with ease of use. Apart from ANOVA, other techniques can also be imposed to verify the relationship gradience between the variables.

Summary Output

Regression Statistics	
R Square	0.089902359
Adjusted R Square	0.087287136
Observations	350

ANOVA

	df	F	Significance F
Regression	1	34.37655443	1.06E-08
Residual	348		
Total	349		

	Coefficients	P-value
Intercept	0.76595744	4.02E-87

Personalized Experience	0.194980053	1.05559E-08

Based on the proposed hypothesis and results generated after simple linear regression analysis, significant results were obtained for the selection of communication tools. According to the results generated by simple linear regression, various tools were chosen as communication tools depending on their ease of use, usefulness, better user experience, and user-friendliness depending on personalized experience. Various statistical techniques like regression analysis, t-test, and two-way ANOVA can be imposed on data for correct inferences through available data.

12.6 DISCUSSION

This paper aims to identify which and why digital learning platforms and tools for communication and learning purposes are used among faculty and students at Indian colleges and universities to support or adopt Education 4.0. This study has identified that Google Meet is widely used as a communication platform and Udemy and Coursera are widely used for learning purposes by the faculty and students. According to [16] few faculty members are not comfortable using digital learning platforms and tools because of difficulties in using online learning platforms. With this issue, our findings have proved that digital learning platforms and tools to support Education 4.0 are chosen because of their flexibility, effectiveness, understanding of the subject matter, personalized experience, usability, ease of use, user-friendliness, and user experience. Hence, we think that digital learning platforms and tools should be used by students and lecturers across India. By implementing digital learning, people can learn and teach individually to support the transformation of Education 4.0.

12.7 CONCLUSION

In this study, we have predicted the selection of digital learning tools and platforms for teaching and learning purposes in India to support Education 4.0. This study showed that the selection of digital learning tools and platforms is done based on their effectiveness, personalized experience, ease of use, user-friendliness, and user experience. The selection of proper digital learning platforms and tools can help students and faculties to improve their self-engagements in learning in line with Education 4.0.

12.8 FUTURE ENHANCEMENT

There were challenges while collecting data. We have observed that the number of responses did not reach the target set across India. In this study, digital learning platforms and tools were referring to the general interest and personal experiences of lecturers and students of any stream, any department, any college, and any interest. However, this survey depicts that out of 350 respondents 338 (96.57%) are using digital platforms and tools for the teaching and learning process to promote Education 4.0, which is executing parallel to Industrial Revolution 4.0 in India. However, our study was able to achieve the aim of which tools are majorly used for communication and learning purposes among faculty and students to strengthen the digital learning practices to support Education 4.0.

12.9 REFERENCES

[1] Siti Dianah Abdul Bujang; Ali Selamat; Ondrej Krejcar; Petra Maresova; Ngoc Thanh Nguyen. Digital Learning Demand for Future Education 4.0—Case Studies at Malaysia Education Institutions. *Informatics*. 2020, 7, 13.

[2] Hussin, A.A. Education 4.0 Made Simple: Ideas for Teaching. *Int. J. Educ. Lit. Stud.* 2018, 6, 92–98.

[3] Mogo,s, R.I.; Bodea, C.N.; Dascalu, I.; Safonkina, O.; Lazarou, E.; Trifan, E.L.; Nemoianu, I.V. Technology Enhanced Learning for Industry 4.0 Engineering Education. *Rev. Roum. Sci. Tech. Ser. Electrotech. Energy.* 2018, 63, 429–435.

[4] Ahmad, A.; Sirajuddin, P.T.S.; Mohamed, A.H. The Effectiveness of Training: Equipping and Enhancing ICT Knowledge and Skills among Polytechnic Lecturers in Producing Quality Highly Skilled Graduates. *Adv. J. Tech. Vocat. Educ.* 2017, 1, 1–5.

[5] Fisk, P. Education 4.0, The Future of Learning Will Be Dramatically Different, in School and Throughout Life. 2017. Available online: http://www.thegeniusworks.com/2017/01/future- education-young-everyone-taught-together (accessed on 27 March 2020).

[6] Puncreobutr, V. Education 4.0: New Challenge of Learning. *St. Theresa J. Humanit. Soc. Sci.* 2016, 2, 2.

[7] Aberšek, B. Evolution of Competences for New Era or Education 4.0. In Proceedings of the XXV Conference of Czech Educational Research Association (CERA/CʹAPV), Czech Budejovice, Czech Republic, 14–16 September 2018.

[8] Sinlarat, P. Education 4.0 Is More Than Education. In Annual Academic Seminar of the Teacher's Council on the Topic of Research of Learning Innovation and Sustainable Educational Management; The Secretariat Oce of Teacher's Council: Bangkok, Thailand, 2016.

[9] Kyriaki Raouna. Best Online Learning Platforms. Available online: https://www.learn-worlds.com/online-learning-platforms/ (accessed on 22 March 2022)

[10] Katherine Boyarsky November 4, 2020. The 10 Best Video Meeting Apps. Available online: https://resources.owllabs.com/blog/best-meeting-apps (accessed on 22 March 2022)

[11] Mohamad, S.N.M.; Salam, S.; Bakar, N. Lecturers' Perceptions and Attitudes Towards the Usage of Online Learning at Polytechnic. *Int. J. Sci. Commer. Humanit.* 2014, 2, 2012–2015.

[12] Desai, D. An Empirical Study of Website Personalization Effect on Users' Intention to Revisit E-commerce Website Through Cognitive and Hedonic Experience. In Balas, V.; Sharma, N.; Chakrabarti, A. (Eds.), *Data Management, Analytics, and Innovation. Advances in Intelligent Systems and Computing* (Vol. 839). Springer, 2019. doi:10.1007/978-981-13-1274-8.

[13] Desai, D. Hyper-Personalization: An AI-Enabled Personalization for Customer- Centric Marketing. In Singh, S. (Eds.), *Adoption and Implementation of AI in Customer Relationship Management.* IGI Global, 2022, pp. 40–53. https://doi.org/10.4018/978-1-7998-7959-6.ch003.

[14] Desai, D. A Study of Personalization Effect on Users' Satisfaction with eCommerce Websites. *Sankalpa- J. Manag. Res.* 2016. ISSN No. 2231–1904.

[15] Abdollahpouri, H.; Adomavičius, G.; Burke, R.; Guy, I.; Jannach, D.; Kamishima, T.; Krasnodebski, J.; Pizzato, L. *Beyond Personalization: Research Directions in Multi Stakeholder Recommendation*, 2019. doi:10.1007/s11257–019–09256.

[16] Desai, Dr. D. Modelling Personalized E-Learning for Effective Distance Education. *IJRASET.* 2020, 8(6), 2428–2435. https://doi.org/10.22214/IJRASET.2020.6390.

[17] Malureanu, A.; Panisoara, G.; Lazar, I. (2021). *The Relationship Between Self-Confidence, Self-Efficacy, Grit, Usefulness, and Ease of Use of eLearning Platforms in Corporate Training During the COVID-19 Pandemic.* https://doi.org/10.3390/su13126633.

[18] Wafiyyah, R.S.; Made, N.; Kusumadewi, W. The Effect of Perceived Usefulness, Perceived Ease of Use, and Trust on Repurchase Intention on E-Commerce Shopee. *IJISET* (Vol. 8), 2021. www.ijiset.com.

[19] Addison, S.; Addison, S. Impact of Advancement of Technology, Competitive Pressure, User Expectation on Continuous Digital Disruption: Mediating Role of Perceived Ease of Use. *Open J. Bus. Manag.* 2021, 9, 2013–2079. https://doi.org/10.4236/ojbm.2021.94109

[20] Zandi Associate Professor, G.; Low Bee Choo Candidate, S.; Ahmed Shahzad, I.; Farid Shamsudin Associate Professor, M. *Extended Practice of Technology Acceptance Model; Impact of Personal Innovation and Ease of Use on Internet Shopping Intentions: A Study on Apparel Buyers' Purchase Intention in Malaysia*, n.d. https://doi.org/10.22059/jitm.2021.86124.

[21] Abubakari, M.S.; Hungilo, G. Evaluating an e-Learning Platform at Graduate School Based on User Experience Evaluation Technique Evaluating an e-Learning Platform at Graduate School Based on User Experience Evaluation Technique Evaluating an e-Learning Platform at Graduate School Based on User Experience Evaluation Technique. *Article J. Phys. Conf. Ser.* 2021, 1737, 12019. https://doi.org/10.1088/1742–6596/1737/1/012019.

13 A Detailed Review on 6G Technology
Online Learning System Applications, Challenges and Research Activities

Arun Agarwal[1], Suvransu Sekhar Mishra[1],
Banoj Kumar Panda[2] and Gourav Misra[3]

1 Department of ECE, ITER, Siksha O Anusandhan
Deemed to be University, Bhubaneswar, Odisha, India,

2 Department of ECE, Gandhi Institute for Education
and Technology, Bhubaneswar, Odisha, India,

3 School of Electronic Engineering, Dublin City
University, Glasnevin, Dublin, Ireland

CONTENTS

DOI: 10.1201/9781003272823-13

13.1 INTRODUCTION

The concept of traditional education has changed dramatically in the last few years. Physical presence in the classroom is not the only way to learn, not with the advent of the internet and new technologies, at least. Nowadays, you can access a quality education anytime and anywhere you want as long as you can connect to the internet. We are now entering a new era: the transformation of online education. E-learning on the internet, mobile devices, and social networking tools have a consistent traditional classroom exchange. This problem will be greatly solved by upcoming 6G networks.

Wireless communication systems are our time's eureka moments, given the incredible pace of technological advancement over the previous several decades and the convergence of Internet of Things (IoT) harmonious technologies. There are five [17] generations of mobile wireless cellular dispatching systems in operation today, with the most recent being the fifth generation (5G) wireless network. Since 1980, a new wireless cellular communication generation has emerged roughly every ten years, with the first-generation analogue FM cellular systems appearing in 1981, the alternate generation in 1992, the third generation [3G] in 2001, and the fourth generation (4G), often referred to as long-term evolution (LTE) in 2011 [1, 2]. A summary of the emerging wireless technologies is shown in Figure 13.1. In general, wireless dispatches have advanced tremendously in the recent decade, resulting in thriving data empty enterprises such as multimedia, online gaming, and high-definition videotape streaming. Mobile internet technology is a catalyst for enabling and spreading colorful state-of-the-art stoner defined services like mobile shopping and payment, smart homes/cities, and mobile gaming [1, 18].

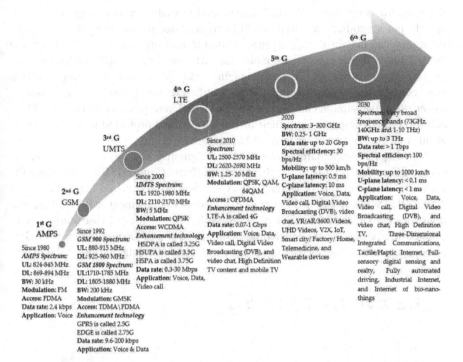

FIGURE 13.1 Major milestones for different generations of communications [1G–6G] [19].

13.2 EVOLUTION OF 5G AND KEY CHALLENGES

13.2.1 EVOLUTION OF 5G

Radio frequencies (sometimes referred to as a spectrum) are used by wireless dispatch systems to transmit information across the air. 5G uses the same technology as 4G, but it does it at a lower frequency, making it less obtrusive. As a result, it's capable of carrying more data at a far faster rate. "Millimeter waves" is the name given to these advanced frequency ranges (mm-Waves). They were formerly unlicensed, but authorities have since made them available for purchase. Due to the outfit's inaccessibility and monetary value, they had mostly gone unnoticed by the general population.

Large distances can be a concern even with sophisticated bands because of how quickly they send information. Physical obstacles, such as trees and structures, effectively hinder their movement. 5G will overcome this problem by utilizing many input and affair antennas to increase wireless network capacity and signal strength. Low-power transmitters will be a part of the technology. Instead of employing single-stage alone masts, mount them on structures and road cabinetry. Most experts believe that 5G will be capable of supporting higher data rates per square foot than 4G.

A physical network can be "sliced" into several virtual networks using 5G technology. To put it another way, drivers will be more suited to managing their networks since they can deliver the appropriate portion of network based on how it is being used. Thus, a driver can, for example, use different slice capacities depending on the importance of the job. Just as managing independent autos is segregated from more complex and time-consuming activities like streaming television, an individual stoner using the same technology would use a different piece of a company. Plans call for letting companies rent their own separated and protected network slices to avoid competition with other internet-based firms.

With dispatches standardized for 5G, the system may now be deployed anywhere. On the 5G commercial network globe content charts (Figure 13.2), you can see the various 5G field testing, trials, and 5G exploration efforts around the world. As of April 2019, South Korea had the most extensive 5G deployment, with 5G base stations in approximately 85 major cities [3]. Still, 85% of the 5G base stations were situated in six major cities, including Seoul, Busan, and Daegu, where a3.5 GHz (sub6) spectrum in distributed architecture with stationed data rate speed tested pets

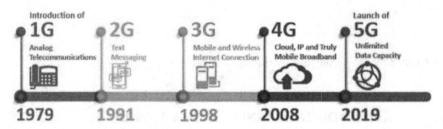

FIGURE 13.2   The evolution of 5G [17].

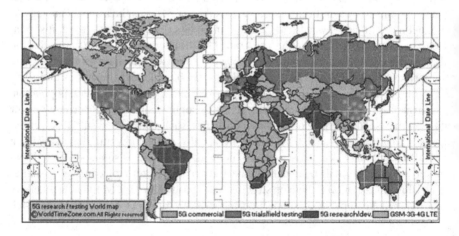

FIGURE 13.3   5G Commercial network world coverage map [December2019] [9].

within the range of 193 to 430 Mbit/s [4]. In general, it is expected that approximately 65 percent of world's population would have access to superfast 5G internet content by the end of 2025 [5].

Continue reading to understand more about 5G's vision, circumstances, and basic features. These networks will offer a wide range of services, including enhanced mobile broadband (eMBB), ultra-reliable and low-latency communications (uRLLC), and large-scale machine dispatching (mMTC). See [2, 6–16] for information on the deployment of 5G wireless cellular mobile communication networks. Wireless data traffic volume and the impact of related impacts are predicted to increase one hundredfold in a given boxy period. Furthermore, data-intensive applications such as holographic video transmission necessitate capacity that is currently unavailable in the millimeter-wave surge spectrum. This situation generates critical challenges in terms of geographical spectral efficacy and the requisite frequency spectrum bands for connectivity. As a result, more radio frequency spectrum bandwidth is needed, which can be found in the sub-terahertz (THz) and terahertz (THz) regions. Recent increases in mobile operations, particularly those aided by AI, have sparked discussions about the future of wireless dispatching [8]. To meet these challenges, researchers and academics have begun conceptualizing the next generation of wireless communication systems (6G), which will provide communication services to meet future demand in the 2030s [8] while also ensuring wireless communication technologies' long-term sustainability and competitiveness. As a result, 6G communication systems are expected to provide a large amount of content, allowing subscribers to interact with one another anywhere at a high-data-rate speed, thanks to the unique technologies that 6G communication systems will promote, similar to an incredibly fast internet connection. High artificial intelligence (AI) and large bandwidths (THz waves) that account for both functional and environmental aspects are required. The extent to which 5G is commercially available around the world is depicted in Figure 13.3.

13.3 KEY CHALLENGES OF 5G

13.3.1 TECHNICAL CHALLENGES

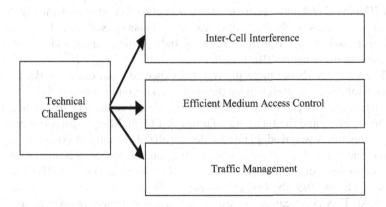

FIGURE 13.4 Technical challenges [20].

13.3.2 COMMON CHALLENGES

FIGURE 13.5   Common challenges [20].

13.4   INTRODUCTION OF 6G

For the sixth generation of telecommunications standards, the 6G standard for wireless dispatch technologies that enable cellular data networks is currently being developed. 6G, which is predicted to be 50 times quicker than 5G, is the planned successor to 5G. 6G networks, like its predecessors, are likely to be broadband cellular networks with service areas separated into smaller geographical pieces known as cells. Both 4G and 5G technologies are used in a 6G network (Figure 13.4 and Figure 13.5). Several companies (including Nokia, Ericsson, Huawei, Samsung, LG, Apple, and Xiaomi) as well as governments (including India, China, Japan, and Singapore) are interested in 6G networks [10, 11, 12].

More diversity [being more different] is expected from 6G networks than their predecessors, with the ability to handle operations beyond existing mobile use scripts, like virtual and stoked reality (VR/AR), omnipresent immediate dispatches, pervasive intelligence, and the Internet of Things (IoT) [15]. Many experts believe mobile network operators would adopt flexible decentralized economic models for 6G, which include spectrum sharing, structure sharing, and intelligent automated operation based on mobile edge computing and artificial intelligence [14] [13] [21] [22].

As of March 2019, the first 6G wireless cellular mobile dispatches council had been held. This event can be regarded as a vision statement for pervasive wireless intelligence [23]. In comparison to earlier generations, the 6G system is predicted

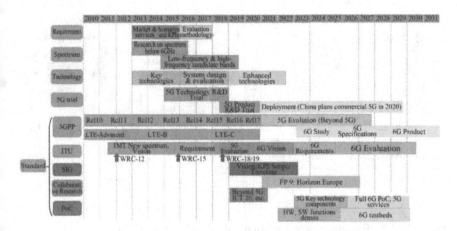

FIGURE 13.6 Timeline of 6G wireless networks [8].

to undergo an enormous shift, reshaping wireless advancement from "connected effects" to "connected intelligence." Further, 6G will go beyond mobile internet and be obliged to provide ubiquitous AI services from the network's core to its bias. 6G will go beyond mobile internet. 6G networks, protocols, and systems will be propelled forward by artificial intelligence (AI) [8, 24]. Figure 13.6 shows the 6G wireless network timeline.

13.4.1 TECHNOLOGIES FOR 6G

The 6G system will be driven by numerous technologies. Many anticipated crucial technologies for 6G are bandied below.

- **Millimetre-Wave Technologies:** Frequencies further out in the frequency spectrum can be used to free up more spectrum. This also permits the utilization of greater channel bandwidths. Due to 6G's enormous data volumes and bandwidth requirements, millimeter-surge technology will be further improved, possibly reaching the Tera Hertz region of the spectrum [25].
- **Terahertz Dispatches:** Sub-THz communication and advanced massive multiple input, multiple output (MIMO) technologies with wide bandwidths can improve spectral efficiency. The RF band has nearly run out due to 6G's intensive usage. The THz band will be used for 6G connectivity. There are two numbers: 100 and 101. The THz band is predicted to represent the next frontier in data transmission rates. THz waves, sometimes referred to as sub millimeter radiation, have wavelengths in the range of 0.03 mm–3 mm and operate in the frequency range of 0.1 THz to 10 THz [27]. ITUR guidelines consider the THz spectrum for cellular dispatches to be the primary component, extending from 275 GHz to 3 THz [27]. Incorporating the THz spectrum (275 GHz to 3 THz) will let 6G cellular transmissions reach their full potential. The 275 GHz—3 THz band, which is currently unallocated in the

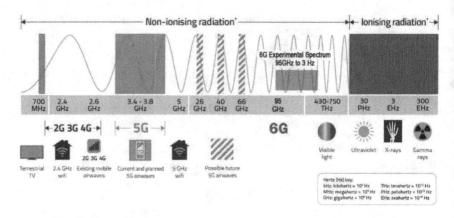

FIGURE 13.7   Electromagnetic spectrum and 6G and spectrum [26].

United States, could be utilized to negotiate extremely high data rates [27]. When the THz band is added to the current millimeter wave band, the overall band capacity increases by at least 11.11 times. THz bands are divided into millimeter wave (275 GHz–3 THz) and far infrared (300 GHz-3 THz) THz bands (IR). A small portion of the optical band, the 300 GHz–3 THz range, is located just outside of the optical band, and it is indistinctly following the RF band in electromagnetic spectrum (Figure 13.7). As a result, the radio frequency spectrum and the 300 GHz–3 THz regions have many similarities. THz enhances high-frequency dispatching capabilities while introducing additional annoyances [28]. THz dispatches require a lot of available bandwidth to enable very high data rates (ii) and a lot of path loss due to the high frequency (most likely a lot of directional antennas are required) [29]. These are critical components. The smaller beamwidths of the directional antennas lessen the impediment. It is more difficult to design effective bias and BSs for THz signals because of the short wavelength. As a result, cutting-edge adaptive array technology can be used to get around range limitations [29].

- **Optic Wireless Technology:** With OWC technologies, 6G dispatches as well as RF-grounded dispatches for all possible device-to-access networks are envisaged for these networks, which further penetrate the network to provide "backhaul/front haul network connectivity." OWC technologies have been in use since the advent of 4G cellular networks. However, 6G communication networks will make more use of it. Some of the more well-known OWC technologies include light devotion, visible light communication, optic camera communication, and FSO communication based on the optical band [30,31]. These technologies now function poorly, but researchers have been experimenting with ways to make them better. Optical wireless communication makes it feasible to communicate at high data rates with little dormancy and secure dispatches. 6G dispatches will be able to perform highly accurate 3D mapping using LiDAR, which is also based on the optic band. For backup transmission system for manned aircraft, a backhaul network using optical fiber communication is not always practical because of geographical distances and other issues. Using the FSO backhaul network for 5 GB communications is quite promising. The following two numbers are intertwined: a number of benefits of the FSO system's transmitter and receiver characteristics can be compared to those of optical fiber networks. Hence, optical fiber-like data transfer is used in the FSO system. When used in conjunction with optical fiber networks, FSO makes an excellent 6G backhaul communication solution. FSO enables long-range dispatches to be sent hundreds of kilometers away. Even remote locations, such as the ocean, outer space, waterways, and isolated islets, can take advantage of FSO's high-capacity backhaul connectivity.

- **Massive MIMO:** Although MIMO (multiple inputs and multiple outputs) is used in a variety of activities from LTE to Wi-Fi and beyond, the number of antennas available is quite limited. When using fryer frequencies, a single article of clothing can utilize numerous counterfeit antennas because to differences in the wavelength widths and lengths of the antennas [25].

- **Blockchain:** Blockchain will play a significant role in future communication networks because of the vast amounts of data they will contain [32–33]. Distributed tally technology comes in many forms, with blockchains being one of them. The term "distributed tally" refers to a database that is spread among numerous bumps or biases. Each tying creates a duplicate of the tally and stores it. Peer-to-peer networks control the blockchain. It doesn't require a server or central authority to run. Blocks are used to organize and store data on a blockchain. Cryptography is used to link and secure the blocks. When it comes to big IoT, blockchain is basically a great match thanks to its improved interoperability and security [34]. Because of this, blockchain technology will enable a wide range of applications, such as interoperability across bias, enormous data traceability, autonomous relationships between different IoT systems, and trustability for 6G communication system immense interconnectedness.

- **3D Networking:** Ground and airborne networks will be integrated into the 6G system to facilitate drug couriers in the perpendicular extension. Low-orbit satellites and unmanned aerial vehicles (UAVs) will deliver the 3D BSs. 3D connectivity differs greatly from ordinary 2D networks due to the presence of new boundaries, such as altitude and associated degrees of freedom.

- **Cell-Free Dispatches:** Many radio frequencies and communication technologies will need to be seamlessly integrated into 6G systems for it to work. As a result, users will not have to make any changes to their device's configuration while switching networks [28]. The network's name will be given to any communication technology that becomes accessible. In terms of cell conception, this will push the envelope on what's feasible with wireless dispatch. A stoner's travel from one cell to another now causes too many handovers in crowded networks, failures in changeover, detention, data loss, and the clunk-pong effect, all of which are undesirable. All these problems can be overcome, and QoS will be improved, thanks to 6G cell-free dispatching (quality of service). Communication without using a cell phone will be feasible via the use of several networking technologies such as multi-league connections and varied and random radios placed throughout the bias [28].

- **Holographic Beam Forming:** Beam forming, a signal processing procedure, can direct a group of antennas to deliver radio signals in a specific direction. Smart antennas include improved antenna systems. This method's benefits include excellent signal-to-noise ratios, low jitter, and good network efficacy. A ground-breaking new method to beam forming, software-defined antennas allow holographic beam forming (HBF), which differs dramatically from current MIMO systems. HBF will be a hugely successful solution in 6G for the efficient and flexible transmission and event of signals in multi-antenna communication bias.

- **Future PHY/MAC:** The new physical sub caste and MAC presents numerous new intriguing possibilities in several areas:

  - **Waveforms:** The development of new waveforms for wireless dispatch is a top priority for scientists. OFDM has proven to be quite successful in mobile dispatch systems such as 4G and 5G as well as other high data rate wireless dispatch systems. It does, however, have severe restrictions when used in specific circumstances, waveforms other than GFDM, Generalized Frequency-Divided Multiplexing, including Filter Bank Multi-Carrier and Universal Filtered Multi-Carrier. Waveforms can be employed differently depending on the context for 6G mobile dispatch systems. Each one has benefits and drawbacks. There will be far more rigidity in 6G dispatches as a result [25].
  - **Multiple Access Schemes:** Again, a variety of new access schemes are being delved for 6G technology.
  - **Modulation:** PSK and QAM (quadrature amplitude modulation) have excelled in spectrum efficiency, adaptability, and capacity thanks to their high peak-to-average power ratios. The use of APSK (amplitude phase-shift keying) as a modulation method can be helpful in some circumstances. Mobile dispatching systems benefit from APSK's reduced peak-to-average power ratio (PAPR), since the final amplifier works better when the PAPR is lower [25].

- **Duplex Methods:** The new 6G wireless dispatch system may make use of several different seeker duplex designs. Time/frequency division duplex systems now in use include FDD and TDD. Sixth-generation (or 6G) wireless networks may use a variety of transmission techniques, including flexible duplex, in which time or frequencies are allotted based on the type of data being sent as well as a new technology known as division-free duplex or single-channel full-duplex. This 6G strategy would allow simultaneous transmission and event holding on the same channel [25].

13.5 REQUIREMENTS

6G-to-5G progression will develop wireless technological requirements [35]. As a result of the advances made possible by 5G, new conditions have emerged, and those that already existed have grown even further. However, new combinations of circumstances will be required for future use cases that haven't been envisioned yet, similar to 5G.

13.5.1 EXTREME-HIGH SPEED DATA AND HIGH-CAPACITY COMMUNICATION

As communication speed improves, new sensitive services with a level of sensitivity equivalent to or greater than factual sensitivity may be created using wireless technology with speeds exceeding 100 Gbps, for example. Spectacles-type outstations are expected to evolve into wearable devices as the stoner interface that makes this service possible. New accompanied activities in cyberspace, equivalent to virtual experience and virtual collaboration, can be predicted as more dopeheads join in new similar real-time experience services. It is becoming increasingly important to increase uplink performance because to trends such as the requirement for diligence and cyber-physical emulsion to deliver colorful real-time information to consumers and AI.

13.5.2 EXTREME COVERAGE

We plan to build "extreme content extension" in the future, which will allow people to communicate in regions like the sky, seas, and space that aren't currently serviced by mobile communication networks. As a result, new levels of effort and diligence will be created for humans and machines alike. There's a good chance this increase will be used in future use cases like flying taxis and trips to outer space.

13.5.3 EXTREME LOW LATENCY

Wireless dispatches that connect AI and bias in cyber-physical emulsion are analogous to the mortal nervous system in that they transfer information. Low latency appears to be an essential need for real-time, interactive, and always stable end-to-end (E2E) services. The target E2E latency for 6G is often 1 millisecond or less. Using this, interactive services that reply carefully like a person by studying a customer's face expression can be built, for example, in a robot-run business.

13.5.4 EXTREME RELIABLE COMMUNICATIONS

It was mentioned in the previous chapter that the evolution of 5G and 6G will move away from merely best-effort communication to incorporate quality assurance communication and other sorts of data as well. Remote control and factory automation, for example, necessitate the transmission of highly reliable control information wirelessly, and 6G is predicted to achieve greater trust ability and security conditions than 5G. A comparative analysis on the same has been presented in Table 13.1. We are seeing an increase in the popularity of robotic devices like drones and robots, and radio programming is expanding into new areas like the sky, so it is possible that reliable dispatches will be required in both small, and large areas like factories and the arrival of reliable dispatches in colorful settings is also expected.

TABLE 13.1

Comparison between 5G and 6G Technologies [36].

Parameters/Aspects	5G	6G
Peak data rate	10 Gbps	1 Tbps
Usage Period	2020–2030	2030–2040
Max Frequency	W-band (<110 GHz)	10 THz
E2E latency	10 ms	1 ms
Connection density	1E5/km^2	1E7/km^2
Maximum spectral efficiency	30 bps/Hz	100 bps/Hz
Mobility support	>500 km/hr	>1000 km/hr
Satellite Integration	Partial	Fully
AI Integration	Partial	Fully
Autonomous Vehicle Support	Partial	Fully
AR/VR/MR Support	Partial	Fully
Haptic Communication/Control	Partial	Fully
Key technologies/aspects	mmW incorporation, small cells, mMIMO, beam forming, antenna arrays, use of non-terrestrial network	THz spectrum, visible light communications (VLC), Intelligent surfaces, data-centric automated process

13.6   APPLICATIONS

13.6.1 ARTIFICIAL INTELLIGENCE

In addition to AI and deep neural networks (DNNs), machine learning (ML) is altering technology and creating new research opportunities in diverse fields such as 6G deployments and the Internet of Things (IoTs). For 6G communication, AI and ML are being used to build the connection and system position outcomes. 6G with AI-enabled capabilities is expected to bring new capabilities such as tone configuration, aggregation, opportunistic setup, and environmental mindfulness [37]. AI-enabled 6G with help from ML algorithms can totally achieve the eventuality of radio signaling and maximum cognitive to intelligent radio transmission [8, 38]. Intelligent and reconfigurable accessories are also expected to lay the groundwork for wireless technology's new foundations [39]; they are known as MIMO2.0 and are extensively discussed in [35, 40].

These are the summaries of ML styles for D2D communication, huge MIMP optimization, and the construction of various networks [42, 43]. Similarly, [44] presented a new mobile communication network armature for examining big data analytics, and comparable analyses can lubricate physical subcaste optimizations. An indication modulation objectification has been proposed by the authors in [45] as a tool to improve 6G network efficacy. High intelligence and machine learning methods, in particular, have the potential to improve performance while also altering the overall

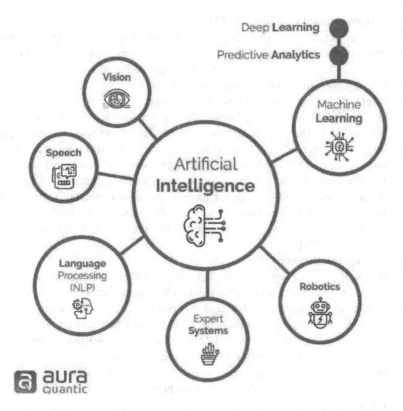

FIGURE 13.8 Features of artificial intelligence [41].

architecture and design of 6G networks (Figure 13.8). The next three sections go into detail on the benefits of intelligent 6G features in wireless and non-wireless communication services:

- **Operational Intelligence [OI]:**
  This technique uses multi-objective optimizations that can work in the vast complicated and dynamic nature of 6G because of its diversity, viscosity, and scalability to efficiently distribute funds (i.e., bands and power) to produce adequate network operations rather than employing standard approaches. It is difficult to optimize for multi-objective performance when dealing with NP-hard problems because of the sensitivity of the measurements. As a result of recent advancements in AI and machine learning (ML) methods, including deep underpinning literacy (DRL), the decision-maker can use the feedback obtained through a DRL-established circle to iteratively refine and finally optimise their opinions [8]. When used in resource allocation, similar learning techniques aid in optimization [46]. A number of recent concerns were addressed by Luong et al. [47], including data dumping, concealing, and adaptive modulation.

- **Environmental Intelligence [EI]:**
  Holistic technology, including wireless communication settings, could make pervasive and dispersed intelligence a reality, including smart radio spaces and accessories [39]. Using intelligence-based services, data centers, IoT bias, unmanned upstanding and road vehicles, and bus robots [48] might all be realized, as could multiple operation scripts involving data centers, IoT bias, unmanned upstanding and road vehicles, and bus robots [49]. Some of the most recent developments are mentioned in [39, 50] as involving adaptive mores based on detecting radio surge tailored metamorphoses with reconfigurable intelligent shells. These advancements lay the groundwork for an e-commerce-friendly technology approach. Although the uprooted original features are communicated to the edge or pall bias in DNNs, processing these features is a difficult operation because of the computation and communication capacities and diversity of the bias. DNNs [8].
- **Service Intelligence [SI]:**
  6G intelligence deployments in a human-centric network include communication services such as e-health, positioning (indoor/outdoor), multi-device operation, information search, and security [51, 52]. As with deep literacy methods that improve position delicacy, SI can help extend all similar human-centric processes in an intelligent and individualized approach to maximize stoner satisfaction [53]. In addition, a multi-model-based structure for intelligent IoT and data collecting can aid with e-health personalization [54]. The high-performance core networks under 6G can be used to improve SI [55, 56].

13.6.2 INTERNET OF THINGS

An IoT is a network of interconnected physical items (or groups of similar objects) that can exchange and exchange data with other systems and biases over the internet or another dispatching network and that are outfitted with sensors, recycling capabilities, software, and other technologies [57] [58] [59] [60]. A broad picture on the same can be found in Figure 13.9.

Technology convergence, including ubiquitous computing and commodity detectors together with decreasingly relevant bed systems and machine literacy, have all contributed to the field's evolution [57]. There are a number of traditional sectors that enable the Internet of Effects, including bed systems, wireless detector networks, control systems, and robotization (including robotics in the home and structure). As a result of consumer demand, IoT technology is most often associated with products that relate to the concept of the "smart home," including bias and appliances (such as home lighting institutions and thermostats and other home appliances) that support one or more common ecosystems and can be controlled through bias associated with that ecosystem, such as smartphones and smart speakers. The Internet of Things (IoT) has applications in healthcare as well.

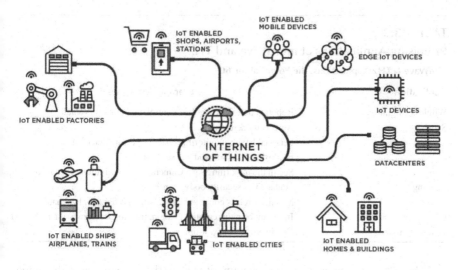

FIGURE 13.9 Usage of IOT [61].

13.6.3 mm-Wave and THz Applications

Wireless original area and cellular networks based on mm-Wave and THz technology will allow for ultra-fast computer communication, autonomous vehicles, robotic controls, the information shower [62], high-definition holographic gaming, entertainment, videotape conferences, and high-speed wireless data distribution in data centers [63]. Beyond the 6G network's probable evolution, there are intriguing activities for future mm-Wave and THz systems as well. Wireless cognition, seeing, imaging, wireless communication, and position/THz navigation (also known as localization or positioning) are all examples of operations that can be divided into these categories. Refer to Table 13.2 for promising applications of mm-Wave and THz.

13.6.3.1 Wireless Cognition

Wireless cognition is the idea of providing a communication link that allows enormous calculations to be carried out continuously from the device or machine performing real-time actions [64]. Consider that a featherlight drone line may not have the power or weight budget to run massive calculations onboard the outfit, but with a wide enough channel bandwidth and fast enough data rate, real-time calculations for extremely complex tasks such as contextual mindfulness and vision and perception can be performed at a fixed base station or edge server that is in wireless connection and supports real-time cognition for the drone line. Cognitive processing can be incorporated into robots, autonomous cars, and other machines using wireless technology, allowing them to complete tasks without relying on the platform's own cognition [64, 65].

TABLE 13.2
Promising Applications at mm-Wave and THz
MmWave & THz Applications: the Potential for 6G

Application	Example Use Cases
Wireless Cognition	Robotic control, drone fleet control, autonomous vehicle
Sensing	Air quality detection
	Personal health monitoring systems, gesture detection
	Explosive detection and gas sensing
	See in the dark (mmWave Camera), high-definition video resolution,
Imaging	radar THz, security body scan
	Mobile wireless communication, wireless fiber for backhaul
Communication	Intra-device radio communication, information shower (≥ 100Gbps)
Positioning	Centimeter-level positioning

When Moore's law is taken into account, it is clear that a computer with computing skills comparable to the human brain will be available for purchase for less than $1,000 USD (the cost of a moment's smartphone) by the year 2036. According to [61, 62], the rise in computing power since 1965 [63] is based on these findings. A new study suggests Terahertz frequencies may be the first to provide the real-time calculations needed for wireless remote control of mortal cognition [59].

Approximately 100 billion (1011) neurons are found in the human brain. Each neuron has a maximum firing rate of 200 times per second (5 ms update rate), and each neuron is connected to about 1,000 others, resulting in a calculation speed of 20 1,015 floating-point operations per second (duds) [61] and Tbps if each operation is assumed to be doubled:

$$\text{Human Brain flops (Computation Speed)}$$
$$= 10^{11} \text{ neurons} \times 200 \text{ flop/sec} \times 10^3 /\text{neuron}$$
$$= 20 \times 10^{15} \text{ flop/sec} = 20 \text{ petaflops/sec} \times 1 \text{ bit/flop}$$
$$= 20,000 \text{Tbps} \tag{13.1}$$

Each neuron has written access to 1,000 bytes resulting in memory size of the human brain of 100 terabytes [66, 67]:

$$\text{Storage} = 10^{11} \text{ neurons} \times 10^3 \text{ bytes/neuron}$$
$$= 10^{14} \text{ bytes} = 100 \text{TB} \tag{13.2}$$

Moment's state-of-the-art 1,000 USD computer technology performs 1 trillion (e.g., 1012) calculations/sec, which are four orders of magnitude lower than the speed of the mortal brain. Unborn wireless generations (e.g., 6G or 7G) are likely to allocate up to 10 GHz RF channels for each stoner in the THz governance, and by assuming that each stoner is suitable to exploit 10 bits/symbol modulation styles and 1,000 times increase in channel capacity using yet to be invented generalities beyond collaborative multipoint (Presentation) and MassiveMIMO, it's readily seen in [3] that data rates of 100 terabytes/sec will be achieved.

$$R = 10\,\text{GHz channel} \times 10\,\text{bits}/(\text{sec} \cdot \text{Hz}) \times 10^3 = 100\text{Tbps}. \tag{13.3}$$

From [1] and [2], it's clear that a 100 Tbps link is presumptive in a 10 GHz channel bandwidth, furnishing 0.5 of real-time mortal computational power. Ambitiously, if 100 GHz channel bandwidths are used, 1 petabits/sec of information, or 5 of the real-time computational power of the mortal brain, could be carried over wireless [59].

13.6.3.2 Sensing

Sensing activities enabled by mm-Wave and THz frequency take advantage of the measured terrain's sub-mm wavelength and frequency selectivity to learn about the terrain's foundation from the propagated signal's seen hand. Over 100 GHz channel bandwidths can be used for sensing activities, as well as the resonant frequencies and immersion of colorful accessories. As frequency rises, the spatial resolution becomes increasingly finer and important as a function of wavelength, enabling sub-millimeter spatial isolation as frequency exceeds 300 GHz. The ability to use veritably high gain antennas in a small physical form factor also enables sensing operations that are veritably directional. To construct photographs of physical areas, ray scanning uses signal autographs entered at a variety of different angles to monitor the signal autographs methodically. It will be possible to measure the parcels of a room, an office, or a complicated terrain in a matter of seconds or less using electrical ray steering techniques that can be implemented in real-time (sub- seconds) and radio multination distances that are short (e.g., on the order of measures in the room). A new dimension of wireless is now available, allowing unborn wireless bias to do "wireless reality sensing" and collect data from any location, resulting in detailed 3D world maps made on the cover and uploaded/participated in on the pall by unborn bias [64], [65]. It's also conceivable to protest the presence of specific particulars anchored on frequency scanning spectroscopy because certain accessories and feasts have a vibration immersion (e.g. resonances) at particular frequency throughout the THz band. There may be a way to detect the presence of particular chemicals or allergens in food, drink, air, or other elements in our environment using spectroscopy, which will be available on smartphones as early as the 6G era. There will be new sensing operations enabled by THz such as miniaturized radars for gesture discovery and touch less smart phones, spectrometers for explosive discovery and gas sensing [56], THz security body scanning, air quality discovery [24], specific health monitoring systems [55], perfection time/frequency transfer, and wireless synchronization in the form of time/frequency transfer and wireless synchronization. A real-time map of any terrain can help predict channel characteristics on a mobile device, support the alignment of directional antennas, provide information on the position of the cover, and modify wireless capabilities [60] by erecting real-time charts. To provide real-time collection capabilities for mapping and sensing the surroundings, this capacity might also be fed into the network and employed in marketable activities for transportation and shopping.

13.6.3.3 Imaging

Radar at a distance of mm Due to rainfall and ambient light having less of an impact on the THz channel than light or infrared frequencies, wave, and THz frequencies are more suitable for ground imaging akin to Light Discovery and Ranging (LIDAR). Even though LIDAR has the ability to provide high resolution, it will not function if it is foggy, pouring, or overcast [68]. It's still possible to employ mm-Wave and THz radar to help with bad weather travel, especially when flying and driving. These technologies are also useful in the military and for public safety. Low-frequency (below 12.5 GHz) circular radars that provide greater range discovery but with poor resolution will be sufficient to give a television-like picture quality and high-description video resolution radars that operate at several hundred gigahertz. Vehicles and aircraft will be able to operate in heavy fog and rain with the use of binary-frequency radar systems [69]. Through the use of THz waves, one can "see" NLOS objects around corners, which allows for new possibilities in delivery and surveillance, navigational self-sufficiency, and localization. THz imaging can see past corners and behind walls if there is enough reflection or scattering routes on a structure's face, which is why walls, floors, and doors act to first order like glasses (e.g., perfect mirrors of THz energy). [70–72] have also proposed NLOS imaging styles based on visible and infrared light. While this is true, the optical wavelength is shorter than the average surface roughness of most rock faces, necessitating the use of computationally expensive reconstruction procedures to achieve short imaging distances (5 m). Because of the weakly scattered signals, short field of view, and long integration periods, practical deployment of visible light systems is still challenging. Alternatively, NLOS radar systems operating at lower frequencies (10 GHz) experience less signal loss, making objects look smoother. There is still semi transparency in the lower-frequency spectrum due to the presence of the edges, and pictures become rapidly crowded due to high multi-reflection propagation [73–77]. There is also accurate information of the static figure in radar systems, and they are confined to item discovery rather than detailed photos of an abandoned scene.

THz waves combine a number of the most useful features of microwaves and visible light in one compact package. High spatial resolution images with relatively tiny imaging devices are possible with Videlicet's narrow wavelengths and large bandwidths [78, 79]. There is also extensive scattering from the utmost structure surfaces, as shown in Figure. 13.10 by THz scattering. As a result of the strong specular element, surfaces become commodities similar to "electrical glasses," allowing images to be captured around barriers while retaining spatial coherency (narrow shafts) and excellent spatial resolution [80]. THz waves are used in radar imaging systems to illuminate the area and calculate the time of flight (ToF) of the backscattered signals to produce 3D images. Performing 3D images are distorted if the scattered signal's path includes many bounces off girding surfaces. However, by using basic mirroring metamorphoses [81], a rectified image of NLOS objects may be rebuilt. Because of the intense specular reflections, the LOS surfaces may act as glasses.

13.6.3.4 Precise Positioning

Unborn mobile bias operating above 100 GHz will most likely include an instigative point such as using mm-wave imaging and dispatching for centimeter-level position

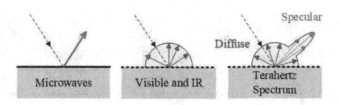

FIGURE 13.10   Scattered EM waves from a flat surface microwave frequency (*specular scattering*) reveal the smoothness of most surfaces; optical spectra reveal the roughness of the same surfaces (*diffuse scattering*). Most building surfaces exhibit significant diffuse scattering and intense specular reflections in the THz regime.

localization [59]. When compared to other methods, mm-Wave and THz imaging for localization have intriguing and distinct advantages. If their journey pathways to the base station/access points see more than one reflection, the mm Wave imaging/communication techniques presented in [57], [60], [65] can locate drug users in NLOS zones (e.g., multiple bounces).

The proposed mm Wave imaging/communication grounded design in [57] also differs from traditional contemporaneous localization and mapping (SLAM) techniques in that it has no prior knowledge of the terrain, whereas traditional SLAM approaches that do. It will be possible for mobile devices that have built-in terrain maps to take advantage of numerous other capabilities, such as predicting the signal position, using real-time point-specific vatic nation, or uploading the map to the pall for physical chart compilation, or using similar maps for mobile operations by erecting or downloading the terrain map. The vast bandwidth available at frequencies above 100 GHz will allow LOS and NLOS drug users to be located to within a centimeter in the future. The cherry on top of the cake will be the ability to use mm-wave imaging and dispatching for precise placement in 6G networks and beyond.

If you use an mm-Wave or THz camera to reconstruct 3D charts of your surroundings in unfamiliar situations, you'll be able to combine sight with imaging and location all at the same time. It's been demonstrated recently that mm-Wave and THz signals reflect explosively from extreme structural accessories, allowing for NLOS imaging of retiring things. Centimeter location localization and mapping are possible with vast bandwidth and big antenna arrays at mm-Wave and THz frequencies [57, 60, 65] based on 3D maps of the physical surroundings and temporal and angular information from a mobile (TOA and AOA).

13.7   CHALLENGES

13.7.1   HIGH INTELLIGENCE VERSUS PRIVACY AND COMPLEXITY

Sixth-generation wireless networks must strike a balance between privacy and intelligence if they are to be creative. AI algorithms must interact with private data in order to improve network functionality, adjust network numbers, and provide higher-quality

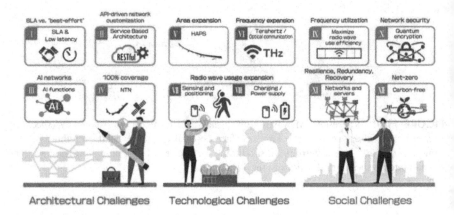

FIGURE 13.11 Challenges of 6G [82].

services [83]. As a result, great intelligence would suffer due to sequestration. Using a central mediator between the final stoner data and AI algorithms yields a sought-after result for seekers. Moderators should be a third party, preferably independent, who work remotely. A central moderator agent will anonymize all specific and sensitive data. In addition, AI algorithms and smart bumps' increased intelligence reduces the amount of freedom that mortals have. AI algorithms are likely to produce an indispensable, but stoner inclination will not be one of them. When a large number of drug addicts are taken into account, the situation becomes much more difficult (Figure 13.11). A good way to think about this problem is to think of it as a place where personalization meets intelligence in 6G deployments [16]. Intelligent algorithms and smart bumps need intelligence over lavish routines and intelligence over sub-routines, and personalization certainly draws more attention. Similar routines and sub-routines should be defined in 6G network abecedarian processes. This approach allows for intelligent portfolios to be offered just within the permissible boundaries.

Highly intelligent systems are expensive in terms of the complexity of the network they require [21], and this could have a significant impact on network drivers and patron budgets. To make low-cost widgets a reality, users will have to pay more for current devices as long as this trend continues. Technology-based intelligent structures are critical in the fight against this issue. New business models are also necessary, if not more so. Security, confidentiality, and sequestration may all be ensured before changing the accessible anonymized data to lower data prices. With the advent of 6G communication networks, it will be possible for electricity customers to trade their own-produced power with electric utility providers.

13.7.2 Security versus Spectral Efficiency

Wireless data connection that is secure enough to be used in an attack involves multiple diapasons bandwidth prevention measures, which reduce the amount of diapason data that can be used to send the data. Trying to come up with a good plan to deal with wireless dispatches' security and spectral effectiveness concerns would require a lot of math, but there are three approaches that could work. First, it's expected that security specialists' encryption methods would be a huge success. Realizing similar algorithms may be awkward now that the encryption algorithm has matured. Second, security specialists should devise a way for implementing PHY security solutions while suffering a spectrum loss. Additionally, AI algorithms are capable of detecting network flaws and might be used in 6G networks to develop a security bastion early warning method.

13.7.3 TRANSCEIVER DESIGN AND THz SIGNAL GENERATORS

In order to successfully train the THz band, the current transceiver structure is considered one of the most challenging challenges to overcome. Current transceivers cannot work at the THz diapason, in other words [73]. Because of the substantial transmission loss in the THz band, high-end signal processing is required. At greater power levels, aspects such noise figure position and perceptivity need to be taken into account more thoroughly. It is also necessary to analyze the transmission power and distance in depth. The use of silicon germanium, gallium nitride, gallium arsenide, and indium phosphide grounded technologies in THz frequency bands is theoretically possible, but researchers must consider the limited power benefits in mobile networks [73]. The broadcast range of similar technology is also limited. The nonlinear amplifier, phase noise, and modulation all need to be considered in the design of a new transceiver armature. Current transceiver infrastructure is not ready to deal with THz sources, and new infrastructure is necessary, especially for the medium to section of THz bands (> 300 GHz) [85, 86]. New transceiver infrastructures for THz-capable outfits can make use of existing reciprocal essence oxide semiconductor technologies and recently introduced nanomaterials like graphene [75].

13.7.4 COST

One of 6G's goals is to make services more affordable. Both non-terrestrial and terrestrial 6G network bumps will be implemented. Despite the fact that terrestrial bumps are very inexpensive, conserving them will help the middle class. Drones and other movable objects, like satellites, are incredibly valuable on the ground. It costs a lot of money to launch satellites into orbit. Another economic consideration is the preservation of their appearance and form. Aquatic communication also necessitates the use of valuable structural elements. For the highest quality of service, 6G needs high-quality bias. Biases that are both sophisticated and high quality can be quite costly. As a result, the smart biases are out of reach from the majority of the population. The objective is to bring down the price so that it is accessible to all.

13.7.5 ENERGY

Like smart bias and APs, every 6G gadget will use advanced signal processing mechanisms. They must also repurpose large amounts of data that have been through a lot of processing and use a lot of energy. As a result, 6G faces energy challenges. In its network bumps, 6G will use emergent technology akin to Edge and AI that is also high in energy. As a result, 6G will have to solve the problems of energy harvesting, charging, and conserving. An additional factor is the coopera- tion of 6G network hiccups in the area of energy consumption. As the transmission method circulates, data transfer also necessitates additional energy consumption. To give high position security, advanced energy is either consumed or advanced energy is generated. On the other hand, using 6G bedding AI reduces the amount of energy you use.

13.7.6 HEAVY COMPUTATION

Sixth-generation wireless networks will integrate communication with computa- tion. 6G's services require a lot of computation. 6G networks are colossal in scope, intricate in design, and multifaceted in functionality. Network topology, consumer demand, business freight, and radio resources all affect how dynamic it is. As a result, wireless connections necessitate automatic network configuration. A smart mobility operation is also required for the 6G network. The moveable knot can be located more easily if there is a calamity or if the knot fails. Nevertheless, each of these duties necessitates much thought and planning. It will take new technologies like edge computing and linked AI to breach the 6G barrier. Enforcing these tech- nologies, however, comes with a host of complications. Problem exists in terms of both 6G technology and the integration of separate technologies.

13.7.7 SENSORY COMMUNICATION

The reason it's called 6G is because it communicates via a sixth sense. Because of this, 6G will be able to support the five senses of the communication system. In order to perceive things, our five senses must be engaged. For 6G to work the data rate must be exceedingly high but quiescence must be extremely low. Additionally, the detectors must be capable of recreating the five senses from distant locations, such as holographic communication, to provide drug users with a realistic experience. As a result, the focus of 6G is on the quality of experience.

13.7.8 POTENTIAL HEALTH ISSUES

Fast communication networks can take advantage of the THz band's huge data rate (terabits/second) and accessible bandwidth. Despite the fact that experts believe that 6G networks and operations are still in their infancy, there is potential for 6G to ben- efit from extremely high frequencies (100 GHz to 1 THz). As a result, it's critical to think about how the spread of THz swells could impair mortal safety.

THz radiation, in particular, lacks ionizing properties due to insufficient photon energy (0.1 to12.4 meV). To put it another way, an ionizing photon has three times the energy of a non-ionizing photon [87,88]. Organizations like this work together to keep people safe from threats such as those to eyes and skin napkins, both of which are very heat-sensitive due to the napkin's low blood inflow location. The FCC [78] and the International Commission on Non-Ionizing Radiation Protection (ICNIRP) [79] are two such organizations. THz radiation's natural and molecular effects on the environment must also be taken into account. Another new idea for addressing health problems will be introduced in 6G: electromotive force transfer [89].

13.8 RESEARCH ACTIVITIES

The following section provides an overview of 6G exploration activities. Sixth-generation activities have been initiated encyclopedically by artificial groups and governments, including the formulation and description of the technology, the re-ad position of the figure, and the wireless system business model. The FCC of the United States has established itself as the leader in 6G research with its plan to utilize the 95 GHz to 3 THz spectrum for 6G exploration. Other countries have begun sifting through 6G networks with only their fingers. Examples include the Finnish Institute's 6Genesis Flagship Program and the Terabit Bidirectional Multi-User Optical Wireless System (MUOWS) for 6G Li-Fi, both of which kicked off in the early months of 2019. In Levi, Finland, in March 2019, the first 6G Wireless Summit kicked off the academic 6G exploration competition [8]. Many mini-shops and conferences have been held encyclopedically to study the prospects of 6G, such the Huawei 6G Factory, the Globecom2018 Wi-UAV Factory, and the Carleton 6G Factory. Thanks to a group based on the EU's Terranova design, dependable 6G connections with 400 Gbit/s alternate transmission capacities in the THz band are now conceivable. LG Electronics also announced that a new 6G exploration center will be built at the Korea Advanced Institute of Science and Technology in Daejeon, South Korea. Samsung launched its 6G research in June of this year. A partnership between SK Telecom and Nokia and Ericsson to investigate 6G technology was announced in 2019. On December 31, 2018, China's Ministry of Industry and Information

TABLE 13.3
Research Initiatives into 6G Communications

Country	Research Initiatives
Finland [2018]	• The University of Oulu coordinates Finnish 6G research, and a 6G programme was initiated there.
United States [2019]	• Open spectrum between 95 GHz and 3 THz was made possible by the Federal Communications Commission (FCC). • "Enabling 5G and beyond" is the tagline for IEEE's new Future Network, which was unveiled this year. • To better understand future network service requirements, the ITU-T Study Group 13 also created the ITU-T Focus Group Technologies for Network 2030.
EU [2019]	• An EU-funded group called Terranova is presently working on a 6G connection that can transmit 400 gigabits per second in the terahertz range. • "Networking Research beyond 5G," a Horizon 2020 ICT-09–2017 EU-Japan project, also looks into the feasibility of utilizing the terahertz spectrum between 100 GHz and 450GHz.

(Continued)

TABLE 13.3 *(Continued)*
Research Initiatives into 6G Communications

Country	Research Initiatives
South Korea [2019]	• According to reports, LG Electronics has partnered with the Korea Advanced Institute of Science and Technology to open a 6G research center, while the E&T Research Institute has reached an agreement to collaborate on 6G network technology with the University of Oulu in Finland. • In order to explore 6G technology and commercial strategies, Samsung and SK Telecom have teamed up. • For the construction of 6G networks, SK Telecom has entered into partnerships with Nokia of Finland and Ericsson of Sweden.
China [2019]	• It's divided into two groups, one made up of government agencies entrusted with pushing 6G development and the other consisting of 37 universities, research organizations, and enterprises that will focus on 6G technology.
Japan	• Japan is ready to provide the industry with US$2 billion to assist 6G technology research. • For the development of 6G mobile network technologies, NTT and Intel have chosen to form a collaboration.

Technology announced plans to increase 6G explorations spending in order to lead in wireless communication demand in the 2030s. As an added bonus, the viability of using the THz spectrum between 100 and 450 GHz was examined as part of an EU-Japan project named "Networking Exploration Beyond 5G" and funded by Horizon 2020 ICT092017. Table 13.3 clearly shows how the exploratory effort can be divided into 6G missions for simplicity's sake. The IEEE Future Network, with the tagline "Enabling 5G and beyond," was also unveiled by IEEE in August 2018. In addition, by 2030, a new ITU-T Study Group 13 will be established to better understand service conditions for future networks [90].

13.9 CONCLUSION

With the advent of 6G, several new technologies, such as holographic communication, will be possible. This will help development of online learning platforms to provide quality education. As a result, we've gathered data on the most frequently asked questions about 6G technologies. The differences and requirements of 6G technologies have been illustrated through a comparison of 5G and 6G mobile communication technologies. Despite this, there are major variations. As a result, 6G faces enormous problems in meeting the specified standards and fulfilling the 6G obligations. Sixth-generation (or 6G) concerns and challenges have been fully exposed from every angle. Finally, we can say that 6G will have a significant impact in many domains and will be a game-changing technology in a variety of industries and academia. Lastly it's going to solve problems faced by faculty members and students related to internet connection services, speed of data, and poor technical support during online learning process.

13.10   REFERENCES

[1]   M.H. Alsharif, and R. Nordin, "Evolution towards fifth generation (5G) wireless net-
      works: Current trends and challenges in the deployment of millimetre wave, massive
      MIMO, and small cells," *Telecommun. Syst.*, vol. 64, pp. 617–637, 2017.

[2]   M.A. Albreem, M.H. Alsharif, and S Kim, "A robust hybrid iterative linear detector for
      massive MIMO uplink systems," *Symmetry*, vol. 12, p. 306, 2020.

[3]   Mobile World Live, https://www.mobileworldlive.com/asia/asia-news/samsung-dominates-
      korea-5g-deployments

[4]   Samsung, "5G Launches in Korea," https://images.samsung.com/is/content/samsung/
      p5/global/business/networks/insights/w hite-paper/5g-launches-in-korea-get-a-taste-of-
      the-future/5G-Launches-in-Korea-Get-a-taste- of-the-future.pdf

[5]   Ericsson Report, "This Is 5G," https://www.ericsson.com/49df43/assets/local/news
      room/media- kits/5g/doc/ericsson_this-is-5g_pdf_2019.pdf

[6]   M. Albreem, M. Juntti, S. Shahabuddin, "Massive MIMO detection techniques: A sur-
      vey," *IEEE Commun. Surv. Tutor*, vol. 21, pp. 3109–3132, 2019.

[7]   M.H. Alsharif, A.H.; Kelechi, K. Yahya, S.A. Chaudhry, "Machine learning algorithms
      for smart data analysis in internet of things environment: Taxonomies and research
      trends," *Symmetry*, vol. 12, p. 88, 2020.

[8]   K.B. Letaief, W. Chen, Y. Shi, J. Zhang, Y.J.A. Zhang, "The roadmap to 6G: AI empow-
      ered wireless networks," *IEEE Commun. Mag.*, vol. 57, pp. 84–90, 2019.

[9]   World Time Zone, https://www.worldtimezone.com/5g.html

[10] Theodore S. Rappaport, "Opinion: Think 5G is exciting? Just wait for 6G," *CNN Business
      Perspectives*, https://edition.cnn.com/2020/02/10/perspectives/6g-future-communications/
      index.html

[11] A. Kharpal, "China starts development of 6G, having just turned on its 5G mobile
      network," *CNBC Work Summit,* 7 Nov. 2019, https://www.cnbc.com/2019/11/07/china-
      starts-6g-development-having-just-turned-on-its-5g-mobile-network.html

[12] Andy Boxall, and Tyler Lacoma, "What is 6G, how fast will it be, and when is it com-
      ing?" *Digital Trends*, 21 Jan. 2021. Retrieved 18 Feb. 2021

[13] W. Saad, M. Bennis, and M. Chen, "A vision of 6g wireless systems: Applications,
      trends, technologies, and open research problems," *IEEE Network*, vol. 34, no. 3,
      pp. 134–142, 2020.

[14] T. Maksymyuk, J. Gazda, M. Volosin, G. Bugar, D. Horvath, M. Klymash, and. Dohler,
      "Block chain-empowered framework for decentralized network management in 6G,"
      IEEE Communications Magazine, vol. 58, no. 9, pp. 86–92, 2020.

[15] M. Dohler, T. Mahmoodi, M.A. Lema, M. Condoluci, F. Sardis, K. Antonakoglou, and
      H. Aghvami, "Internet of skills, where robotics meets AI, 5G and the Tactile Internet,"
      2017 European Conference on Networks and Communications (EuCNC), 2017.

[16] N.K. Mallat, M. Ishtiaq, A.U. Rehman, A. Iqbal, "Millimeter-wave in the face of 5G
      communication potential applications," *IETE J. Res.*, pp. 1–9, 2020.

[17] https://www.systemoneservices.com/5g-what-you-need-to-know/5g-timeline-graphics-01/

[18] S.L. Mohammed, M.H. Alsharif, S.K. Gharghan, I. Khan, and M. Albreem, "Robust
      hybrid beamforming scheme for millimeter-wave massive-MIMO 5G wireless net-
      works," *Symmetry*, vol. 11, p. 1424, 2019.

[19] https://www.mdpi.com/2073-8994/12/4/676/html(figure 1)

[20] https://www.tutorialspoint.com › 5g › 5G - Challenges.

[21] Chathuranga Basnayaka, and Dushantha Nalin K. Jayakody, "Age of information in
      an URLLC-enabled decode-and-forward wireless communication system," 2021 IEEE
      93rd Vehicular Technology Conference.

[22] Chamitha De Alwis, Anshuman Kalla, Quoc-Viet Pham, Pardeep Kumar, Kapal Dev,
      Won-Joo Hwang, Madhusanka Liyanage, "Survey on 6G frontiers: Trends, applications,

requirements, technologies and future research," *IEEE Open J. Commun. Soc.*, vol. 2, pp. 836–886, 2021.

[23] 1st 6G Wireless Summit, http://www.6gsummit.com/2019

[24] S. Chen, Y.C. Liang, S. Sun, S. Kang, W. Cheng, M. Peng, "Vision, requirements, and technology trend of 6G: How to tackle the challenges of system coverage, capacity, user data-rate and movement speed. IEEE Wirel," *Commun.*, pp. 1–11, 2020.

[25] https://www.electronics-notes.com/articles/connectivity/6g-mobile-wireless-cellular/technology-basics.php

[26] https://www.miwv.com/what-is-6g.

[27] ITU-R SM.2352–0, Technology trends of active services in the frequency range 275–3000 GHz, June 2015.

[28] M. Giordani, M. Polese, M. Mezzavilla, S. Rangan, and M. Zorzi, "Toward 6G networks: Use cases and technologies," *IEEE Commun. Mag.*, vol. 58, no. 3, pp. 55–61, 2020, doi: 10.1109/MCOM.001.1900411.

[29] Shahid Mumtaz, Josep Miquel Jornet, Jocelyn Aulin, Wolfgang H. Gerstacker, Xiaodai Dong, and Bo Ai, "Terahertz communication for vehicular networks," *IEEE Trans. Veh. Technol.*, vol. 66, no. 7, pp. 5617–5625, July 2017, doi: 10.1109/TVT.2017.2712878.

[30] M.Z. Chowdhury, M.T. Hossan, A. Islam, and Y. Min Jang, "A comparative survey of optical wireless technologies: architectures and applications," *IEEE Access*, vol. 6, pp. 9819–10220, Jan. 2018.

[31] M.T. Hossan, M.Z. Chowdhury, M. Shahjalal, and Y.M. Jang, "Human bond communication with head-mounted displays: Scope, challenges, solutions, and applications," *IEEE Commun. Mag.*, vol. 57, no. 2, pp. 26–32, Feb. 2019.

[32] R. Henry, A. Herzberg, and A. Kate, "Blockchain access privacy: Challenges and directions," *IEEE Secur. Priv.*, vol. 16, no. 4, pp. 38–45, July/Aug. 2018.

[33] D. Miller, "Blockchain and the internet of things in the industrial sector," *IT Professional*, vol. 20, no. 3, pp. 15–18, May/June 2018.

[34] H.-N. Dai, Z. Zheng, and Y. Zhang, "Blockchain for internet of things: A survey," *IEEE Internet of Things Journal*, vol. 6, no. 5, pp. 8076–8094, October 2019, doi: 10.1109/JIOT.2019.2920987.

[35] Y. Kishiyama, and T. Nakamura, "Real and future for 5G evolution and 6G," *MWE2018Workshop FR2A-1*, Nov. 2018.

[36] https://electronics360.globalspec.com/images/assets/447/16447/Table_2_-_Comparing_5G_and_6G.PNG

[37] M. Albreem, M.H. Alsharif, S. Kim, "A low complexity near-optimal iterative linear detector for MassiveMIMO in realistic radio channels of 5g communication systems," *Entropy*, vol. 22, p. 388, 2020.

[38] S.J. Nawaz, S.K. Sharma, S. Wyne, M.N. Patwary, M. Asaduzzaman, "Quantum machine learning for6G communication networks: State-of-the-art and vision for the future," *IEEE Access*, vol. 7, pp. 46317–46350, 2019.

[39] M. di Renzo, M. Debbah, D.T. Phan-Huy, A. Zappone, M.S. Alouini, C. Yuen, V. Sciancalepore, G.C. Alexandropoulos, J. Hoydis, H. Gacanin, et al., "Smart radio environments empowered by reconfigurable meta-surfaces: An idea whose time has come," *Eurasip J. Wirel. Commun. Netw*, vol. 129, 2019.

[40] Q.U.A. Nadeem, A. Kammoun, A. Chaaban, M. Debbah, and M.S. Alouini, "Large intelligent surface assisted MIMO communications," arXiv 2019.

[41] https://www.auraquantic.com/artificial-intelligence-technologies-and-their-categories

[42] C. Jiang, H. Zhang, Y. Ren, Z. Han, K.C. Chen, L. Hanzo, "Machine learning paradigms for next-generation wireless networks," *IEEE Wirel. Commun*, vol. 24, pp. 98–105, 2016.

[43] H. Fang, X. Wang, S. Tomasin, "Machine learning for intelligent authentication in 5G and beyond wireless networks," *IEEE Wirel. Commun*, vol. 26, pp. 55–61, 2019.

[44] S. Han, I. Chih-Lin, G. Li, S. Wang, and Q. Sun, "Big data enabled mobile network design for 5G and beyond," *IEEE Commun. Mag*, vol. 55, pp. 150–157, 2017.

[45] E. Basar, "Reconfigurable intelligent surface-based index modulation: A new beyond MIMO paradigm for 6G," *IEEE Trans. Commun.*, vol. 68, no. 5, 3187–3196, May 2020, doi: 10.1109/TCOMM.2020.2971486.

[46] Q. Mao, F. Hu, and Q. Hao, "Deep learning for intelligent wireless networks: A comprehensive survey," *IEEE Commun. Surv. Tutor*, vol. 20, pp. 2595–2621, 2018.

[47] N.C. Luong, D.T. Hoang, S. Gong, D. Niyato, P. Wang, Y.C. Liang, D. In Kim, "Applications of deep reinforcement learning in communications and networking: A survey," *IEEE Commun. Surv. Tutor*, vol. 21, pp. 3133–3174, 2019.

[48] I. Yaqoob, L.U. Khan, S.A. Kazmi, M. Imran, N. Guizani, and C.S. Hong, "Autonomous driving cars in Smartcities: Recent advances, requirements, and challenges," *IEEE Netw*, vol. 34, pp. 174–181, 2020.

[49] G. Gui, M. Liu, N. Kato, F. Adachi, F. Tang, "6G: Opening new horizons for integration of comfort," *Securityand Intelligence. IEEE Wirel. Commun.*, vol. 1–7, 2020.

[50] E. Basar, M. di Renzo, J. de Rosny, M. Debbah, M.S. Alouini, R. Zhang, "Wireless communications through reconfigurable intelligent surfaces," *IEEE Access*, vol. 7, pp. 116753–116773, 2019.

[51] S. Dang, G. Ma, B. Shihada, and M.S. Alouini, "Enabling smart buildings by indoor visible light communications and machine learning," arXiv 2019.

[52] N. Javaid, A. Sher, H. Nasir, and N. Guizani, "Intelligence in IoT-based 5G networks: Opportunities and challenges," *IEEE Commun. Mag*, vol. 56, pp. 94–100, 2018.

[53] A. Belmonte-Hernández, G. Hernández-Peñaloza, D.M. Gutiérrez, and F. Álvarez, "SWiBluX: Multi-Sensor Deep Learning Fingerprint for precise real-time indoor tracking," *IEEE Sens. J*, vol. 19, pp. 3473–3486, 2019.

[54] N. Zhu, T. Diethe, M. Camplani, L. Tao, A. Burrows, N. Twomey, D. Kaleshi, M. Mirmehdi, P. Flach, and I. Craddock, "Bridging e-health and the internet of things: The sphere project," *IEEE Intell. Syst.*, vol. 30, pp. 39–46, 2015.

[55] M. Alzenad, M.Z. Shakir, H. Yanikomeroglu, M.S. Alouini, "FSO-based vertical backhaul/fronthaulframework for 5G+ wireless networks," *IEEE Commun. Mag*, vol. 56, pp. 218–224, 2018.

[56] M.A. Kishk, A. Bader, and M.S. Alouini, "Capacity and coverage enhancement using long-endurance tethered airborne base stations," arXiv 1906.11559, https://arxiv.org/pdf/1906.11559

[57] Alexander Gillis, "What is internet of things (IoT)?" *IOT Agenda*. Retrieved 17 Aug. 2021.

[58] Brown, Eric, "21 open source projects for IoT," *Linux.com*, 20 Sept. 2016. Retrieved 23 October 2016.

[59] "Internet of things global standards initiative," ITU. Retrieved 26 June 2015.

[60] D. Hendricks, "The trouble with the internet of things," London Datastore. Greater London Authority. Retrieved 10 Aug. 2015.

[61] fig 9 https://www.tibco.com/sites/tibco/files/media_entity/2020-05/IoT.png.

[62] V. Petrov, D. Moltchanov, and Y. Koucheryavy, "Applicability assessmentof terahertz information showers for next-generation wireless networks," in *Proceedings IEEE International Conference on Communications (ICC)*, pp. 1–7, May 2016.

[63] I.F. Akyildiz, J.M. Jornet, and C. Han, "Terahertz band: Next frontier for wireless communications," *Phys. Commun.*, vol. 12, pp. 16–32, Sept. 2014.

[64] S. Garg, et al., "Enabling the next generation of mobile robotics using 5Gwireless," *IEEE Access*, submitted for publication.

[65] S. Chinchali, A. Sharma, J. Harrison, A. Elhafsi, D. Kang, E. Pergament, E. Cidon, S. Katti, and M. Pavone, "Network offloading policies for cloudrobotics: A learning-based approach," Feb. 2019, arXiv:1902.05703.

[66] R. Kurtzweil, *The Age of Spiritual Machines: When Computers Exceed Human Intelligence*. New York: Penguin Books, 1999.

[67] H. Moravec, "When will computer hardware match the human brain," *J. Evol. Technol.*, vol. 1, no. 1, p. 10, 1998.

[68] H. Aggrawal, P. Chen, M.M. Assefzadeh, B. Jamali, and A. Babakhani, "Gone in a picosecond: Techniques for the generation and detection ofpicosecond pulses and their applications," *IEEE Microw. Mag.*, vol. 17, no. 12, pp. 24–38, Dec. 2016.

[69] M.J.W. Rodwell, Y. Fang, J. Rode, J. Wu, B. Markman, S.T.Š. Brunelli, J. Klamkin, and M. Urteaga, "100–340 GHz systems: Transistors and applications," in *IEDM Technical Digest*, pp. 14.3.1–14.3.4, Dec. 2018.

[70] A. Velten, T. Willwacher, O. Gupta, A. Veeraraghavan, M.G. Bawendi, and R. Raskar, "Recovering three-dimensional shape around a corner using ultrafast time-of-flight imaging," *Nature Commun.*, vol. 3, Mar. 2012, Art. no. 745.

[71] M. O'Toole, D.B. Lindell, and G. Wetzstein, "Confocal non-line-of-sightimaging based on the light-cone transform," *Nature*, vol. 555, no. 7696, pp. 338–341, Mar. 2018.

[72] F. Xu, G. Shulkind, C. Thrampoulidis, J.H. Shapiro, A. Torralba, F.N.C. Wong, and G.W. Wornell, "Revealing hidden scenes by photonefficient occlusion-based opportunistic active imaging," *Opt. Express*, vol. 26, no. 8, pp. 9945–9962, Apr. 2018.

[73] A. Sume, M. Gustafsson, M. Herberthson, A. Janis, S. Nilsson, J. Rahm, and A. Orbom, "Radar detection of moving targets behind corners," *IEEE Trans. Geosci. Remote Sens.*, vol. 49, no. 6, pp. 2259–2267, June 2011.

[74] K.-P.-H. Thai, O. Rabaste, J. Bosse, D. Poullin, I. Hinostroza, T. Letertre, and T. Chonavel, "Around-the-corner radar: Detection and localization of a target in non-line of sight," in *Proceedings IEEE Radar Conference (RadarConf)*, pp. 842–847, May 2017.

[75] P. Setlur, T. Negishi, N. Devroye, and D. Erricolo, "Multipath exploitation in non-LOS urban synthetic aperture radar," *IEEE J. Sel. Topics Signal Process.*, vol. 8, no. 1, pp. 137–152, Feb. 2014.

[76] R. Zetik, M. Eschrich, S. Jovanoska, and R.S. Thoma, "Looking behinda corner using multipath-exploiting UWB radar," *IEEE Trans. Aerosp. Electron. Syst.*, vol. 51, no. 3, pp. 1916–1926, July 2015.

[77] T.S. Rappaport, G.R. MacCartney, Jr., S. Sun, H. Yan, and S. Deng, "Small-scale, local area, and transitional millimeter wave propagation for5G communications," *IEEE Trans. Antennas Propag.*, vol. 65, no. 12, pp. 6474–6490, Dec. 2017.

[78] G.C. Trichopoulos, H.L. Mosbacker, D. Burdette, and K. Sertel, "A broadband focal plane array camera for real-time THz imaging applications," *IEEE Trans. Antennas Propag.*, vol. 61, no. 4, pp. 1733–1740, Jan. 2013.

[79] T. Chi, M.-Y. Huang, S. Li, and H. Wang, "A packaged 90-to-300 GHztransmitter and 115-to-325 GHz coherent receiver in CMOS for full-band continuous-wave mm-wave hyper spectral imaging," in *Proceedings IEEE International Solid- State Circuits Conference (ISSCC)*, pp. 304–305, Feb. 2017.

[80] S. Ju, S. Shah, M. Javed, J. Li, G. Palteru, J. Robin, Y. Xing, O. Kanhere, and T.S. Rappaport, "Scattering mechanisms and modeling for terahertz wireless communications," in *Proceedings Under IEEE International Conference on Communications*, pp. 1–7, May 2019.

[81] S.K. Doddalla, and G.C. Trichopoulos, "Non-line of sight terahertz imaging from a single viewpoint," in *IEEE MTT-S International Microwave Symposium (IMS)*, pp. 1527–1529, June 2018.

[82] https://www.free6gtraining.com/2021/07/softbanks-12-challenges-for-beyond-5g-6g.html.

[83] J. Parikh, A. Basu, "Technologies assisting the paradigm shift from 4G to 5G," *Wirel. Pers. Commun*, pp. 1–22, 2020.

[84] Y. Shi, J. Zhang, K.B. Letaief, B. Bai, W. Chen, "Large-scale convex optimization for ultra-dense cloud-RAN," *IEEE Wirel. Commun*, vol. 22, pp. 84–91, 2015.
[85] K.M.S. Huq, S.A. Busari, J. Rodriguez, V. Frascolla, W. Bazzi, D.C. Sicker, "Terahertz-enabled wireless system for beyond-5G ultra-fast networks: A brief survey." *IEEE Netw.*, vol. 33, pp. 89–95, 2019.
[86] I.F. Akyildiz, J.M. Jornet, and C. Han, "Terahertz band: Next frontier for wireless communications," *Phys. Commun.*, vol. 12, pp. 16–32, 2014.
[87] T. Wu, T.S. Rappaport, and C.M. Collins, "Safe for generations to come: Considerations of safety for millimeter waves in wireless communications." *IEEE Microw. Mag.*, vol. 16, pp. 65–84, 2015.
[88] T. Wu, T.S. Rappaport, and C.M. Collins, "The human body and millimeter-wave wireless communication systems: Interactions and implications." In *Proceedings of the 2015 IEEE International Conference on Communications (ICC)*, London, UK, 8–12 June 2015.
[89] M.Z. Chowdhury, M. Shahjalal, M. Hasan, and Y.M. Jang, "The role of optical wireless communication technologies in 5G/6G and IoT solutions: Prospects, directions, and challenges," *Appl. Sci.*, vol. 9, p. 4367, 2019.
[90] S. Dang, O. Amin, B. Shihada, and M.-S. Alouini, "What should 6G be?" *Nat. Electron.*, vol. 3, pp. 20–29, 2020.
[91] P. Horn, Former IBM SvP and Director of Research of New York University, Private Communications, 201.
[92] S. Mumtaz, J.M. Jornet, J. Aulin, W.H. Gerstacker, X. Dong, and B. Ai, "Terahertz communication for vehicular networks." *IEEE Trans. Veh. Technol.*, vol. 66, pp. 5617–5625, 2017.
[93] S. Chen, Y. Liang, S. Sun, S. Kang, W. Cheng, and M. Peng, "Vision, requirements, and technology trend of 6g: How to tackle the challenges of system coverage, capacity, user data- rate and movement speed," *IEEE Wirel. Commun.*, pp. 1–11, 2020.
[94] T.S. Rappaport, "6G and beyond: Terahertz communications and sensing," 2019 Brooklyn 5G Summit Keynote, Apr. 2019, https://ieeetv.ieee.org/conference-highlights/keynote-tedrappaport-terahertz-communication- b5gs-2019?
[95] H. Wang and T.S. Rappaport, "A parametric formulation of the UTDdiffraction coefficient for real-time propagation prediction modeling," *IEEE Antennas Wireless Propag. Lett.*, vol. 4, pp. 253–257, Aug. 2005.
[96] C. Cho, M. Maloy, S.M. Devlin, O. Aras, H. Castro-Malaspina, L.T. Dauer, A.A. Jakubowski, R.J. O'Reilly, E.B. Papadopoulos, M.-A. Perales, et al., "Characterizing ionizing radiation exposure after T-cell depletedallogeneic hematopoietic cell transplantation." *Biol. Blood Marrow Transplant.*, vol. 24, pp. 252–253, 2018.
[97] T. Kleine-Ostmann, "Health and safety related aspects regarding the operation of THz Emitters." Towards Terahertz Communications Workshop; European Commission: Brussels, Belgium, 2018, https://ec.europa.eu/digital-single-market/events/cf/towards-terahertz-communications-workshop/item-display.cfm?id=21219.
[98] T. Kleine-Ostmann, "Health and safety related aspects regarding the operation of THz emitters," Towards Terahertz Communications Workshop; European Commission: Brussels, Belgium, 2018, https://ec.europa.eu/digital-single- market/events/cf/towards-terahertz-communications-workshop/item-display.cfm?id=21219.
[99] M. Aladsani, A. Alkhateeb, and G. C. Trichopoulos, "Leveraging mmWave imaging and communications for simultaneous localization and mapping," in *Proceedings Under International Conference on Acoustics, Speech, and Signal Processing* (ICASSP), pp. 4539–4543, May 2019.
[100] I.F. Akyildiz, J.M. Jornet, and C. Han, "Terahertz band: Next frontier for wireless communications," *Phys. Commun.*, vol. 12, pp. 16–32, Sept. 2014.
[101] K. Tekbıyık, A.R. Ekti, G.K. Kurt, and A. Görçinad, "Terahertz band communication systems: Challenges, novelties and standardization efforts," *Phys. Commun.*, vol. 35, Aug. 2019.

[102]   O. Kanhere, S. Ju, Y. Xing, and T.S. Rappaport, "Map assisted millimeter wave local-
        ization for accurate position location," submitted to *IEEE Global Communication
        Conference (GLOBECOM)*, Dec. 2019, pp. 1–6.
[103]   D.M. Mittleman, R.H. Jacobsen, R. Neelamani, R.G. Baraniuk, and M.C. Nuss, "Gas
        sensing using terahertz time-domain spectroscopy," *Appl. Phys. B*, vol. 67, no. 3,
        pp. 379–390, Sept. 1998.
[104]   M. Tonouchi, "Cutting-edge terahertz technology," *Nature Photon.*, vol. 1, no. 2,
        pp. 97–105, Feb. 2007.
[105]   X.-F. Teng, Y.-T. Zhang, C. C. Y. Poon, and P. Bonato, "Wearable medical systems for
        p- health," *IEEE Rev. Biomed. Eng.*, vol. 1, no. 1, pp. 62–74, Jan. 2008.
[106]   D.M. Mittleman, "Perspective: Terahertz science and technology," *J. Appl. Phys.*, vol.
        122, no. 23, Dec. 2017, Art. no. 230901.
[107]   Z. Gu, J. Zhang, Y. Ji, L. Bai, and X. Sun, "Network topology reconfiguration for FSO-
        based front haul/backhaul in 5G+ wireless networks," *IEEE Access*, vol. 6, pp. 69426–
        69437, 2018.
[108]   A. Douik, H. Dahrouj, T. Y. Al-Naffouri, and M. Alouini, "Hybrid radio/free-space
        optical design for next generation backhaul systems," *IEEE Trans. Commun.*, vol. 64,
        no. 6, pp. 2563–2577, June 2016.
[109]   B. Bag, A. Das, I.S. Ansari, A. Prokeš, C. Bose, and A. Chandra, "Performance analy-
        sis of hybrid FSO systems using FSO/RF-FSO link Draft adaptation," *IEEE Photonics
        J.*, vol.10, no. 3, pp. 1–17, June 2018, Art no. 7904417.
[110]   O. Kanhere and T.S. Rappaport, "Position locationing for millimeter wave systems,"
        in *Proceedings IEEE Global Communcation Conference*, pp. 206–212, Dec. 2018.
[111]   T. Aste, P. Tasca, and T. Di Matteo, "Blockchain technologies: The foreseeable impact
        on society and industry," *Computer*, vol. 50, no. 9, pp. 18–28, 2017.
[112]   J. Harvey, M.B. Steer, and T.S. Rappaport, "Exploiting high millimeter wave bands for
        military communications, applications, and design," *IEEE Access*, vol. 7, pp. 52350–
        52359, Apr. 2019.
[113]   D.M. Mittleman, "Twenty years of terahertz imaging," *Opt. Express*, vol. 26, no. 8,
        pp. 9417–9431, Apr. 2018.
[114]   C. Pan, J. Yi, C. Yin, J. Yu, and X. Li, "Joint 3D UAV placement and resource allo-
        cation in software-defined cellular networks with wireless backhaul," *IEEE Access*,
        vol. 7, pp. 104279–104293, 2019.
[115]   M. Mozaffari, A. Taleb Zadeh Kasgari, W. Saad, M. Bennis, and M. Debbah, "Beyond
        5Gwith UAVs: Foundations of a 3D wireless cellular network," *IEEE T. Wirel.
        Commun.*, vol. 18, no. 1, pp. 357–372, Jan. 2019.
[116]   M.J.W. Rodwell, "Sub-mm-wave technologies: Systems, ICs, THz transistors," in
        Proceedings Asia-Pacific Microwave Conference (APMC), pp. 509–511, Nov. 2013.

Index

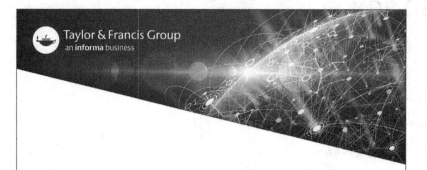

Printed in the United States
by Baker & Taylor Publisher Services

Printed in the United States
by Baker & Taylor Publisher Services